WORLDCOMP'13
July 22-25, 2013
Las Vegas Nevada, USA
www.world-academy-of-science.org

PROCEEDINGS OF THE 2013 INTERNATIONAL CONFERENCE ON GRID & CLOUD COMPUTING & APPLICATIONS

GCA 2013

Editors

Hamid R. Arabnia
George A. Gravvanis
Ashu M. G. Solo

FIREWALL MEDIA
(An Imprint of Laxmi Publications Pvt. Ltd.)
An ISO 9001:2008 Company
BENGALURU • CHENNAI • COCHIN • GUWAHATI • HYDERABAD
JALANDHAR • KOLKATA • LUCKNOW • MUMBAI • RANCHI • NEW DELHI
BOSTON (USA) • ACCRA (GHANA) • NAIROBI (KENYA)

This volume contains papers presented at The 2013 International Conference on Grid & Cloud Computing & Applications (GCA'13). Their inclusion in this publication does not necessarily constitute endorsements by editors or by the publisher.

Branches

Bengaluru	080-26 75 69 30	
Chennai	044-24 34 47 26,	24 35 95 07
Cochin	0484-237 70 04,	405 13 03
Guwahati	0361-254 36 69,	251 38 81
Hyderabad	040-27 55 53 83,	27 55 53 93
Jalandhar	0181-222 12 72	
Kolkata	033-22 27 43 84	
Lucknow	0522-220 99 16	
Mumbai	022-24 91 54 15,	24 92 78 69
Ranchi	0651-220 44 64	

PUBLISHED IN INDIA BY

FIREWALL MEDIA
(An Imprint of Laxmi Publications Pvt. Ltd.)

An ISO 9001:2008 Company
113, GOLDEN HOUSE, DARYAGANJ,
NEW DELHI - 110002, INDIA
Telephone : 91-11-4353 2500, 4353 2501
Fax : 91-11-2325 2572, 4353 2528
www.laxmipublications.com info@laxmipublications.com

C—
Printed at:

Foreword

It gives us great pleasure to introduce this collection of papers to be presented at the 2013 International Conference on Grid & Cloud Computing and Applications (GCA'13) July 22 through 25, 2013, at The New Tropicana Hotel, Las Vegas, USA.

An important mission of the World Congress in Computer Science, Computer Engineering, and Applied Computing (a federated congress to which this conference is affiliated with) includes *"Providing a unique platform for a diverse community of constituents composed of scholars, researchers, developers, educators, and practitioners. The Congress makes concerted effort to reach out to participants affiliated with diverse entities (such as: universities, institutions, corporations, government agencies, and research centers/labs) from all over the world. The congress also attempts to connect participants from institutions that have* ***teaching*** *as their main mission with those who are affiliated with institutions that have* ***research*** *as their main mission. The congress uses a quota system to achieve its institution and geography diversity objectives."* By any definition of diversity, this congress is among the most diverse scientific meeting in USA. We are proud to report that this federated congress has authors and participants from 82 different nations representing variety of personal and scientific experiences that arise from differences in culture and values. As can be seen (see below), the program committee of this conference as well as the program committee of all other tracks of the federated congress are as diverse as its authors and participants.

The program committee would like to thank all those who submitted papers for consideration. Each submitted paper was peer-reviewed by two experts in the field for originality, significance, clarity, impact, and soundness. In cases of contradictory recommendations, a member of the conference program committee was charged to make the final decision; often, this involved seeking help from additional referees. In addition, papers whose authors included a member of the conference program committee were evaluated using the double-blinded review process. One exception to the above evaluation process was for papers that were submitted directly to chairs/organizers of pre-approved sessions/workshops; in these cases, the chairs/organizers were responsible for the evaluation of such submissions. The overall paper acceptance rate for regular papers was 32%; 9% of the remaining papers were accepted as poster papers (at the time of this writing, we had not yet received the acceptance rate for a few individual tracks.)

We are very grateful to the many colleagues who offered their services in organizing the conference. In particular, we would like to thank the members of the Program Committee of GCA'13, members of the congress Steering Committee, and members of the committees of federated congress tracks that have topics within the scope of GCA. Many individuals listed below, will be requested after the conference to provide their expertise and services for selecting papers for publication (extended versions) in journal special issues as well as for publication in a set of research books (to be prepared for publishers including: Springer, Elsevier, BMC, and others).

- *Dr. Alireza Abbasi; School of Eng. & IT, University of New South Wales (UNSW), Canberra, Australia*
- *Dr. Selim Aissi (World Congress Steering Committee); formerly, Chief Strategist - Security, Intel Corporation, USA; Senior Business Leader & Head of Global Enterprise Security Architecture, Visa Corporation, USA*
- *Prof. Babak Akhgar (World Congress Steering Committee); Fellow of the British Computer Society, CITP; Professor of Informatics; Co-Director of CENTRIC (Centre of Excellence in Terrorism, Resilience, Intelligence & organised Crime research), Sheffield Hallam University, Sheffield, UK*
- *Prof. Nizar Al-Holou (World Congress Steering Committee); Professor and Chair, Electrical and Computer Engineering Department; University of Detroit Mercy, Detroit, Michigan, USA*
- *Prof. Hamid R. Arabnia (World Congress Steering Committee); Professor, Computer Science; Editor-in-Chief, The Journal of Supercomputing (Springer); Elected Fellow, Int'l Society of Intelligent Biological Medicine (ISIBM); The University of Georgia, Department of Computer Science, USA*
- *Peyman Arebi; Assistant Professor, Department of Computer Engineering, Technical and Vocational University, Bushehr, Iran*
- *Prof. Ezendu Ariwa (Publicity Vice-Chair); Chair, IEEE Consumer Electronics Chapter, UK&RI; Visiting Professor, Gulf University, Bahrain*

- *Prof. Juan Jose Martinez Castillo; Director of The Acantelys Research Group and Coordinator of the Computer Engineering Department, Universidad Gran Mariscal de Ayacucho, Venezuela*
- *Dr. Hsi-Ya (Jerry) Chang; Division Chief, National Center for High-Performance Computing, Taiwan; Secretary General of ACCTA; Member, Council of the Taiwan Association of Cloud Computing (TACC); Taiwan, ROC*
- *Prof. Juan Cuadrado-Gallego; Universidad de Alcala, Edificio Politecnico, Madrid, Spain; Ecole de technologie superieure, University of Quebec, Canada*
- *Prof. Kevin Daimi (World Congress Steering Committee); Director, Computer Science and Software Engineering Programs; Department of Mathematics, Computer Science and Software Engineering; University of Detroit Mercy, Detroit, Michigan, USA*
- *Prof. George A. Gravvanis (Vice-Chair GCA); Democritus University of Thrace, Greece*
- *Prof. Houcine Hassan; Universitat Politecnica de Valencia, Spain*
- *Prof. George Jandieri (World Congress Steering Committee); Georgian Technical University, Tbilisi, Georgia; Chief Scientist, The Institute of Cybernetics, Georgian Academy of Science, Georgia; Editorial Board Member: International Journal of Microwaves and Optical Technology, The Open Atmospheric Science Journal, American Journal of Remote Sensing, Georgia*
- *Prof. Dong Hwa Kim; Department of Electronic and Control Engineering, Hanbat National University, Korea; Visiting Professor, Budapest University of Technology and Economic, Hungary; International Einstein awardee for Scientific achievement (2010)*
- *Prof. Dattatraya V. Kodavade (World Congress Steering Committee); Head of Computer Science and Engineering, D.K.T.E Society's Textile & Engineering Institute, Ichalkaranji, Maharashtra State, India*
- *Prof. Kun Chang Lee (World Congress Steering Committee); Professor of MIS and WCU Professor of Creativity Science, Business School and Department of Interaction Science, Sungkyunkwan University, Seoul, South Korea*
- *Dr. Bala Krishna Maddali; University School of IT, GGS Indraprastha University, India*
- *Muhammad Naufal Bin Mansor; Intelligent Signal Processing Group (ISP), University Malaysia Perlis, Kangar, Perlis, Malaysia*
- *Prof. Gevorg Margarov; Head of Information Security and Software Development Department, State Engineering University of Armenia, Armenia*
- *Prof. George Markowsky (World Congress Steering Committee and SAM Session Chair); Professor and Associate Director, School of Computing and Information Science; Chair International Advisory Board of IEEE IDAACS; Director 2013 Northeast Collegiate Cyber Defense Competition; Chair Bangor Foreign Policy Forum; Cooperating Professor Mathematics and Statistics Department UMaine; Cooperating Professor School of Policy & International Affairs UMaine; University of Maine, Orono, Maine, USA*
- *Dr. Sara Moein; Editorial Board, International Journal of Science and Technology; Faculty of Engineering, MultiMedia University, Malaysia*
- *Dr. Ali Mostafaeipour; Industrial Engineering Department, Yazd University, Iran*
- *Dr. Saurabh Mukherjee; Associate Professor, Department of Computer Science, Banasthali University, Banasthali, Rajasthan, India*
- *Prof. Noel De Palma; Associate Vice President for Research, Computer Science; Leader, ERODS Research, LIG Labs.; Board of Directors, OW2 Consortium; Department of Computer Science; University Joseph Fourier (UJF), Grenoble, France*
- *Prof. G. N. Pandey (World Congress Steering Committee); Vice-Chancellor, Arunachal University of Studies, Arunachal Pradesh, India; Adjunct Professor, Indian Institute of Information Technology, Allahabad, India*
- *Prof. James J. (Jong Hyuk) Park (World Congress Steering Committee); Professor of Computer Science and Engineering, Seoul National University of Science and Technology (SeoulTech), Korea; President, KITCS; President, FTRA; Editor-in-Chiefs: HCIS, JoC and IJITCC Journals*
- *Dr. Satish Penmatsa; Computer Science, University of Maryland - Eastern Shore, Maryland, USA*
- *Prof. Junfeng Qu; Clayton State University, Morrow, Georgia, USA*
- *Dr. Liang Shi; Senior Researcher, McAfee, USA*
- *Dr. Kok Swee Sim; Faculty of Engineering and Technology, Jalan Ayer Keroh Lama, Melaka, Malaysia*
- *Ashu M. G. Solo, (Publicity Chair); Fellow of British Computer Society, Principal/R&D Engineer, Maverick Technologies America Inc., USA*
- *Dr. Alain Tchana; Grenoble University, France*
- *Prof. Fernando G. Tinetti (World Congress Steering Committee); School of Computer Science, Universidad Nacional de La Plata, La Plata, Argentina; Co-editor, Journal of Computer Science and Technology (JCS&T)*
- *Dr. Predrag Tosic (World Congress Steering Committee); Microsoft, Washington, USA*

- *Prof. Vladimir Volkov (World Congress Steering Committee & Vice-Chair of IPCV); The Bonch-Bruevich State University of Telecommunications, Saint-Petersburg, Russia*
- *Dr. Wei Wei; School of Computer Science & Engineering, Xi'an University of Technology, Xi'an, P. R. China*
- *Dr. Alexander Wohrer; Program Manager ICT at Vienna Science and Technology Fund, Schlickgasse, Vienna, Austria*
- *Prof. Jongwook Woo; Director, High-Performance Information Computing Center (HiPiC), Computer Information Systems Department, California State University, Los Angeles, California, USA*

As Sponsors-at-large, partners, and/or organizers each of the followings (separated by semicolons) provided help for at least one track of the World Congress: Aldebaran Robotics Inc., USA (http://www.aldebaran-robotics.com); Altera Corporation, USA (http://www.altera.com/); Computer Science Research, Education, and Applications Press (CSREA); Impulse Accelerated Technologies, Inc., USA (http://www.impulseaccelerated.com/); NVIDIA Corporation, USA (http://www.nvidia.com/object/about-nvidia.html); Parallella Community, Supercomputing for Everyone, USA (http://forums.parallella.org/); Pico Computing, Inc., USA (http://picocomputing.com/); SemiWiki.com, The Semiconductor Wiki Project, USA (http://www.semiwiki.com/); Solarflare Communications, Inc., USA (http://www.solarflare.com/); Stream Computing, Performance Engineers, The Netherlands (http://streamcomputing.eu/); Taylor & Francis, UK (http://www.taylorandfrancis.com/); US Chapter of World Academy of Science (http://www.world-academy-of-science.org/) ; and WEBestSOL & Webest Solutions Ltd, UK (http://webestsol.com/). In addition, a number of university faculty members and their staff (names appear on the cover of the set of proceedings), several publishers of computer science and computer engineering books and journals, chapters and/or task forces of computer science associations/organizations from 5 countries, and developers of high-performance machines and systems provided significant help in organizing the conference as well as providing some resources. We are grateful to them all.

We express our gratitude to keynote, invited, and individual conference/tracks and tutorial speakers - the list of speakers appears on the conference web site. We would also like to thank the followings: UCMSS (Universal Conference Management Systems & Support, California, USA) for managing all aspects of the conference; Dr. Tim Field of APC for managing the printing of the proceedings; and the staff of the New Tropicana Hotel in Las Vegas for the professional service they provided. Last but not least, we would like to thank the Co-Editors of GCA'13: Prof. Hamid R. Arabnia, Dr. George A. Gravvanis, and Ashu M. G. Solo.

We present the proceedings of GCA'13.

Steering Committee, 2013
http://www.world-academy-of-science.org/

Contents

SESSION: PARALLEL AND DISTRIBUTED ALGORITHMS AND APPLICATIONS + GRID COMPUTING

SESSION: CLOUD COMPUTING AND RELATED ISSUES

SESSION: VIRTUAL MACHINES AND CLOUD COMPUTING

SESSION

PARALLEL AND DISTRIBUTED ALGORITHMS AND APPLICATIONS + GRID COMPUTING

Chair(s)

TBA

VM Migration Approach for Autonomic Fault Tolerance in Cloud Computing

Anju Bala[1] Inderveer Chana[2]
[1]CSED, Thapar University, Patiala, Punjab, India
[2]CSED, Thapar University, Patiala, Punjab, India

Abstract - *VM Migration for Autonomic Fault Tolerance provides the continuous availability for applications in the event of virtual machine failures along with the benefits of improved performance and manageability. Multipath correlation coefficient approach for VM migration has been proposed, which takes into account the overutilization of CPU without performance degradation based on work variability. The proposed approach has been validated through CloudSim toolkit. The experimental results demonstrate that the proposed approach is effective for handling VM migration or VM Reallocation. Further the proposed algorithm considerably reduces the VM Reallocation execution time, VM Reallocation time standard deviation and number of VM migrations.*

Keywords—VM Migration, autonomic, fault tolerance, cloud computing, overutilization.

1 Introduction

Cloud computing has revolutionized the ICT industry by enabling on-demand provisioning of computing resources based on a pay-as-you-go model. An organization can either outsource its computational needs to the Cloud avoiding high up-front investments in a private computing infrastructure and consequent maintenance costs, or implement a private Cloud data center to improve the resource management and provisioning processes [1]. Many computing service providers including Google, Microsoft, Yahoo, facebook and IBM are rapidly deploying their data centers in various locations around the world to deliver cloud computing services [2].

Autonomic fault tolerance has become very popular, especially in scenarios of Cloud Computing. The goal of autonomic fault tolerance is to overcome the management complexity and improves the performance of today's cloud services. As cloud provides various services to the user like software as service, platform as service, hardware as a service and infrastructure as a service. Therefore, Cloud requires security, reliability, robustness and high performance. The reliability models for software or hardware failures cannot be simply applied to increase the cloud reliability [19].To handle the failures proactively; autonomic tolerance policies can be used. Virtual machine migration policy can be used to proactively move the computation away from faulty or suspicious machines. Memory, storage, and network connectivity of the virtual machine are transferred from the original host machine to the destination. In virtualization community, live migration of virtual machines is pretty much considered a "default" mature feature [3].

In order to predict a failure due to an overutilization of CPU it is usually sufficient to simply employ a threshold on CPU utilization, whereas the prediction of overloaded host requires more sophisticated algorithms. One way to such issues is to design algorithms that can detect over utilization of resources and predict any adversity in datacenter. After the detection of overutilization of virtual machines, fault tolerance mechanism or fallback virtual machine policy is required that may be reactive or proactive in nature. Therefore there is a need to build VM migration policy that works as fault tolerance algorithm to migrate and consolidate the virtual machines dynamically and efficiently based on non-linear nature of distribution of workflow jobs in tasks. VMs utilize fewer resources according to the workload data, creating opportunities for dynamic consolidation but if there is overloading or adversity it again forms another type of challenge in terms of defining the VM reallocation or migration policy after the overloading and adversity has been detected.

The main objective of the research work is to implement VM migration policy for handling faults autonomically.The local regression technique used for identifying overloading or over subscription of VMs. In this research work, improvement in Maximum Correlation Policy is improvised as correlation cannot explain the cause of two random variable's association. There might be two or more machines working together and therefore there may be higher correlation among them. So, there is a need to find the intercorrelation among overloaded machines. To address this issue, this research proposes a VM migration policy namely multipath correlation coefficient approach is proposed which is an extension of multiple correlation coefficient approach [4]. The proposed approach reduces the VM reallocation time, number of VM migrations.

The remainder of the paper is organized as follows. Section 2 discussed the related work. A section 3 presents a thorough analysis of the VM migration policies. Section 4 discussed the proposed VM migration policy to handle fault tolerance. Section 5 demonstrates the experimental results. Section 6 discusses the future research directions and concludes the paper.

2 Related Work

Power consumption is one of the most important design constraints for high-density servers. Charles Lefurgy [15] presented a control-theoretic peak power management system for servers by implementing feedback controller. Further the datacenter operators may use power control to match server power consumption to the available rack cooling capacity.Nathuji et al. [12] have proposed architecture of a data center's resource management system where resource management is divided into local and global policies. At the local level the system leverages the guest OS's power management strategies. The global manager gets the information on the current resource allocation from the local managers and applies its policy to decide whether the VM placement needs to be adapted. However, the authors have not proposed a specific policy for automatic resource management at the global level.

Beloglazov et al. [2] proposed a heuristic for deciding the time to migrate VMs from a host based on utilization thresholds. It is based on the idea of setting upper and lower utilization thresholds for hosts and keeping the total utilization of the CPU by all the VMs between these thresholds. But, fixed values of utilization thresholds are unsuitable there can be dynamic threshold values. Anton Beloglazov et al. [4] proposed various heuristics to detect the overload. An Adaptive Utilization Threshold Median Absolute Deviation which is a measure of statistical dispersion. It is a more robust estimator of scale than the sample variance or standard deviation, as it behaves better with distributions without a mean or variance. In the MAD, the magnitude of the distances of a small number of outliers is irrelevant. They proposed second method An Adaptive Utilization Threshold: Interquartile Range is a measure of statistical dispersion, being equal to the difference between the third and first quartiles [12][13]. The main idea of the method of local regression is fitting simple models to localized subsets of data to build up a curve that approximates the original data [5]. Cleveland [5] has proposed the addition of the robust estimation method bisque to the least-squares method for fitting a parametric family .This modification transforms Loess into an iterative method. The initial fit is carried out with weights defined using the tricube weight function. This overloading detection algorithm is called Local Regression Robust (LRR).After detecting the overload, VM Selection policy is used to select which VM can be migrated.

Beloglazov et al. [4] proposed VM selection policies like minimum migration time policy, random choice policy, the maximum Correlation Policy. The Minimum Migration Time (MMT) policy migrates a VM that requires the minimum time to complete a migration relatively to the other VMs allocated to the host. The Random Choice (RC) policy selects a VM to be migrated according to a uniformly distributed discrete random variable. Maximum correlation policy finds if the correlation is higher between the resource usages by applications running on an oversubscribed server, the higher the probability of the server overloading. According to this idea, VMs is to be selected to migrate that have the highest correlation of the CPU utilization with other VMs. It is used in multiple regression analysis to assess the quality of the prediction of the dependent variable. The multiple correlation coefficients [16] generalize the standard coefficient of correlation. It is used in multiple regression analysis to assess the quality of the prediction of the dependent variable. It corresponds to the squared correlation between the predicted and the actual values of the dependent variable.Maximun correlation policy cannot explain the cause of two random variables association, why these variables are negatively or positively correlated. This policy only shows the association between same levels of virtual machines. Anton Beloglazov [2] proposed a Highest Potential Growth Policy migrates VMs that have lowest CPU utilization relative to the CPU capacity defined by VM parameters in order to the potential increase of the host's utilization and prevent an SLA violation. Jing Tai et al. [10] introduced Network Aware VM migration approach that places the VMs on physical machines with consideration of the network conditions between the physical machines and the data storage. This approach could improve the task execution time. But this approach does not guarantee the enforcement of SLA [10].

Red Hat's System Scheduler [17], and Platform's VM Orchestrator [18] provide placement policies with the aim of load balancing and energy consumption saving. They continuously monitor the utilization of available hosts and, if necessary, perform a re-mapping using live migration [14], which guarantees the fulfillment of policies during runtime. Priorities and other parameters for the placement can be defined by the user, but it is not possible to change the policies.

3 VM Migration Policies

VM Migration policies are implemented first by applying the overloading detection algorithm to check whether a host is overloaded or not. The general flow of VM Migration policies as shown in Figure 1.VM overloaded detection algorithm is used, if the host is overloaded, then VM selection policy is used to select VMs that need to be migrated from the host. Once the list of VMs to be migrated from the overloaded hosts is built, the VM placement algorithm is invoked to find a new placement for the VMs to be migrated.

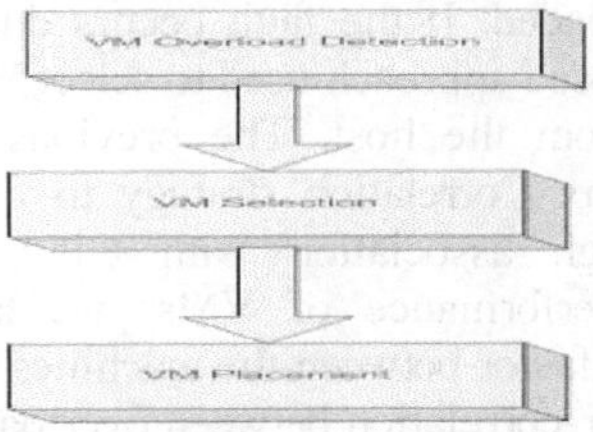

Figure 1: Flow of VM Migration

3.1 Overload Detection Algorithms

Overload detection is based on the idea of setting upper and lower utilization thresholds for hosts and keeping the total utilization of the CPU by all the VMs between these thresholds. Therefore, novel techniques are used for the auto-adjustment of the utilization thresholds based on a statistical analysis of historical data collected during the lifetime of VMs.An Adaptive Utilization Threshold Median Absolute Deviation is a measure of statistical dispersion. An Adaptive Utilization Threshold: Interquartile Range method is used for setting an adaptive upper utilization threshold based on another robust statistician descriptive statistics [12].Local regression is used for fitting simple models to localized subsets of data to build up a curve that approximates the original data.

3.2 VM Selection Policies

After selecting the host which is overloaded, the next step is to select particular VMs to migrate from the host. After the selection of a VM to migrate, the host is checked again for being overloaded. If it is still considered being overloaded, the VM selection policy is applied iteratively. This is repeated until the host is considered as being not overloaded. There are various VM Migration Policies which can be used for detecting overloading like minimization of migrations policy [2],Highest Potential Growth Policy[2],Minimum Migration Time Policy[5],Random Choice Policy, Maximum Correlation Policy , Network Aware VM migration approach [6][7][8].

3.3 VM Placement

VM Placement guarantees the SLA enforcement for migrated machines [10].

4 Problem Description and Proposed Approach

Our propose approach is an extension of the multiple correlation coefficient approach [4]. It is a method of describing complex sequential relationship between measurements. These measurements are assigned to different levels in a sequence or cascade of influence, where the earlier levels affect the subsequent ones, but the reverse does not happen. In this sequence, all measurements in prior levels affect all subsequent levels, and the scale of the influence is described by the path coefficient, and partial correlation between measurements in the same level assumes that there are as yet unexplained common preceding influences. Since, for experiment it is considered Planet Lab work flow, but at the same time, the assumption is that some machines are working together or are dependent on each other completing the complete tasks, so therefore, we need to find which is machine which has least influence on others in terms of work load, second which VM located on a host has maximum utilization, so that it is not considered for migration and the one which has least expected work is considered for migration.

For example the table 1 shows the Correlation matrix which has the data of CPU utilization with respect to VMs in datacenter; this forms the data to be processed for taking VM migration decision when over utilization occurs. Because the CPU consumes the main part of energy, and the CPU utilization is typically proportional to the overall system load. Therefore the relationship between the CPU usage and VMs has been considered.

Table 1: Correlation Matrix

	VM1	VM2	VM3	VM4	VM5	VM6	VM7
VM1	1	0.5	0.2	0.2	0.3	0.6	0.4
VM2	0.5	1	0.1	0.1	0.3	0.7	0.5
VM3	0.2	0.1	1	0.4	0.5	0.1	0.5
VM4	0.2	0.1	0.4	0.6	0.6	0.1	0.4
VM5	0.3	0.3	0.5	0.6	1	0.3	0.7
VM6	0.6	0.7	0.1	0.1	0.3	1	0.8
VM7	0.4	0.5	0.5	0.4	0.7	0.8	1

Virtual machine VM7 represents one of the VMs which can be currently considered for being avoided for migration.CPU utilization of VM1, VM2 may be correlated with those of VM3 and VM4 as also have similar pattern of CPU utilization and VM5 and VM6 also may have similar CPU utilization pattern to VM1 and VM2. Figure 2 depicts that the CPU utilization of VM1, VM2 may be correlated with those of VM3 and VM4 as also have similar pattern of CPU utilization, we need a multiple correlation analysis to correct for all the inter-correlations, and identify the direct influence on other machines. If the CPU utilization pattern is same as with other machines, then these machines might be working together.

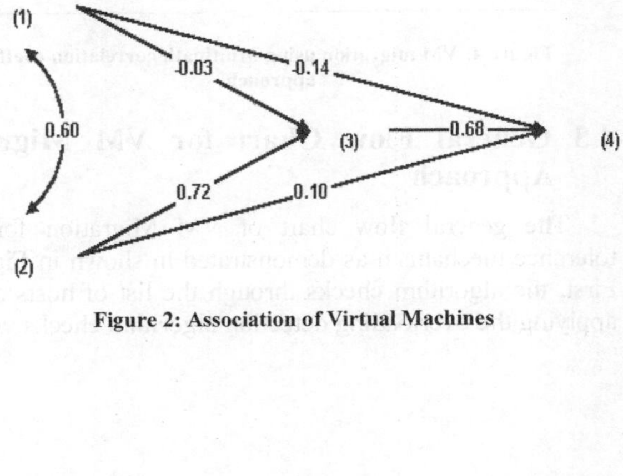

Figure 2: Association of Virtual Machines

4.1 Optimization of Virtual Machines

To optimize the performance of virtual machines, we have implemented the correlation between occupied and standby machines and intercorrelation between occupied machines which is shown in Figure 3. First it will check the correlation between V1 and VM1, if the correlation factor is one then intercorrelation factor is calculated between VM1 and VM2, If the inter-correlation factor is one then it means there is a perfect correlation and these machines are working together. These machines are not migratable, because it may degrade the overall performance. In the similar way the intercorrelation can be found between VM1 and other VM's.

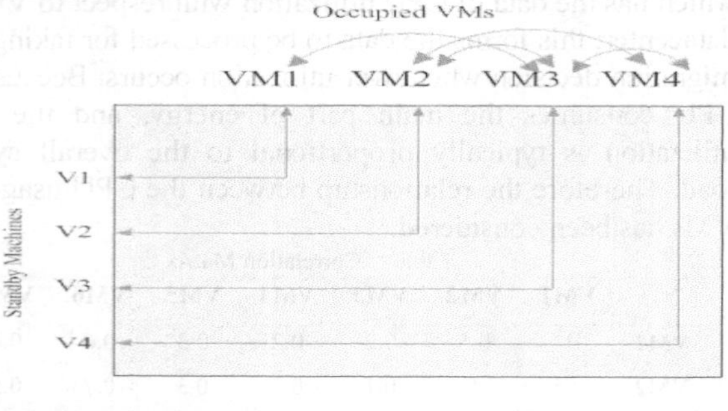

Figure 3: Intercorrelation between occupied and standby machines

4.2 VM Migration from Overloaded Host

Figure 4 shows the migration of virtual machine from overloaded host to another host. If the CPU utilization exceed than the demand then host is overloaded. Then overloaded virtual machines from the host need to be migrated to another host by finding the correlation and intercorrelation between virtual machines. If inter-correlation factor between overloaded virtual machines is zero, then that machines can be migratable.

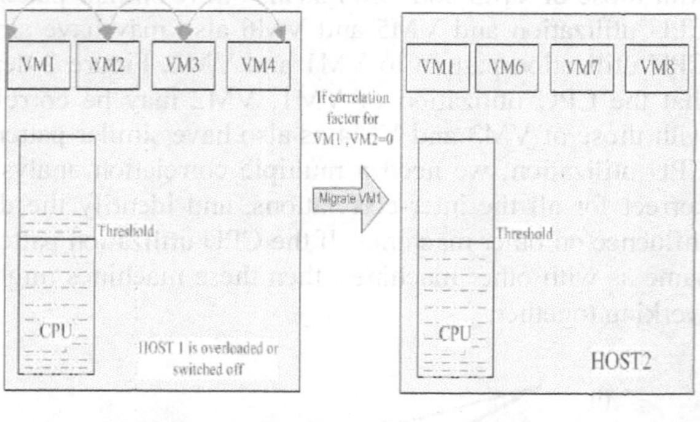

Figure 4: VM migration using Multipath correlation coefficient approach

4.3 General Flow Chart for VM Migration Approach

The general flow chart of VM Migration for fault tolerance mechanism as demonstrated in shown in Figure 5. First, the algorithm checks through the list of hosts and by applying the overloading detection algorithm checks whether a host is overloaded. If the fault occurs due to overloaded host, then proposed approach used to select VMs that need to be migrated from the host. The previous algorithm was working on Max Correlation strategy to find which VMs have some high association with CPU utilization. To improve the performance of VMs, we have found the intercorrelation factor between the machines VM (i) and VM (i+1), if the inter-correlation between overloaded machines is one then there is a strong association between occupied machines and these machines are in group, and put these machines into ignore list, then there is no need to find out the association of VM (i+1) with other standby macines.So it will reduce the VM reallocation time, number of migrations. If the intercorrelation factor is one then put these machines into migration list.

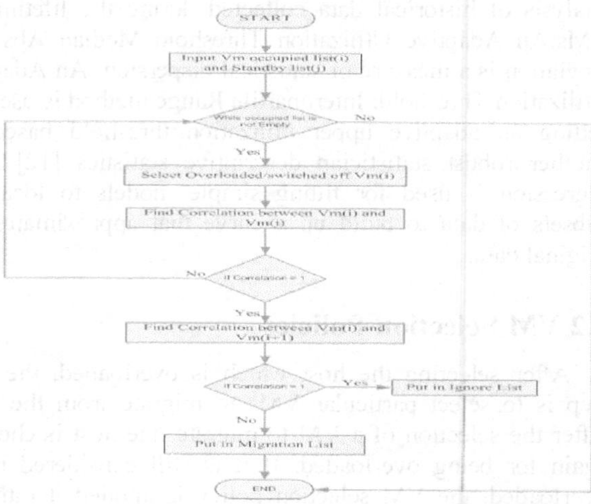

Figure 5: Flowchart for the proposed approach

5 Experimental Results of the Proposed Approach

It is essential to evaluate the proposed approach on a large-scale virtualized data center infrastructure. However, it is extremely difficult to conduct repeatable large-scale experiments on a real infrastructure, which is required to evaluate and compare the proposed algorithms. The usefulness of proposed VM Migration approach is implemented and tested using Cloudsim 4.0 which supports modeling and stimulating one or more VMs on a stimulated data centers [9][2]. In the experiment, we focused on to reduce the VM Reallocation time and no. of migrations. The comparative analysis of proposed approach is implemented with the multiple correlation coefficient approach.

5.1 Simulation Results

We have simulated the data center that comprises 25 heterogeneous nodes and 25 virtual machines. Half of the nodes are HP ProLiant ML110 G4 servers, and the other half consists of HP ProLiant ML110 G5 servers. We have evaluated our results by using 14 experiments with safety parameter as threshold value from 0.1 to 1.1.Results are evaluated by using overload detection algorithm local regression and proposed approach. The simulation results in cloudsim 4.0 is shown in Table 2.The results shows that proposed VM migration approach can bring better results in comparison to the Multiple coefficient approach(MC).

Table 2: Simulation results of the proposed algorithm with MC

Exp. No.	Safety Parameter(Threshold value)	Algorithm	Energy	No. of Migrations	Execution Time VM Reallocation Mean	Execution Time VM Reallocation Standard Deviation
1	0.1	MC	6.06534	101	0.00089	0.00089
2.	0.2	MC	7.57247	114	0.00011	0.00133
3	0.3	MC	9.03644	121	0.00005	0.00089
4	0.5	MC	10.00375	128	0	0
5	0.7	MC	12.64221	287	0.00016	0.0016
6	0.9	MC	14.05626	780	0.0006	0.00299
7	1.1	MC	16.33943	1199	0.00157	0.0047
8	0.1	Proposed	6.02803	92	0.00011	0.00129
9	0.2	Proposed	7.49453	98	0.00006	0.00094
10	0.3	Proposed	8.51442	108	0	0
11	0.5	Proposed	9.98966	130	0	0
12	0.7	Proposed	12.55814	242	0.00006	0.00094
13	0.9	Proposed	13.95547	626	0.00043	0.00144
14	1.1	Proposed	16.31823	1037	0.00108	0.00397

5.2 Performance Metrics

Several metrics are used to evaluate the performance and efficiency of proposed approach. The selection of performance parameters should be done in such a manner that it is able to find the efficiency of the algorithm in terms of reallocation time and must be able to reduce failures and help in running of datacenters smoothly without any loss of energy. These parameters give an overall picture of the nature of the fault tolerance mechanism for each step it performs. For example, it helps us to understand how much average time it takes for the algorithm to give response for reallocating or migrating the workload to a new VM and if there is some variation in doing this process we also get how much is the variation by calculating standard deviation and variance. Another metric is the number of VM Migrations.

Case 1: VM Migration places the virtual machine into a saved state during the migration from faulty or overloaded host to other host. Figure 6 shows that no. of VM Migrations is less in proposed approach as compared to previous one. However, it can optimize the performance during live migration.

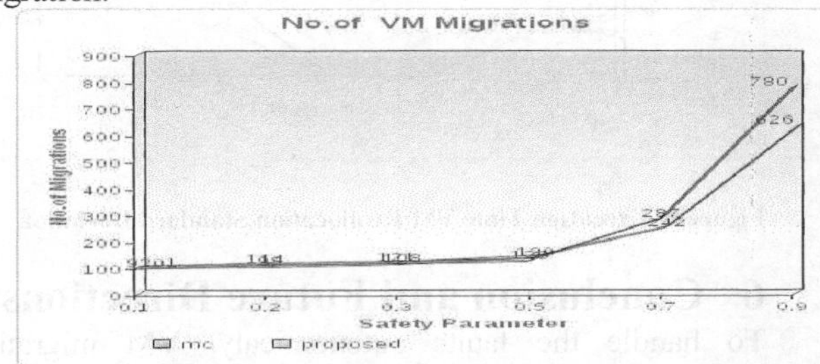

Figure 6: Number of VM Migrations

Case 2: This is the graph [Figure 7] showing how much time it takes on average for the fault tolerance algorithm to finally get the migration or the reallocation of VMs, it can be seen the average time has improved due to new algorithm as it is working for reselecting the machines based on intercorrelation factor affecting the VM migration decision making process.

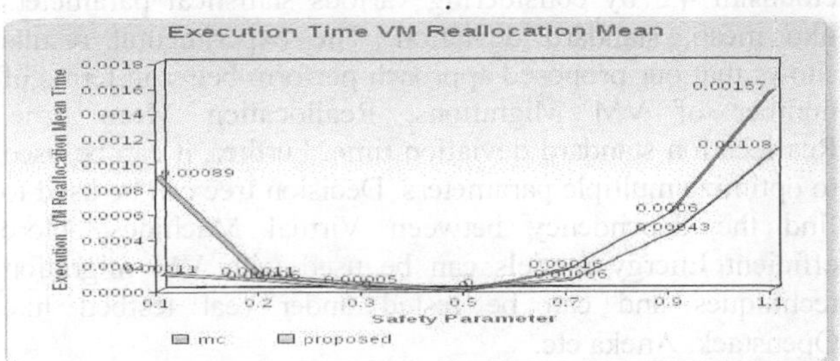

Figure 7: Execution Time VM Reallocation Mean

Case 3: Standard deviation is a measure of how much the data is distributed around both sides of the mean. The wider the difference between the maximum and minimum values in a distribution, the bigger the standard deviation. In this case for safety parameter 0.1, the standard deviation is around 0.0129 of the mean which is analyzed in Figure 8. But for other safety parameters the standard deviation is small for the proposed algorithm, which means that this the proposed algorithm will not be much erratic in nature and will not disturb the overall process of migration during reallocation of VMs due to some over load utilization or some adversity issue.

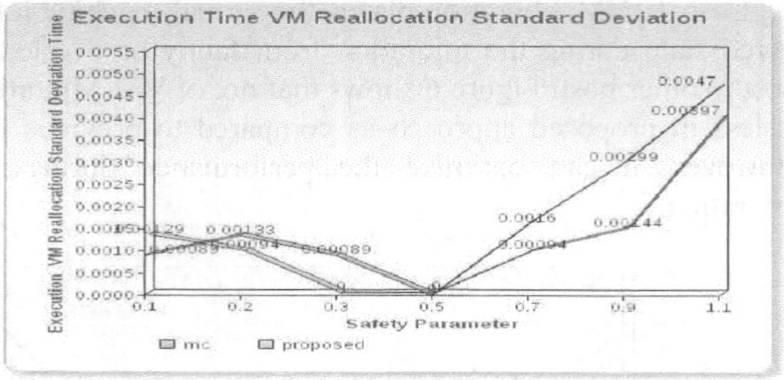

Figure 8: Execution Time VM Reallocation Standard Deviation

6 Conclusion and Future Directions

To handle the faults autonomicaly, VM migration approach has been proposed and implemented. The proposed policy automatically moves computation away from faulty or overloaded machines to other machines. Because the CPU consumes the main part of energy and the CPU utilization is typically proportional to the overall system load. So, overloading detection has been implemented using local regression by considering the CPU utilization parameter. The proposed multipath correlation coefficient approach has been implemented to select the virtual machine which needs to be migrating. Performance evaluation has been done using cloudsim 4.0 by considering various statistical parameters like mean, standard deviation. The experimental results shows that our proposed approach perform better in terms of number of VM Migrations, Reallocation Mean time, Reallocation standard deviation time. Further, it can be used to optimize multiple parameters. Decision tree can be used to find the dependency between Virtual Machines. More efficient Energy models can be used with VM migration techniques and can be tested under real testbed like Openstack, Aneka etc.

7 References

[1] Anton Beloglazov, Rajkumar Buyya, "Managing Overloaded Hosts for Dynamic Consolidation of Virtual Machines in Cloud Data Centers Under Quality of Service Constraints," IEEE Transactions on Parallel and Distributed Systems, 15 Aug. 2012.

[2] Anton Beloglazov , Jemal Abawajy, Rajkumar Buyya," Energy-aware resource allocation heuristics for efficient management of data centers for Cloud computing," in Future Generation Computer Systems 28 (2012) 755–768.

[3] Understanding Live Migration at http://ppadala.net/blog/2010/06/understanding-live-migration-of-virtual-machines.

[4] Anton Beloglazov_ and Rajkumar Buyya," Optimal Online Deterministic Algorithms and Adaptive Heuristics for Energy and Performance Efficient Dynamic Consolidation of Virtual Machines in Cloud Data Centers" in concurrency Computat.: Pract. Exper. 2012; 24:1397–1420.

[5] Cleveland WS.," Robust locally weighted regression and smoothing scatterplots." Journal of the American statistical association 1979; 74(368):829–836.

[6] Verma A, Dasgupta G, Nayak TK, De P, Kothari R.," Server workload analysis for power minimization using consolidation" in Proceedings of the 2009 USENIX Annual Technical Conference, San Diego, CA, USA, 2009; 28–28.

[7] Abdi H. ," Multiple correlation coefficient. Encyclopedia of Measurement and Statistics (edited by Neil J. Salkind), "Sage, Thousand Oaks, CA, USA, 2007; 648–651.

[8] Kendall MG, Ord JK.," Time-series. Oxford University Press, "Oxford, 1973.

[9] Calheiros RN, Ranjan R, Beloglazov A, Rose CAFD, Buyya R. ,"CloudSim: a toolkit for modeling and simulation of Cloud computing environments and evaluation of resource provisioning algorithms " in Software: Practice and Experience 2011; 41(1):23–50.

[10] Jing Tai Piao, Jun Yan," A Network-aware Virtual Machine Placement and Migration Approach in Cloud Computing" in 2010 Ninth International Conference on Grid and Cloud Computing IEEE.

[11] Franco Travostinoa,Paul Daspitb," Seamless live migration of virtual machines over the MAN/WAN" in Future Generation Computer Systems 22 (2006) 901–907.

[12] Feitelson," DG.Workload modeling for performance evaluation" in Lecture notes, computer science 2002; 2459:114–141.

[13] Barford P, Crovella M.Generating representative web workloads for network and server performance evaluation.

[14] C. Clark, K. Fraser, S. Hand, J. G. Hansen, E. Jul,C. Limpach, I. Pratt, and A. Warfield, " Live migration ofVirtual machines," in Proceedings of the 2nd Symposium on Networked Systems Design & Implementation (NSDIS).Berkeley, CA, USA: USENIX Association, 2005.

[15] C. Lefurgy, X. Wang, and M. Ware. Server-level power control. In Proceedings of the IEEE International Conference on Autonomic Computing (ICAC), June 2007.

[16] Abdi H. Multiple correlation coefficient. Encyclopedia of Measurement and Statistics (edited by Neil J. Salkind).

[17] .RedHat, "RedHat Enterprise Virtualization: System Scheduler. Data sheet" [Online]. Available: http://www.redhat.com/f/pdf/rhev/doc060-

[18] Platform, "Platform VM Orchestrator" [Online]. available:. http://www.platform.com/resources/datasheets/vmov4-ds.pdf

[19] M. Xie, Y.S. Dai, K.L. Poh.," Computing System Reliability: Models and Analysis", NewYork, Kluwer: Academic Publishers, (2004).

Adaptive Data Replication Scheme Based on Access Count Prediction in Hadoop

Jungha Lee, JongBeom Lim,
Daeyong Jung, HeonchangYu§
Dept. of Computer Science Education
Korea University
Seoul, Korea
{jungha07, jblim, karat, yuhc}@korea.ac.kr

KwangSik Chung
Dept. of Computer Science
Korea National Open University
Seoul, Korea
kchung0825@knou.ac.kr

JoonMin Gil§
School of Information Technology Engineering
Catholic University of Daegu
Daegu, Korea
jmgil@cu.ac.kr

Abstract— **Hadoop, an open source implementation of the MapReduce framework, has been widely used for processing massive-scale data in parallel. Since Hadoop uses a distributed file system, called HDFS, the data locality problem often happens (i.e., a data block should be copied to the processing node when a processing node does not possess the data block in its local storage), and this problem leads to the decrease in performance. In this paper, we present an Adaptive Data Replication scheme based on Access count Prediction (ADRAP) in a Hadoop framework to address the data locality problem. The proposed data replication scheme predicts the next access count of data files using Lagrange's interpolation with the previous data access count. With the predicted data access count, our adaptive data replication scheme determines whether it generates a new replica or it uses the loaded data as cache selectively, optimizing the replication factor. Furthermore, we provide a replica placement algorithm to improve data locality effectively. Performance evaluations show that our adaptive data replication scheme reduces the task completion time in the map phase by 9.6% on average, compared to the default data replication setting in Hadoop. With regard to data locality, our scheme offers the increase of node locality by 6.1% and the decrease of rack and rack-off locality by 45.6% and 56.5%, respectively.**

Hadoop, Data locality, Access prediction, Data replication, Data placement

I. INTRODUCTION

Due to the increasing demands for processing massive-scale data with the use of Internet-based services (e.g., search engines, e-commerce, social networks, and web maps), the concept of "big data" has emerged. To process big data, an efficient programming model is required. MapReduce is a simple and flexible parallel programming model proposed by Google to process large scale data in a distributed computing environment [1].

Hadoop is an open source implementation of the MapReduce and includes a distributed file system (HDFS), where application data can be stored with replication. With replication, Hadoop provides high degrees of availability and fault-tolerance. Hadoop is also increasingly gaining popularity and has proved to be scalable and of production quality by Facebook, Amazon, Last.fm, etc. In HDFS, data are split in a fixed size (e.g., 32MB, 64MB, and 128MB) and the split data blocks (chunks) are distributed and stored in multiple data nodes with replication. Hadoop divides each MapReduce job into a set of tasks according to the number of data blocks. Basically, the Hadoop scheduler assigns a task to a node storing the data block preferentially, but it may assigns a task to a node not storing the data occasionally according to the Hadoop scheduling policy.

In the latter case, the data locality problem occurs; that is, the assigned node should load the data block from a different node storing the data block. An informal description of data locality in Hadoop refers to the degree of distance between data and the processing node for the data, and there are three types of data locality in Hadoop: node, rack, and rack-off locality. We describe the data locality problem and the three types of data locality in more detail in Section 3.B.

In this paper, we propose an Adaptive Data Replication scheme based on Access count Prediction (ADRAP) to reduce the data transfer overhead associated with the data locality problem in a Hadoop framework. Our adaptive data replication scheme aims at improving the data locality in the map task phase, and reducing the total processing time. The proposed data replication scheme adaptively determines whether increasing the replication factor is required for a particular data file, avoiding the unnecessary data replication by analyzing data access patterns and the current replication factor.

The contributions of this paper are as follows.

- **It optimizes and maintains the replication factor effectively.** Thus, unnecessary overhead caused by data replication can be avoided because it dynamically determines whether the data replication is required or not during runtime.
- **It minimizes the data transfer load between racks.** If data replication is required, it replicates the data block in the rack that does not have the data block, or distributes it to nodes evenly. Hence, it tries to increase a probability that a data block is located in the rack in which the node reside, for the case when concurrent MapReduce jobs are running in a Hadoop environment.

§ Corresponding authors

- **It reduces the processing time of MapReduce jobs.** By improving the data locality, it results in the decrease of the frequency of data loading due to the poor data locality, which causes low throughput.

The rest of this paper is organized as follows. In Section II, we discuss related studies on data locality in a MapReduce framework. Section III provides the system model of a Hadoop cluster and the description of the data locality problem. The proposed adaptive data replication scheme based on access count prediction is presented in Section IV. In Section V, we evaluate the performance of our scheme, comparing it with the default data replication setting. Finally, Section 6 gives our conclusions.

II. Related Work

There are several purposes of data replication in HDFS. In [3, 4, 5, 6], data replication in HDFS is used mainly for availability of data. These research efforts have focused on improving fault tolerance of data in the presence of failures. Recently, a few studies attempted to improve data locality with data replication in Hadoop.

In DARE[7], the authors proposed a dynamic data replication scheme based on access patterns of data blocks during runtime to improve data locality. Note that the default Hadoop distribution provides the fixed data replication in the phase of data storing. DARE allows to increase the data replication factor automatically by replicating the data to the fetched node. However, removing the replicated data is performed when only the available data storage is insufficient. Thus, it has a limit to provide the optimized replication factor with data access patterns.

In PHFS[8], the authors proposed a data placement scheme that balances the data load, considering the processing speed of nodes. PHFS provides the initial data placement and data redistribution algorithms to improve data locality in heterogeneous cluster environments. In PHFS, however, the performance is dependent on applications because it considered data locality on scientific applications only. As far as data locality is concerned, it is more important to consider applications that share data across the nodes in the system.

In HPMR[9], the authors proposed a data prefetching scheme based on the predictor that copies the predicted data block to the local rack. HPMR collects and analyzes data access logs of the system. By using the logs, it uses a data mining method to predict the access patterns of data files. On the other hand, HPMR cannot be used at the initial stage, at which no log information is available. Hence, HPMR is also particularly suited for scientific applications, which require a long processing time.

As well as data replication, some scheduling methods are proposed to improve data locality. In [10], authors proposed a data locality aware of scheduling method in heterogeneous environments. It uses the waiting time estimation and the data transfer time to schedule tasks. It dynamically determines whether to reserve the task for the node storing the data or to schedule the task to the requesting node by transferring the data to the requesting node.

In [11], the authors proposed a delay scheduling method for both data locality and fairness. If the job cannot launch a local task due to the data locality reason, it waits for a while to allow other jobs to launch tasks. Although the delay scheduling method is designed to improve data locality, it let the jobs wait for a small amount of time, resulting in violating the fairness for jobs.

III. System Model and Problem Description

A. *System model of Hadoop cluster*

Hadoop is an open source software framework that supports data intensive distributed applications. Hadoop was derived from Google's MapReduce and Google File System papers and was originally created by Yahoo.

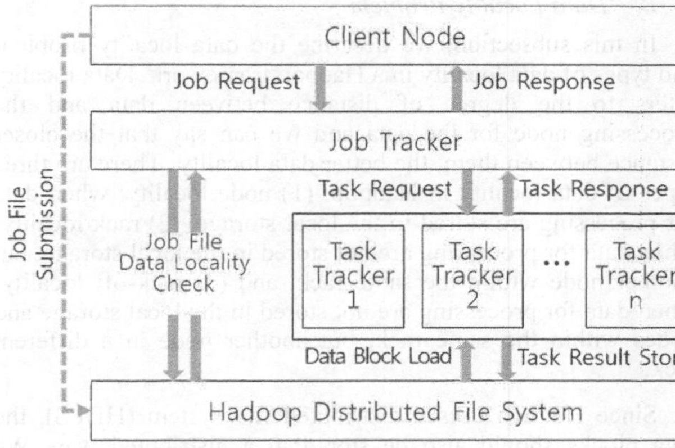

Figure 1 Architecture of Hadoop-based Cluster

The architecture of a Hadoop cluster can be divided into two layers as shown in Figure 1: MapReduce and HDFS (Hadoop Distributed File System). The MapReduce layer maintains MapReduce jobs and their tasks, and the HDFS layer is responsible for storing and managing data blocks and their metadata.

A job tracker in the master node splits a MapReduce job into several tasks and the split tasks are scheduled to task trackers by the job tracker. For the purpose of monitoring the state of task trackers, the job tracker aggregates the heartbeat messages from the task trackers. When storing input data into the HDFS, the data are split in fixed sized data blocks with replication (the default replication factor is 3) and the split data blocks (chunks) are stored in slave nodes. The name node maintains and keeps track of information about locations associated with data blocks.

A task tracker of a slave node is in charge of scheduling tasks in the node. A task tracker requests a task from a job tracker by sending a heartbeat message when it has an empty task slot. While a task is in progress, it also sends a heartbeat message periodically and the message includes information about the state of the node and the status of tasks that the node executes. A data node maintains data blocks stored in the local storage, and local disk information associated with HDFS.

The basic flow of a Hadoop application is as follows. When storing input data from a client, the data are divided into chunks and the chunks are stored to nodes. The job tracker deals with a MapReduce job request from a client. Upon reception of a job request, the job tracker divides a job into tasks, and then, the tasks are assigned to task trackers. At this stage, it schedules tasks by considering data locality with metadata of the job. Next, each task tracker assigns a task to a node, and then, the node performs the task by loading the data block from HDFS when needed. A task tracker keeps track of the state of the node about the task. When a task is completed, this information is sent to the job tracker and the result of the map task is stored at the local storage temporarily. After all tasks of the job are completed, the job tracker informs the client of the completion of the job and the client can check the result of the job, which is stored in HDFS.

B. *Data Locality Problem*

In this subsection, we describe the data locality problem and types of data locality in a Hadoop framework. Data locality refers to the degree of distance between data and the processing node for the data and we can say that the closer distance between them, the better data locality. There are three types of data locality in Hadoop: (1) node locality: when data for processing are stored in the local storage, (2) rack locality: when data for processing are not stored in the local storage, but another node within the same rack, and (3) rack-off locality: when data for processing are not stored in the local storage and nodes within the same rack, but another node in a different rack.

Since Hadoop uses a distributed file system (HDFS), the data blocks should also be stored in a distributed way. We define the data locality problem as follows. The data locality problem is a situation where a task is scheduled with rack or rack-off locality; that is, a node should load data from another node, causing poor throughput [13]. With regard to data locality, the overhead of rack-off locality is greater than that of rack locality.

More precisely, when it comes to rack locality, the node receives the data block from another node using a high speed/bandwidth interconnection network. On the other hand, in rack-off locality, the data block should be passed from a rack to another, and this may incur the latency of data processing due to data transfer time. To alleviate the data locality problem, we propose an adaptive data replication scheme, which predicts the access count of data files using Lagrange's interpolation and uses a data replication placement algorithm to reduce an extent of rack and rack-off locality effectively.

IV. Adaptive Data Replication Scheme based on Access count Prediction

Individual nodes are supposed to perform the fixed number of tasks in accordance with task slots configured in Hadoop. When a task tracker notices that there are one or more empty task slots, it sends request messages for tasks to job trackers. A job tracker preferentially assigns a task to the node that holds the data block. If there is no such node with node locality, it assigns the task to a node with rack or rack-off locality.

When the data locality problem arises, for such a reason, some data blocks should be transferred to nodes with overhead. This problem can be alleviated by using a data replication scheme. The proposed data replication scheme adaptively determines whether it replicates a data file or not, according to the current replication factor value and the predicted access count for the data file.

To this end, it is necessary to maintain and analyze metadata for data blocks. HDFS supports write-once-read-many semantics on files and files are divided into fixed sized data blocks with replication. A typical size of a block and a replication factor used by HDFS are 64MB and 3, respectively. However, the default replication factor in HDFS is fixed at an initial stage and the replication factor does not be changed during runtime, regardless of the current access count and data locality of data files.

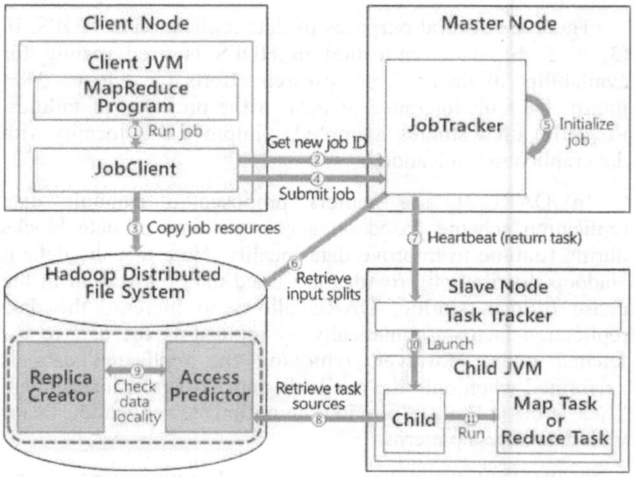

Figure 2 Flow Diagram of Adaptive Data Replication

Figure 2 shows the flow diagram of a MapReduce job. The modules proposed in this paper for data replication are marked with the dotted rectangle box. A job submitted by a client is assigned to task trackers by the job tracker. Task trackers make use of HDFS for data blocks and their metadata. Each time access is made to data blocks then the access predictor calculates the predicted access count and the threshold value. With this threshold value, the replica creator determines whether it replicates a data file or not. As it turns out, it will improve data locality and optimize the replication factor.

A. *Access Prediction*

The basic idea of deciding replication is to maintain the different replication factor per data file. Roughly speaking, maintaining the larger replication factor than the current access count for a data file does not always guarantee the better data locality for all data blocks. However, if the replication factor is greater than the current access count, the probability of being processed with node locality is higher than that of the opposite case.

To determine the replication factor, a method that predicts the next access count for a data file is required. To accomplish this work, the amount of changes of access counts with time can be expressed as a mathematical formula. However, because the access for a data file can be made at random, a constant function is inappropriate. Therefore, we adopt Lagrange's interpolation using a polynomial expression to obtain a predicted access count for a data file.

$$g(x)=\frac{(x-x_1)(x-x_2)(x-x_3)...(x-x_N)}{(x_0-x_1)(x_0-x_2)(x_0-x_3)...(x_0-x_N)}f_0 +\frac{(x-x_0)(x-x_2)(x-x_3)...(x-x_N)}{(x_1-x_0)(x_1-x_2)(x_1-x_3)...(x_1-x_N)}f_1 \\ \vdots \\ +\frac{(x-x_0)(x-x_1)(x-x_3)...(x-x_{N-1})}{(x_N-x_1)(x_N-x_2)(x_N-x_3)...(x_N-x_{N-1})}f_N \quad (1)$$

Equation (1) shows the Lagrange's interpolating polynomial. In the equation, N is the number of points, x_i is the i-th point, and f_i is the function of x_i. To calculate the predicted access count, we substitute x by time t at which the access is made and y by an access count at t.

```
AccessPrediction()

/* Step 1. Initialization of the variables */
initialize sum to 0
initialize Threshold to 0
initialize tempX to 1.0

/* Step 2. Calculation of the average time interval */
for t_i in t_0...t_{n-1}
    temp = t_{i+1} - t_i
    sum = sum + temp
end for

avg = sum / N

/* Step 3. Prediction of the next access */
t_next = t_{n-1} + avg

/* Step 4. Calculation of the number of future access */
for t_i in t_0...t_{n-1}
    for t_j in t_0...t_{n-1}
        if i is not equal to j then
            temp = (t_next - t_j)/(t_i - t_j)
            tempX = tempX x temp
        end if
    end for
    temp = tempX x NUM^i_Access
    Threshold = Threshold + temp
end for
```

Figure 3 Access Prediction Algorithm

Figure 3 shows our access prediction algorithm. In the algorithm, t_i is the time at which i-th access is made, *avg* is the average time interval between accesses, and NUM^i_{Access} is the access count at t_i. After initializing the variables (Step 1), it calculates the average time interval between access of data files (Step 2). Afterwards, it calculates the predicted access count for the next predicted access time using Lagrange's interpolation (Step 3 and Step 4).

B. Adaptive Data Replication and Replica Placement

In this subsection, we describe the adaptive data replication algorithm based on access count prediction. The proposed algorithm compares the predicted access count with the current replication factor, and then determines the replication factor. In addition, to effectively reduce the number of nodes with rack or rack-off locality, we also introduce the replica placement algorithm that chooses the nodes where the replica will be placed.

```
AdaptiveDataReplication()

/* Step 1. Requesting a task */
if a TaskTracker has one more idle slot then
    request a task to JobTracker
end if

/* Step 2. Checking the data locality of tasks */
if there are one more tasks with the node locality then
    assign a task of them
else if there are one more tasks with the rack locality then
        assign a task of them
    else
        assign a task with the rack-off locality
    end if
end if

/* Step 3. Increasing the number of accesses */
if the assignment in Step 2 is the first assignment for the job then
    for F_i in F_0...F_{n-1} belong to the job files
        increase Access_i of F_i by one
    end for
end if

/* Step 4. Obtaining the value of Threshold */
set Threshold to AccessPrediction(NUM^i_Access)

/* Step 5. Creating the caches or replicas */
for F_i in F_0...F_{n-1} belongs to the job files
    if Replica_i is equal or greater than Threshold then
        create some of the cache when task has no node locality
    else if Replica_i is less than Threshold then
            create the replica of the corresponding file
        end if
    end if
end for
```

Figure 4 Adaptive Data Replication Algorithm

```
ReplicaPlacement()
/* Step 1. Selection of a rack to store the replica*/
for Rack_i belong to the circular linked list of racks
    if Replica_n does not exist in theRack_i
        set Rack_selected to Rack_i
        goto Step 2
    end if
    if all the racks have Replica_n
        set Rack_selected to the first rack to be searched
    end if
end for
/* Step 2. Selection of a node to store the replica */
select the Node_inturn belong to the circular linked list of nodes
on the Rack_selected

/* Step 3. Store of the replica */
store Replica_n to Node_inturn
register the information of Replica_n to NameNode
```

Figure 5 Replica Placement Algorithm

As discussed, when a task is assigned without node locality, an input data block should be loaded from a different node. At this stage, the adaptive data replication scheme considers the loaded data block as cache when the replication factor is greater than the predicted access count. In such a situation, the cache and the replicated data are similar from the perspective that the data block is loaded from another node. However, the loaded data block is abandoned after its use when the data block is used as cache, whereas if the data block is used as replica, the data block is stored in HDFS and that can be used many times afterwards. If a data block is replicated like in the latter case, the information about the location and the data block is maintained by the name node, and thenceforth the data block can be used by nodes.

Figure 4 shows the adaptive data replication algorithm based on access count prediction. In the algorithm, F_i means the i-th file, $Access_i$ means the access count of the i-th file, and $replica_i$ means the replication factor of the i-th file. Each time access is made for a data file, the algorithm determines whether the data file will be replicated or it will be used as cache, by comparing the predicted access count with the replication factor. Determining of replication is made when the first task is assigned from a job tracker because all data blocks of a job file may be accessed equally as the job is being processed. For this reason, the replication is also made by a data file for a job.

Of types of data locality in Hadoop, the rack-off locality introduces the largest overhead as discussed. To improve data locality especially for the rack-off locality, the adaptive data replication scheme uses the replica placement algorithm as shown in Figure 5. In the algorithm, $Rack_i$ means the i-th rack in the circular linked list of racks, $Rack_{selected}$ means the current rack selected by the algorithm, $node_{inturn}$ means the current node selected by the algorithm in the circular linked list of nodes, and $Replica_n$ means the n-th replica.

When replicating a data block, in turn, it traverses the circular linked list of racks to check whether the rack has the data block or not. If the rack has the data block, it traverses the next rack in the circular linked list of racks until it finds the rack that does not have the data block. If it cannot find a satisfied rack after traversing all the elements in the circular linked list of racks, it replicates the data block to the rack which it selected first.

Conversely, if the rack does not possess the data block, it selects a node whose number of data blocks is minimal, and then replicates the data block to the node. With the replica placement algorithm, the data blocks to be replicated will be distributed evenly throughout the nodes. In addition to this, the algorithm will reduce the number of tasks with rack-off locality effectively.

V. EVALUATION

A. Experiment Environment

To evaluate our adaptive data replication scheme based on access count prediction(ADRAP), we generated the real job traces of MapReduce jobs for the WordCount application and the logs are used in our event-driven simulator. The physical Hadoop cluster comprises one master node and four slave nodes and the version of a Hadoop distribution is 0.20.2. Each node is equipped with Intel Core i5 (3.30GHz, quad core) CPU and 8GM RAM. Nodes within a rack is connected by giga-bit ethernet switches, and fast ethernet routers are used between racks.

We run the WordCount application for varying sizes of input data: 1.3GB, 1.9GB, 2.5GB, 3.2GB, and 4.4GB. Based on the real job trace logs, we evaluate our adaptive data replication scheme compared with the default Hadoop replication setting. The simulation environment is configured to have three racks, and 100 slave nodes if it is not noted. Note that if there are only one or two racks in the Hadoop system, the rack-off locality does not happen. As such, at least three racks are required in Hadoop environments to figure out node, rack, and rack-off locality comprehensively.

As a baseline, the replication factor and the size of data block are set to 3 and 64MB, respectively. Since we consider the shared MapReduce computation environment, the FIFO scheduler is not used in our experiments. Instead, we configured the experimental environment to be more concerned with realistic operations using the fair scheduler. Specifically, 6 jobs are configured to be processed concurrently, resulting that about 5 data files are shared among the jobs.

In addition, because data locality in Hadoop is associated with map tasks, we show the results of the map phase only. The experimental results are about the completion time and data locality (node, rack, and rack-off) of the map phase and those are averaged over 10 runs. As mentioned, in terms of throughput, the greater number of tasks with node locality is better, while the greater number of tasks with rack or rack-off locality is worse.

B. Results

In the first experiment, we evaluate the map phase completion time according to completion rates for our adaptive data replication scheme and the default setting, as shown in Figure 6. For 6 jobs, 216 map tasks are spawned. The average completion time of the map phase in the default setting is about 137 seconds, while that of our adaptive data replication scheme is about 124 seconds, which offers 9.6% of performance improvement. Figure 7 shows the number of map tasks with node, rack, and rack-off locality. Our scheme provides the increase of node locality by about 6.1% and the decrease of rack and rack-off locality by about 45.6% and 56.5%, respectively, in comparison with the default setting.

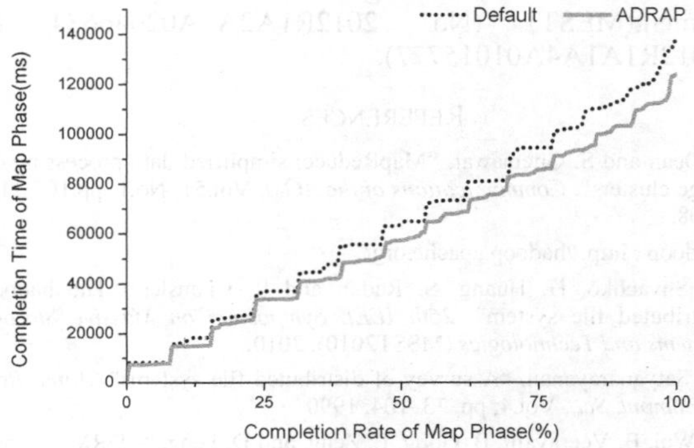

Figure 6 Comparison of the completion time of map phase between ADRAP and default

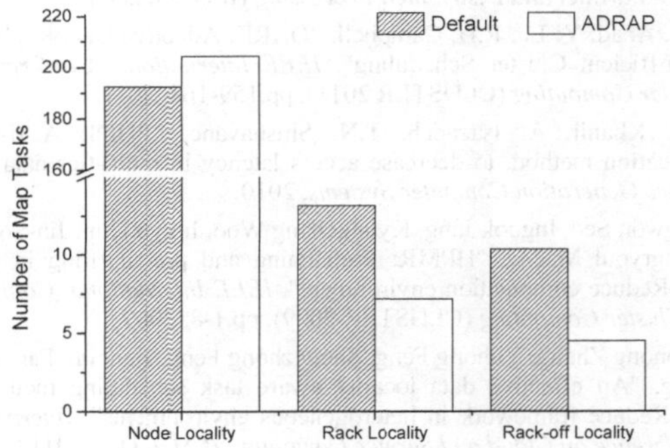

Figure 7 Comparison of data locality between ADRAP and default

In the second experiment, we varied the size of data blocks, retaining the rest of experimental settings. In other words, we compared the completion time and data locality of the map phase between adaptive data replication scheme and the default setting, by varying sizes of data blocks: 32MB, 64MB, and 128MB. In these cases, the numbers of map tasks generated are 432, 216, and 109 for 32MB-, 64MB-, and 128MB-sized data blocks, respectively.

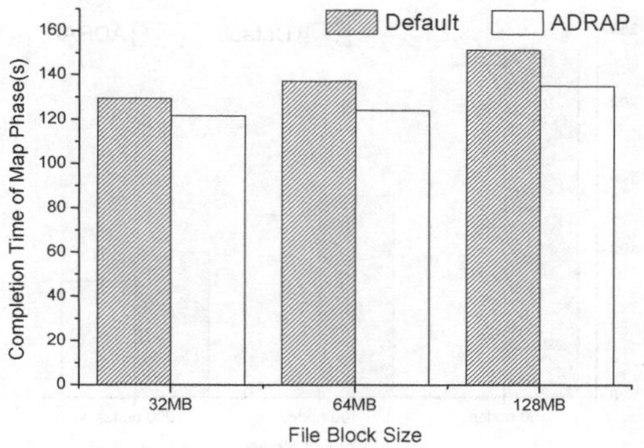

Figure 8 Comparison of the completion time of map phase with varying sizes of data blocks

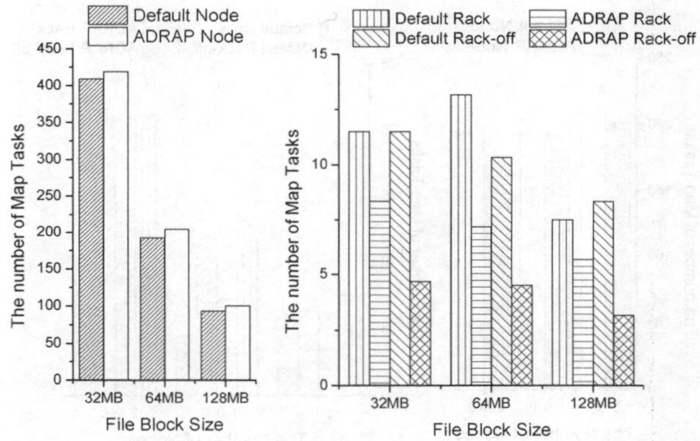

(a) Node locality(higher is better) (b)Rack and Rack-off locality(lower is better)

Figure 9 Comparison of data locality with varying sizes of data blocks

Figure 8 shows the completion time of the map phase when sizes of data blocks are 32MB, 64MB, and 128MB in both our proposed scheme and the default setting. In the result, the completion time of our scheme is less than that of the default setting by about 5.9%, 9.6%, and 10.8% when the sizes of data blocks are 32MB, 64MB, and 128MB, respectively. Note that the performance gain of our scheme increases as the size of data blocks grows. Since the greater size of data blocks leads to the fewer number of data blocks, the probability of node locality becomes lower as the size of data blocks grows.

Figure 9 shows the result of data locality with varying sizes data blocks. The largest performance difference in percentage can be found in the case that the size of data blocks is 128MB. Comparing with the default setting, the performance improvement of node, rack, and rack-off locality in our scheme is approximately equal to 7.5%, 24,4%, and 62%, respectively.

Besides the size of data blocks, we varied the number of slave nodes in the third experiment. In this experiment, the experimental settings are same as the first experiment except for the number of slave nodes. Like in the first experiment, the number of map tasks is 216, regardless of the number of slave nodes.

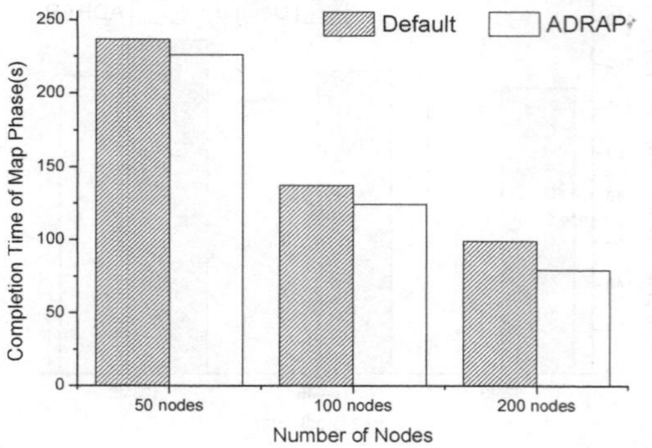

Figure 10 Comparison of the completion time of map phase with varying numbers of nodes

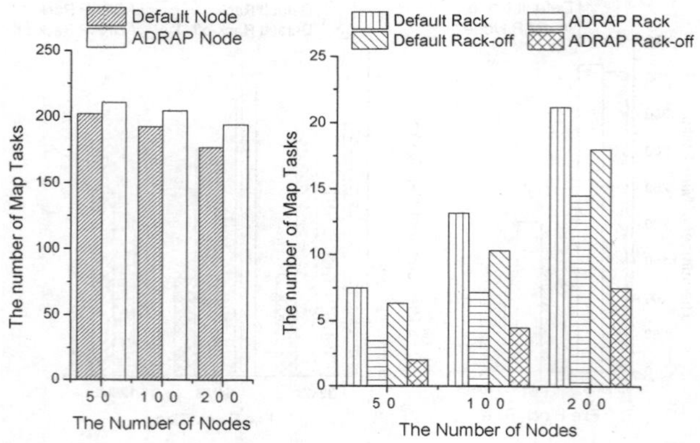

(a) Node locality(higher is better) (b)Rack and Rack-off locality(lower is better)

Figure 11 Comparison of data locality with varying numbers of nodes

Figure 10 shows the completion time of the map phase with varying numbers of slave nodes. It is worth noting that the reduction of the completion time of the map phase increases as the number of slave nodes increases. The percentages of reduction of completion time compared with the default setting are 4.5%, 9.6%, and 19.8% when the numbers of slave nodes are 50, 100, and 200, respectively. Thus, our scheme can help us to address the scalability issue well in terms of the number of nodes over the existing Hadoop environment.

Finally, Figure 11 shows the number of map tasks in regard to data locality with varying numbers of slave nodes. As expected, the largest enlargement of node locality takes place when the number of slave nodes is 200, in comparison with the default setting. In this case, node locality is increased by about 9.7% and rack and rack-off locality is decreased by about 31.5% and 58.3%, respectively.

VI. Conclusions

In this paper, we proposed an Adaptive Data Replication scheme based on Access count Prediction (ADRAP) in a Hadoop framework to address the data locality problem. Through prediction of access counts of data files using Lagrange's interpolation, it optimizes the replication factor per data file. Our adaptive data replication scheme determines whether it generates a new replica or it uses the loaded data as cache dynamically during runtime. Furthermore, we provide a replica placement algorithm to improve data locality effectively. Performance evaluations show that our scheme reduces the completion time of the map phase by 9.6% on average, compared with the default data replication setting in Hadoop. In terms of data locality, the number of map tasks with node locality is increased by 6.1%, while the number of map tasks with rack and rack-off locality is decreased by 45.6% and 56.5%, respectively.

Acknowledgment

This work was supported by the National Research Foundation of Korea(NRF) grant funded by the Korea government(MEST) (No. 2012R1A2A2A02046684 & No. 2012R1A1A4A01015777).

References

[1] J. Dean and S. Ghemawat, "MapReduce: simplified data processing on large clusters", *Communications of the ACM*, Vol.51, No.1, pp.107-113, 2008.

[2] Hadoop : http://hadoop.apache.org/

[3] K. Shvachko, H. Huang, S. Radia, and R. Chansler, "The hadoop distributed file system", *26th IEEE Symposium on Massive Storage Systems and Technologies* (MSST2010), 2010.

[4] M. Satyanarayanan, "A survey of distributed file systems", *Annu. Rev. of Comput. Sci.*, Vol.4, pp. 73–104, 1990.

[5] Q. Wei, B. Veeravalli, B. Gong, L. Zeng, and D. Feng, "CDRM: A cost-effective dynamic replication management scheme for cloud storage cluster", *IEEE International Conference on Cluster Computing* (CLUSTER 2010), pp.188–196, 2010.

[6] J. Xiong, J. Li, R. Tang, and Y. Hu, "Improving data availability for a cluster file system through replication," *In Proceeding of IEEE Int'l Symp. Parallel and Distributed Processing* (IPDPS), 2008.

[7] C.L. Abad, Yi Lu, R.H. Campbell, "DARE: Adaptive Data Replication for Efficient Cluster Scheduling", *IEEE International Conference on Cluster Computing* (CLUSTER 2011), pp.159-168, 2011.

[8] L.M. Khanli, A. Isazadeh, T.N. Shishavanc, "PHFS: A dynamic replication method, to decrease access latency in multi-tier data grid", *Future Generation Computer Systems*, 2010.

[9] Sangwon Seo, Ingook Jang, Kyungchang Woo, Inkyo Kim, Jin-Soo Kim, Seungryoul Maeng, "HPMR: Prefetching and pre-shuffling in shared MapReduce computation environment", *IEEE International Conference on Cluster Computing* (CLUSTER 2009), pp.1-8, 2009

[10] Xiaohong Zhang, Yuhong Feng, Shengzhong Feng, Jianping Fan, Zhong Ming, "An effective data locality aware task scheduling method for MapReduce framework in heterogeneous environments", *International Conference on Cloud and Service Computing (CSC)*, Dec. 2011

[11] M. Zaharia, D. Borthakur, J. Sen Sarma, K. Elmeleegy, S. Shenker, and I. Stoica, "Delay scheduling: A simple technique for achieving locality and fairness in cluster scheduling", *In Proceeding of European Conference Computer System* (EuroSys), 2010.

[12] T. White, Hadoop: The Definitive Guide. O'Reilly Media, Yahoo! Press, 2009.

[13] JungHa Lee, HeonChang Yu, Eunyoung Lee, "Data Replication Technique for Improving Data Locality of MapReduce", *Proceedings of The Korea Computer Congress 2012*, Vol.39, No.1(A), pp.218-220 2012.

Elastic Integration of a Dedicated Grid Site with an Opportunistic Cloud Infrastructure

Harold Castro, Nathalia Garcés, Mario Villamizar
Department of Systems and Computing Engineering
Universidad de los Andes
Bogotá, Colombia
{hcastro, n.garces26, mj.villamizar24}@uniandes.edu.co

***Abstract*— this work aims to extend and integrate a dedicated grid infrastructure based on the middleware gLite with opportunistic IaaS resources provided by the UnaCloud project. The extension takes place during the periods of time when the current demand exceeds the base resources capacity. The integration is done elastically, allowing the grid site to dynamically change the processing capabilities according to the current workload, using opportunistic resources when needed. To manage the elastic integration different implementation strategies are proposed and different testing scenarios are analyzed to validate a good reactiveness to workload spikes.**

***Keywords-** Elastic Integration; Opportunistic Cloud; Infrastructure as a Service; Grid Computing; gLite; Cloud Computing*

I. INTRODUCTION

Computing tasks delivered by scientific communities have regularly been executed on grids based on dedicated servers, gathering resources from multiple important sites across the world. EGI, OSG, Pragma, etc. are examples of such infrastructures and as impressive as their number of servers can be, each individual site may be in short of resources when a peak of load arrive to a site. Of course, small sites are more prone to suffer this problem.

On the other hand levering computing power from the unused computing capabilities of desktops present in organizations has become a common area of research. The reasons to exploit opportunistic resources (i.e. desktops being used by regular students in a campus) encompass reducing infrastructural and administrative costs, optimal use of desktop resources and the possibility of executing jobs with higher computing requirements.

Even though one institution may have both kind of infrastructures (dedicated and non-dedicated), the tight SLAs and configuration requirements present on grid collaborations have kept both worlds apart. Resources available to jobs arriving to a grid site are limited to the available dedicated servers on that site, no matter how many free nodes may have their opportunistic environment.

This work presents a successful integration of a gLite [1] grid site with an open source opportunistic infrastructure. We take advantage of the IaaS model to recreate the particular configuration requirements of grid solutions on desktop servers, allowing those desktops to be dynamically aggregated to the grid site. Our validation results show that the elastic integration provides to the grid site a good reactiveness to unexpected spikes in the workload, being able to satisfy the demands of the associated scientific organizations with a minimum delay.

This paper is organized as follows: section II discusses the related work for integration of infrastructures and the mechanisms used to provide elastic features; section III briefly describes the architecture and characteristics of both the grid site and the opportunistic solution; section IV describes three different strategies to manage the elastic integration with IaaS resources, followed by the implementation of the most suited in the next section; section VI presents testing scenarios and issues observed; finally section VII concludes and presents future work.

II. RELATED WORK

The classic approach to overcome the shortage of resources of a site is to overprovide computing resources, trying to satisfy researchers demand during peak periods but remaining underutilized most of the time. Of course, this approach is expensive from the economic and administrative point of view. In this section we focus on solutions integrating different kinds of infrastructures as well as those solutions implementing elastic features to adapt resource provisioning to load requirements. We are particularly interested in solutions integrating with an open production infrastructure where changes on configuration must be kept as limited as possible. In the case of grid computing, a grid site must comply with strict tests in order to be part of international collaborations.

We identify three categories of solutions aimed to integrate different infrastructures: the first one covers integration of physical and virtualized resources [2], the second group covers integration of different dedicated resources [3] [4] and the last category covers integration of dedicated and opportunistic resources [5] [6] [7].

VioCluster [2] is a borrowing-lending implementation of the University of Purdue that dynamically extend resources between the university clusters. This implementation uses virtual machines (VMs) as the extended resources while the base are physical resources. Each cluster expands when queue jobs overcome the cluster available resources and there are available resources in other clusters; this is achieved establishing some policies among them. The present work has a wider and scalable implementation and uses available resources in campus-wide desktops. Oracle Grid Engine [8] is a solution by itself. It enables the automatic provision of additional resources from the Amazon EC2 service to process peak application workloads. Unfortunately, it represents a closed solution with no applicability to international collaborations.

Zhang et al. [3] propose an implementation that integrates a cluster infrastructure with cloud resources when the current demand of the application reach a given threshold. The elasticity is achieved by the cloud infrastructure and the integration is application dependent. The extended resources are dedicated and no opportunism is allowed. SlapOS [9] is a proof of concept aimed at developing a distributed cloud operating system allowing different kinds of infrastructures to be integrated under a cloud model. SlapOs allows turning any solution to its correspondent cloud model but it does not offer integration of already established infrastructures neither it supports using opportunistic resources.

The EDGeS project [7] aims to close the gap between service grids (based on gLite) and opportunistic grids. For this objective the 3G-bridge was developed and three implementations so far integrates gLite sites with BOINC, ExtremeWeb and OurGrid infrastructures. This scheme integrates the middleware gLite with specific opportunistic middlewares, which differs from the present work because the goal is to recreate a gLite cluster in the opportunistic infrastructure making it middleware independent.

The second set of solutions presents two approaches to manage an elastic feature. Elasticity is the ability to dynamically adapt the computing resources according to the current demand. The most well-known approach is Elastic Compute Cloud (EC2) by Amazon [10]. EC2 is a product that provides an elastic system based on rules and real time monitoring to manage systems and applications. Each user defines a group of rules that specifies how the infrastructure must adapt to the current demand. These rules are condition-action specified, where the condition is checked periodically using real time metrics and actions are taken upon them.

On the other hand, Tirado et al. [11] use prediction models based on historic data instead of real time monitoring. The models anticipate and predict the demand, adapting the infrastructure based on their results. The solution does not react to events but anticipates them.

Workload spikes are characterized by being unpredictable, becoming a common practice to combine both mechanisms [12] [13]. In the present paper it was decided to use the first technique, in particular monitoring IT infrastructure metrics.

III. Site Uniandes and UnaCloud

This work is aimed at integrating two infrastructures currently on production: site Uniandes and Unacloud. Site Uniandes [14] is a resource provider of EGI, an international grid infrastructure based on gLite, sharing its resources with other grid sites all around the world. In production since 2009, site Uniandes provides dedicated computing capabilities to different scientific communities, mainly High Energy Physics and biology.

Site Uniandes integrates clusters from different academic units: the administrative middleware components are located in a central cluster while the worker nodes (WNs) are distributed among the rest of the clusters. Because the number of WNs accounts for less than 200 processing cores, it is considered a small site within EGI. As any site in the EGI collaboration, site uniandes uses dedicated servers to run the jobs sent by its communities. These resources are however static and limited and cannot handle efficiently its demand during peak loads.

On the other hand UnaCloud [5] is an implementation of the IaaS cloud computing model that provides computational resources such as CPU, RAM, storage and network using the idle capabilities of desktop computer labs present in a university campus. The main concept in UnaCloud is that resources are shared by applications of different research groups through the creation, deployment and execution of customized virtual clusters (CVCs). A CVC is a set of interconnected virtual machines (VMs) that are deployed in a non-dedicated distributed infrastructure. The idea of a CVC is to allow the customization of computing resources according to the needs of each research group at the university. Each VM within a CVC can be configured with the operating system, libraries and applications that each research project requires.

UnaCloud bases its functionality through the use of VMs. These VMs may be dedicated or opportunistic. Mainly, they are opportunistic resources obtained by taking advantage of the unused capabilities of desktop computer rooms at a university campus. Although most of the resources in UnaCloud are based on desktop systems, UnaCloud requires the use of some dedicated resources in order to guarantee stability and availability when needed. The goal of the project is to expand the gathering of opportunistic resources around the campus. It currently has access to three computer rooms with 105 desktop computers, whose aggregate capacity can deliver 572 processing cores, 572 GB of RAM, 8 TB of storage and a shared storage system of 1TB in a Network Attached Storage (NAS).

Resources are shared by applications from different research groups at the university through the use and deployment of Customized Virtual Clusters (CVCs). A CVC is a collection of interconnected physical desktop computers, each one executing a single VM in low priority and as a background process. Each VM can take advantage of the unused capabilities while students do their daily activities on the computers. Additionally, the VM is a template created by each research group, specifying the operating system, libraries and applications they require, forming customized execution environments. The deployment of a CVC is done on-demand by researchers through the UnaCloud web portal or through the connection to its web services (WS). When a CVC is deployed UnaCloud is in charge of copying and configuring the set of VMs on a group of specified resources.

A. CPU consumption

To estimate the processing capabilities that UnaCloud can provide to the gLite site through an elastic integration, it is necessary to measure the average CPU consumption of the desktop computers available in computer labs while students do their daily activities.

In [15], the author collected the CPU consumption of every desktop machine used by UnaCloud. Metrics were collected during a one-month period, during which every physical machine reported their CPU status to a central database with a periodicity of a minute. The collected data are plotted in Fig. 1, showing the average CPU usage only when the laboratories are opened to students. As expected, CPU consumption remains low most of the time (i.e. at around 6%), making these computer labs a suitable environment to run an opportunistic infrastructure.

B. Services

Since the project implements a cloud model, this research can leverage services such as usability, access through the network, on-demand service personalization, self-service, automation and scalability. In spite of this, current implementation of UnaCloud does not provide an elastic feature and users have to specify the number of VMs to be deployed as well as the duration of the deployment.

In order to limit the number and duration of resources allocated to a single user, in this work we modified the UnaCloud Web Service (WS) API to allow gathering information about the physical resources available in UnaCloud. Thanks to this update, we are now able to implement allocation policies from an external component.

CVCs facilitate the integration of site Uniandes with UnaCloud because they allow recreating the same execution environments. As a result, the integration can be done with a CVC composed of gLite components, turning on VMs (IaaS resources) when needed to balance the workload of the site. The CVC can be deployed from an external program with a connection to UnaCloud WS.

IV. STRATEGIES

Although Uniandes site participates on different international collaborations, exposing services from different middleware, in this work we focus on extending only resources from the gLite middleware, so new capabilities will be only available to EGI communities.

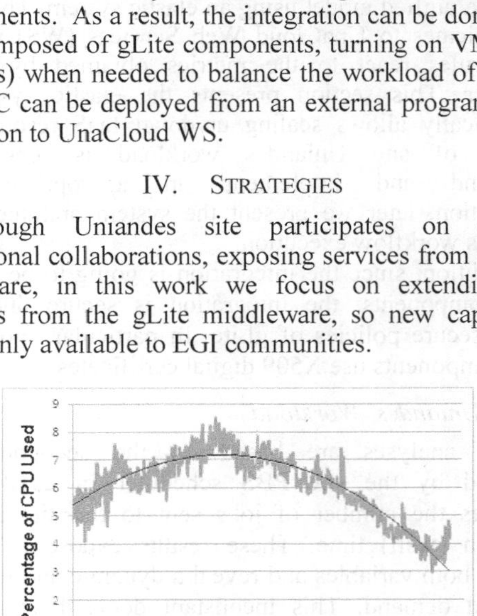

Figure 1. CPU usage of the computer labs

In order to accomplish an elastic integration of site Uniandes with IaaS resources, this section presents two different strategies we identified to achieve the integration of the infrastructures as well as three different approaches to carry out the monitoring needed to achieve elasticity.

A. Integration model

The first idea was to recreate a full gLite site using UnaCloud. We created site Sistemas, a gLite site with services running on a dedicated infrastructure, and WNs running on the opportunistic infrastructure. This model allows each site to handle independent information of its resources so it avoids overloading the scheduler component of the original site.

Although we have now a new site to process jobs, jobs sent directly to the Uniandes CreamCE (Computer Element) will not benefit of this new site. Only jobs sent to the WMS (Workload Management System) may be assigned to either two sites. As our primary goal is to unload site Uniandes of jobs no matter where these jobs come from, we added a connection between the schedulers on both systems (Fig. 2). This connection puts the opportunistic site as a subset of site Uniandes, allowing site Uniandes to consume resources from site Sistemas when needed. Fig. 2 shows the WN cluster of site Sistemas as a white dotted oval because of its opportunistic nature.

Besides being a complex configuration, management in this scenario becomes difficult because opportunistic nodes must be turned on to provide resources to both sites. Also administration costs of gLite environments are known to be high; having a whole new site to be managed leads us to look for a simpler solution.

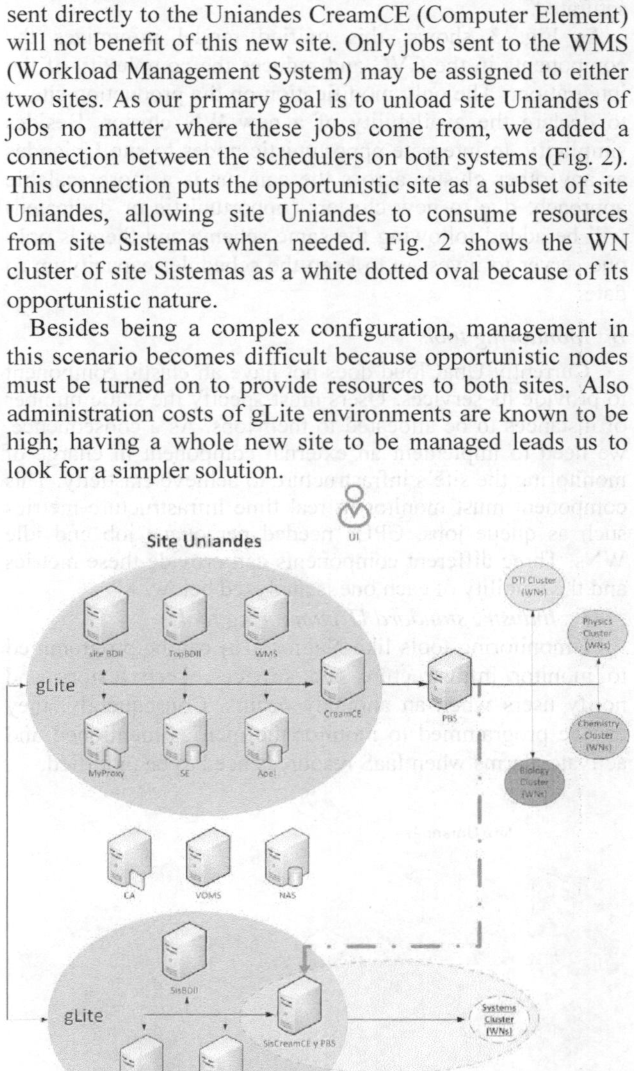

Figure 2. Two gLite sites integration

We decided then not to build a new site but a new Worker Node cluster. We created a complete cluster of WNs by building a CVC of gLite WNs. The stack of software running on this new cluster is an exact replica of the software running in any other cluster of site Uniandes. The only difference is that instead of running these new VMs on dedicated servers, they are running on desktops managed by UnaCloud. The CVC adds up to the site's infrastructure as a new WN cluster. These new WNs appear to the scheduler as available resources to assign jobs. This new cluster appears to the infrastructure as a normal cluster but we configure it in such a way, dedicated clusters are always preferred as WNs. These new IaaS resources are turned on only during peak loads, when the based infrastructure becomes saturated.

As Fig. 3 shows, this unified model minimizes the components in the CVC and reduces the complexity of the integration. The only modification on the production site is to declare the availability of a new WN cluster. Besides simplicity, to integrate opportunistic nodes to site Uniandes as any other cluster across the campus is a more scalable approach, due to new clusters (opportunistic or dedicated) will be added following the same schema and there is only one server to invest in to keep the scheduler capacity up to date.

B. *Monitoring tools*

Currently UnaCloud does not have an elastic component to provide its services. Users must specify the static number of instances to be allocated to their jobs. As a consequence, we need to implement an external component in charge of monitoring the site's infrastructure to achieve elasticity. This component must monitor in real time infrastructure metrics such as queue jobs, CPUs needed per queue job and idle WNs. Three different components can provide these metrics and the viability of each one is analyzed below.

1) Industry standard IT monitoring tools

IT monitoring tools like Nagios [16] can be programmed to monitor infrastructure and services, keep history and notify users when an anomaly occurs. Consequently, they can be programmed to monitor the metrics mentioned and activate alarms when IaaS resources need to be modified.

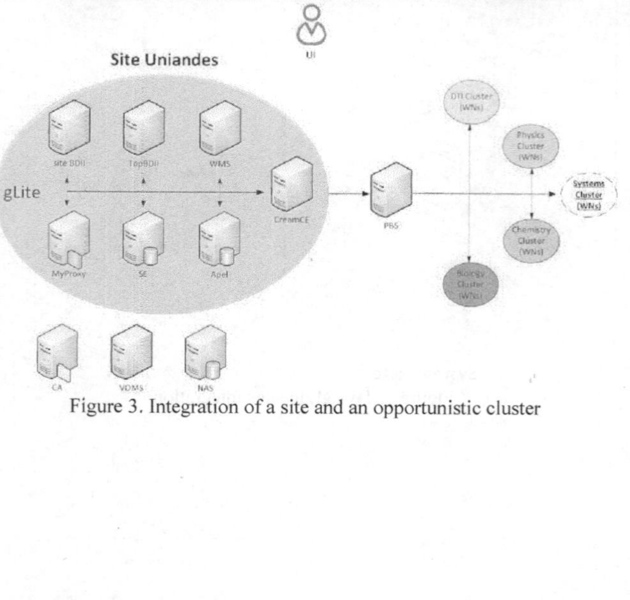

Figure 3. Integration of a site and an opportunistic cluster

These systems are normally available to monitor clusters on any grid site so they can be easily deployed on the new WN cluster.

2) Information systems for Grid Infrastructures

Site BDII is a gLite component managing all the information of a grid infrastructure, including the proposed metrics. However, as BDII must offer a view of the whole infrastructure, it obtains the information through reports from other components which adds important delays to the information gathering (3 to 5 minutes latency).

3) Internal site scheduler

A simpler solution is to use the same component that is currently providing some infrastructure metrics: the scheduler of the site, in this case a Torque PBS implementation. Using this component the elastic system can obtain the metrics in real time without intermediary components and without extra configurations.

We decided then to collect the necessary metrics from the scheduler to determine and adjust the IaaS resources of site Uniandes when needed. The elasticity is achieved through the definition of a set of elastic rules.

V. IMPLEMENTATION

Currently site Uniandes does not have an environment to carry out experiments with the infrastructure; therefore a new site was implemented to play the role of a development site. Again, we built a UnaCloud CVC using a simplified version of Uniandes site, deploying only gLite components.

The previous section established an elastic integration of a dedicated site known as site Uniandes with an opportunistic cloud infrastructure known as UnaCloud through a unified model using an elastic system. This system communicates to UnaCloud Web Services (WS) when the elastic rules react to the metrics obtained by the site scheduler. This section presents the elastic system that automatically allows scaling up/down IaaS resources. An analysis of site Uniandes workload is presented to understand and implement an appropriate elastic composition, later we present the system architecture and finally its workflow execution.

In addition, since the integration is going to be made by gLite components, the integration is secure due to the strictly secure policies of gLite. In particular, most of the CVC components use X509 digital certificates.

A. *Site Uniandes' Workload*

These analyses are based on the accounting logs generated by the site PBS scheduler in 2012. Fig. 4 elucidates the number of jobs sent to the site and their execution (wall) time. These results expose no relation between both variables and reveal a dynamic and inconstant workload demand. This inconstant demand supports the need for the elastic integration proposed in this work. Moreover, Table I presents the average queue time of the jobs executed by the site. These results also support the need for the elastic integration, which primary objective focus on dropping the waiting time to zero.

Current queue times are useful to determine a limit on the frequency to monitor the workload of the site, as we need to be able to react while jobs are waiting to be dispatched. Finally, jobs were analyzed in clusters, each cluster representing a scientific community. We wanted to find time patterns that would help predicting the kind of demand to be received by the site. Result patterns were not conclusive, reinforcing the need to monitor the infrastructure in order to undertake elastic actions.

Due to our decision of using the internal scheduler to monitor the infrastructure, we achieved a minimum overhead monitoring, allowing us to trigger the monitoring with a frequency of 5 minutes. This high frequency balances the workload of the site without filtering any type of jobs in the queue, and also allows us to turn off opportunistic resources when their idle time exceeds 10 minutes. Returning idle resources to the opportunistic pool is important because these resources may be needed for projects directly running on UnaCloud (or may generate a cost if integrating with public infrastructures).

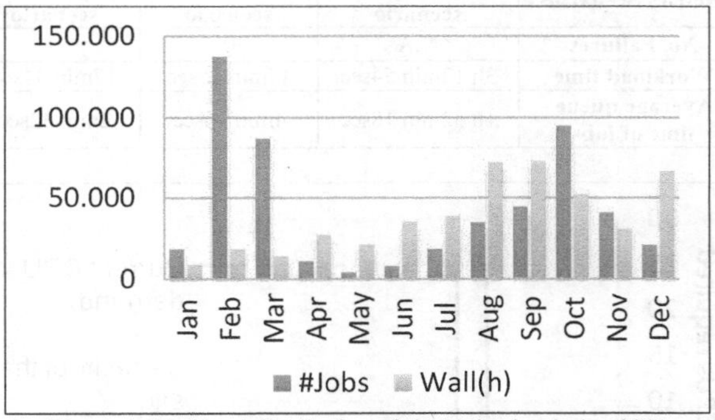

Figure 4. Workload distribution of site Uniandes during 2011

TABLE I. AVERAGE QUEUE TIME OF JOBS SENT TO SITE UNIANDES DURING 2011

Month	Queue Time (hours)
January	3.12
February	0.96
March	1.44
April	9,84
May	2.16
June	5.76
July	0.48
August	5.52
September	1.2
October	2.4
November	0.96
December	1.44

B. Architecture

The elastic system is a Java program that connects to site Uniandes scheduler (Torque PBS) every 5 minutes to gather real time data. When these metrics activate the elastic rules, the program connects to UnaCloud WS to adjust IaaS resources (WNs) necessary to balance the site's demand. The opportunistic IaaS resources forms a CVC composed of gLite components. The program runs onto the scheduler server to avoid communication delay.

The program components are illustrated in Fig. 5, where *Monitoring* is the component in charge of monitoring the infrastructure metrics to define the current demand. This component communicates with the scheduler consuming *CommandExec* services. *ElasticComponent* applies the elastic rules using *Monitoring* information in order to determine if the site's workload is above or below a threshold, and if so, it communicates with *UnaCloudWS* to adjust the number of IaaS opportunistic resources. In other words, the elastic system calculates, based on the current demand and certain policies, the number of opportunistic instances needed to lighten the load.

As UnaCloud opportunistic resources are also to be shared among several researchers, this system implements the "80 Percent" policy which avoids UnaCloud to deliver WNs if its own utilization ratio is above 80 percent. This rule guarantees a minimum of available resources to UnaCloud's users during massive spikes in site Uniandes' workload.

Since UnaCloud current limitation does not support the execution of more than one VM on a desktop computer, the "Fully Optimize Resources" strategy tries to optimize the use of the desktop capacities. For this reason the elastic system only turns on resources to extend the site capacity when they can be fully utilized. In other words, when the number of queue jobs trespass a given threshold related to the desktop physical capabilities.

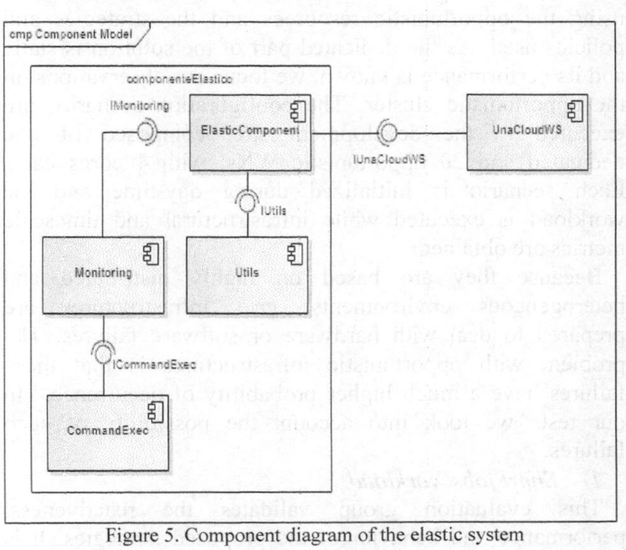

Figure 5. Component diagram of the elastic system

Finally, to guarantee that the extension of opportunistic resources will only take place when site Uniandes is fully loaded, the policy "Offline/Online" is intended for dedicated resources to take precedence over opportunistic resources when available. The strategy consists in changing the opportunistic WNs state to offline when fully loaded. An offline state implies a WN continuing to process their assign tasks but not accepting any more. Eventually the WN will become idle and shut down after 10 minutes (or just before complete an hour in case of using a public IaaS [17], due to in most public IaaS CPU costs are based in an hour period). This translates into a quick increase and a slow decrease in IaaS resources. In addition, the system always checks offline resources before turning on new WNs.

C. *Workflow*

The elastic workflow can be divided into three major activities. The first is in charge of monitoring metrics required to turn on (or online) IaaS resources. This activity applies the "80Percent", "Offline/Online" and "Fully Optimize Resources" strategies. The second major activity is in charge of monitoring the opportunistic infrastructure. Due to its volatility, the elastic system checks for failures and if detected, redirects the jobs that were being executed on failed WNs. Also it applies "Offline/Online" to WNs when fully loaded. Finally the third activity monitors the metrics needed to shut-down opportunistic resources, looking for current WNs in idle state for more than 10 minutes.

VI. Validation

The evaluation of the elastic integration is divided in two parts. The first aims to evaluate the performance and reactiveness of the integration while the second analyses the behavior of the elastic system workflow.

A. *Performance of test site*

Three evaluation groups were designed to analyze the reactiveness and performance of the system, the viability for using the opportunistic resources and the strategies and policies used. As the dedicated part of the solution is static and its performance is known, we focus our observations on the opportunistic cluster. The configuration scenarios are executed in the development site, composed of one dedicated and 20 opportunistic WNs, with 4 cores each. Each scenario is initialized during day-time and the workload is executed while infrastructural and timescale metrics are obtained.

Because they are based on highly distributed and heterogeneous environments, grid infrastructures are prepared to deal with hardware or software failures. The problem with opportunistic infrastructures is that these failures have a much higher probability of occurrence. In our tests we took into account the possibility of such failures.

1) *Short jobs workload*

This evaluation group validates the reactiveness, performance and behavior of the proposed strategies. It is composed of two tests, each one with a workload of approximately 10 minutes jobs. The first test executes 22 jobs at once (1 core each) and these are the only jobs executed in 3 scenarios. The first scenario does not utilize the elastic integration, the second utilizes it during the night, reproducing a dedicated environment and the third one, utilized in all the tests, is executed during day-time. Table II presents the evaluation metrics measured in the different scenarios and Fig. 6 shows the reactiveness of the site during the last scenario.

Table II shows no failures during the tests, making short jobs suitable for opportunistic infrastructures. The workload time and the average queue waiting time decreases drastically with the elastic feature, showing a good performance of the site. This can also be seen graphically in Fig. 6, where the opportunistic resources are turned on to balance the workload of the site and are turned off once the spike is over.

TABLE II. Evaluation metrics of the scenarios of test 1

Metrics Scenarios	Dedicated scenario	Night-time scenario	Day-time scenario
No. Failures	N.A	0	0
Workload time	3h 12min 54sec	17min 25sec	17min 34sec
Average queue time of jobs	1h 32min 18sec	4min 16sec	2min 32sec

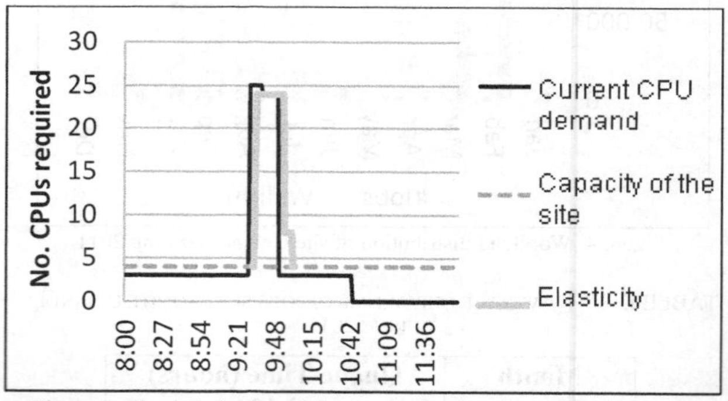

Figure 6. Elastic behavior of the site during day-time scenario in test 1

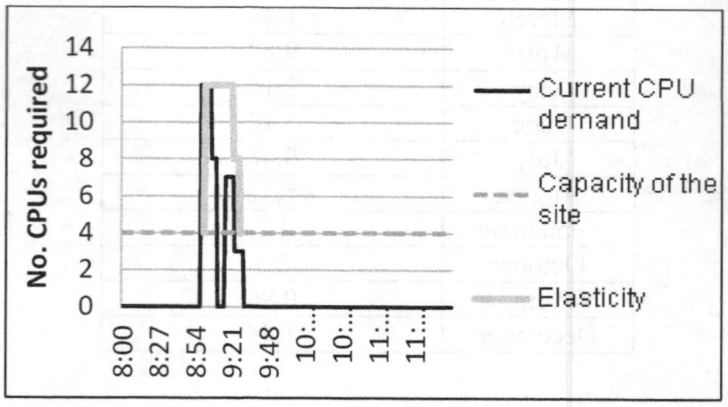

Figure 7. Elastic behavior of the site in test 2

The second test executes 12 jobs (1 core each), waits 13 minutes and executes 7 jobs (1 core each). The idea of this test is to evaluate "Offline/Online" and the strategy to increase rapidly and decrease slowly. The 13 minutes are broken down in 10 minutes short job execution plus 3 minutes where the resources remain idle but active. Fig. 7 clarifies the execution test and shows a good reaction to the workloads. From this it can be concluded that the strategies are a good practice. In addition, no failures where presented during this test.

2) Medium jobs workload

This group of medium jobs has the goal of examining the viability for using opportunistic resources in grid infrastructures. It executes a workload of 5 jobs (4 cores each, one job per WN) of approximately 3 hours. Table III shows the metric wall time in order to compare the computing capability of a dedicated versus opportunistic resources. When the workload is launched, 4 opportunistic WNs are turned on to balance the site. The execution time varies in the IaaS resources due to its opportunistic feature. Moreover the worst execution time belongs to the dedicated WN, which implies that opportunistic resources are better, mainly because they are more frequently updated. Table IV exposes the processor features of the WNs of both sites (Uniandes and test). These tests confirm the statement that in some grid environments opportunistic resources can be faster. Opportunistic resources may be volatile but the better capacity makes them a good choice to help balance the site. Lastly, no failures where executed during this test.

3) Extended jobs workload

The last experiment was built to analyze the site behavior during IaaS resources failures. A workload of 10 jobs (4 cores each) with an execution time of 8 hours was carried out. Although no natural failure occurred, we induced one for the purpose of this work. Results showed that elastic system has also a good reactiveness to detect failures. A job executed by a down WN is re-launched to the queue so it can be processed again by an active resource. The major drawback is the loss of all the previous processing data.

TABLE III. EVALUATION METRICS OF TEST 3

Resources	Wall Time	No. Failures
Dedicated	3h 27min 16sec	N.A
Opportunistic 1	2h 50min 34sec	0
Opportunistic 2	2h 55min 25sec	0
Opportunistic 3	3h 04min 36sec	0
Opportunistic 4	3h 00min 12seg	0

TABLE IV. CHARACTERISTICS OF THE WN PROCESSORS

Resources	Processor
Opportunistic	Intel core i5@ 3.33 GHz
Dedicated site test	Intel Xeon @ 2.27 GHz
Dedicated1 site Uniandes	Intel Xeon @ 1.6 GHz
Dedicated 2 site Uniandes	Intel Xeon @ 2.93 GHz
Dedicated 3 site Uniandes	Intel Xeon @ 3.00 GHz

B. Behaviour of the elastic workflow

This section analyzes the time spent by the three major activities of the elastic workflow presented early. The time of each activity was taken in all the evaluation tests. Three common scenarios were identified and are shown in Table V. The first is the execution of a normal cycle where nothing happens to the IaaS resources; the second is when the site is fully loaded and needs to turn on WNs; the third scenario is when the workload spike ends and opportunistic resources need to be turned off.

Results show that turning on IaaS resources is a costly activity compared to monitor or even to turn them off. This increase is proportional to the IaaS resources needed but an average measure indicates it is in the order of a few minutes. In contrast, the order to turn down IaaS resources is in the order of seconds. The results also support the strategy to decrease slowly the resources, because it prevents incurring in initialization costs when IaaS resources are available.

The resource consumption of the elastic system where also monitored to see if it incurred in extra costs to the host machine. Results show that CPU and RAM consumption are really low.

VII. Conclusion and Future Work

In this work we implemented a secure elastic integration of a production gLite based grid site with an opportunistic infrastructure implementing the IaaS model. In this way, the grid site may dynamically extend its processing capabilities with opportunistic IaaS resources, according to its current workload and utilizing only extra resources when needed. The integration is achieved by configuring the IaaS resources as a replica of a WN cluster of the production site. The size of this virtual opportunistic cluster varies according to the dynamic needs of the grid site. This elastic integration address to enlarge the collaboration between research groups at a local, national and international arena without incurring in infrastructural extra costs and utilizing the minimum number of resources. It also shows that organizations with low budget to provision grid initiatives with dedicated resources can also support them with opportunistic resources.

Our validation results show that the elastic integration provided site Uniandes a good reactiveness to unexpected spikes in the workload, being able to satisfy the demands of the associated scientific organizations with a minimum delay. This integration is transparent to the users, has a low computational cost and is scalable by itself allowing the integration of new clusters with minimum intrusion on the grid site.

TABLE V. EVALUATION OF THE ELASTIC WORKFLOW

Scenarios	First Activity Monitoring Dedicated gLite Resources to Scale Them	Second Activity Monitoring Opportunistic UnaCloud Resources	Third Activity Turning off UnaCloud Resources non-used by gLite Site
Normal	29 sec	35 sec	1 sec
Overload site	3min 20sec	35 sec	1 sec
Weigh down site	30 sec	35 sec	10 sec

The elasticity is achieved by elastic rules based on infrastructure metrics obtained by the batch scheduler. The site's workload was analyzed to determine the parameters of the elastic rules. An idle period of 10 minutes was established in order to shutdown IaaS resources and a frequency of 5 minutes was determined to monitor the scheduler of the site. The validation showed that the elastic integration provided the site a good reactiveness to unexpected spikes in the workload, being able to satisfy the demands of the users with a minimum delay. The scaling and monitoring strategies turned out adequate.

For future work, UnaCloud must be extended to overcome its limitation of deploying only 1 VM per desktop. This will allow a more efficient sharing of its resources. Also, the dedicated resources could be used in an opportunistic approach to support UnaCloud's jobs when they require a special SLA. The workload analysis of the site suggests that sometimes the site resources may be used in an opportunistic way. In addition, the analysis of the site's workload must be done constantly to update the parameters of the elastic system, as well to validate a good reactiveness to the workload in all times. The elastic system may implement other strategies, and could be evaluated in a non-controlled workload environment. The integration can also be tested with another IaaS provider, like Amazon Web Services [18].

References

[1] gLite. (2012, November) gLite - Lightweight Middleware for Grid Computin. [Online]. http://glite.cern.ch/

[2] P. Ruth, P. McGachey, and Dongyan Xu, "VioCluster: Virtualization for Dynamic Computational Domains," in *Cluster Computing, 2005. IEEE International* , Burlington, MA , 2005, pp. 1-10.

[3] Hui Zhang, Guofei Jiang, Kenji Yoshihira, Haifeng Chen, and Akhilesh Saxena, "Intelligent Workload Factoring for A Hybrid Cloud Computing Model," *SERVICES '09 Proceedings of the 2009 Congress on Services*, 2009.

[4] Paul Marshall, Kate Keahey, and Tim Freeman, "Elastic Site: Using clouds to elastically extend site resources," in *Cluster, Cloud and Grid Computing (CCGrid), 2010 10th IEEE/ACM International Conference on* , Melbourne, Australia , 2010, pp. 43-52.

[5] Eduardo Rosales, Mario Villamizar Harold Castro, "UnaCloud: A Desktop Grid and Cloud Computing Solution," in *The Second International Conference on Parallel, Distributed, Grid and Cloud Computing for Engineering*, Ajaccio, France, 2011.

[6] Andrei Goldchleger, Fabio Kon, Alfredo Goldman, and Marcelo Finger, "InteGrade: Object-Oriented Grid Middleware Leveraging Idle Computing Power of Desktop Machines," *Concurrency and Computation: Practice & Experience - Middleware for Grid Computing*, vol. 16, no. 5, April 2004.

[7] EDGES. (2012, November) EDGES: Enabling Desktop grids for e-science. [Online]. http://www.edges-grid.eu/

[8] Moreno-Vozmediano R., Montero R.S., and Llorente I.M., "Multicloud Deployment of Computing Clusters for Loosely Coupled MTC Applications," *IEEE Transactions on Parallel and Distributed Systems*, vol. 22, no. 6, pp. 924-930, June 2011.

[9] J.P. Smets-Solanes and R. Courteaud, "SlapOS: A Multi-Purpose Distributed Cloud Operating System Based on an ERP Billing Model," in *2011 IEEE International Conference on Services Computing (SCC)*, 2011, pp. 765-766.

[10] Amazon Web Services. (2012, November) Amazon Elastic Compute Cloud. [Online]. http://aws.amazon.com/es/ec2//190-2014314-7227319/

[11] J.M. Tirado, D. Higuero, F. Isaila, and J. Carretero, "Predictive Data Grouping and Placement for Cloud-Based Elastic Server Infrastructures," *2011 11th IEEE/ACM International Symposium on Cluster, Cloud and Grid Computing*, pp. 285-294, May 2011.

[12] David Meisner, Brian T. Gold, and Thomas F. Wenisch, "PowerNap: eliminating server idle power," *ACM SIGPLAN Notices - ASPLOS 2009*, vol. 44, March 2009.

[13] Peter Bodík et al., "Statistical machine learning makes automatic control practical for internet datacenters," *HotCloud'09 Proceedings of the 2009 conference on Hot topics in cloud computing*, p. 12, June 2009.

[14] Universidad de los Andes. (2012, November) Grid Universidad de los Andes. [Online]. http://tibana.uniandes.edu.co/wikigrid/doku.php?id=infraestructura_sitio

[15] Arthur Alejandro Oviedo, Plataforma basada en UNACLOUD para la generación y análisis de alineamientos múltiples de secuencias, 2011, Tesis de Maestría de Ingeniería de Sistemas y Computación.

[16] Nagios Enterprises. (2012, November) Nagios. [Online]. http://www.nagios.org/

[17] João Nuno Silva, Luís Veiga, and Paulo Ferreira, "A2HA—automatic and adaptive host allocation in utility computing for bag-of-tasks," *Journal of Internet Services and Applications*, vol. 2, no. 2, pp. 171-185, September 2011.

[18] amazon.com. (2012, November) Amazon Web Services. [Online]. http://aws.amazon.com/es/

Instantaneous Availability-Aware Scheduling Method for Parallel Task in Cloud Environment

Jie Cao ,Guosun Zeng
Department of Computer Science and Technology, Tongji University, Shanghai, China
Tongji Branch, National Engineering & Technology Center of High Performance Computer
Shanghai, China

Abstract - *Cloud computing is a new emerging computing paradigm that advocates supplying users everything as a service. High availability is a key requirement in design and development of cloud computing systems where processors operate at different speeds and are not continuously available for computation. This paper addresses the main factors of availability requirement for parallel tasks based on the graph structure of parallel task. We present the formulas to quantify the availability requirements of parallel tasks and availability support of computing resources. Through being aware of availability, we realize the availability matching between availability requirement and availability support, and develop an availability aware scheduling algorithms, that is Availability-DLS.*

Keywords: *cloud computing, availability requirement availability support, task scheduling*

1 Introduction

Cloud computing is a new emerging computing paradigm that advocates supplying users everything as a service. Cloud computing becomes more and more popular in large scale computing and data store recently due to it enables the sharing of computing resources that are distributed all over the world. Cloud computing may become the dominant enterprise and business-to-consumer computing paradigm within the next many years.

Large scale cloud computing infrastructure are unified computing platform which tries to connect and shares all resources in the Internet, including computation resource, storage resource, information resource, knowledge resource and equipment for scientific research. However, with the characteristics of dynamic join and exit, hardware or software failure, operating maintenance, system upgrade, how to obtain available computing resource becomes a key issue in large-scale cloud computing research.High availability is a key requirement in the design and development of cloud computing systems where processors operate at different speeds and are not continuously available for computation.Some work has been done to investigate resource allocation schemes for tasks with availability constraints. Smith introduced a mathematical model for resource availability and then proposed a method to maintain availability information as new reservations or assignments are made [1]. Adiri et al. addressed the scheduling issue in a single machine with availability constraints [2].Qi et al. developed three heuristic algorithms to tackle the problem of scheduling jobs while maintaining machines simultaneously [3].Very recently, Kacem et al. investigated a branch-and-bound method to solve the single-machine scheduling problem with availability constraints [4]. Lee studied the two-machine scheduling problem in which an availability constraint is imposed on one machine as well as on both machines[5].The problem was optimally solved by Lee using pseudopolynomial dynamic programming algorithms. Mosheiov addressed the scheduling issue in the context of identical parallel machines with availability constraints [6]. Qin et al. propose a scheduling algorithm to improve the availability of heterogeneous systems while maintaining good performance in the response time of tasks[7].

Although the above schemes considered scheduling problems with availability constraints, they are inadequate for multiclass applications running in cloud computing systems because they either focused on a single machine[2],[3],[4], two machines[5], or a homogeneous system [6].Besides, most of task types are most independent tasks [7] and the availability of computing resources is fixed. To remedy this issue, in this paper, we address the problem of scheduling parallel tasks with availability constraints in heterogeneous systems whose computational resources are dynamic change in availability. Specifically, we present the formulas to compute availability requirement of parallel tasks and availability support of computing resources. Through being aware of availability, we develop an availability aware scheduling algorithms, that is Availability-DLS. The simulation experimental results show that such algorithm is significant to improve the success rate of parallel task scheduling in practice.

The rest of this paper is organized as follows. Section 2 introduces the parallel tasks and system modeling and assumptions. Section 3 describes availability requirement and availability support. Section 4 describes the details of the proposed Availability-DLS. The evaluation of our approach by simulations is given in Section 5. Finally we conclude this paper with future works in Section 6.

2 Task and system modeling and assumptions

2.1 Parallel task modeling

In cloud computing environment, there may be constraints priority between tasks, for instance, a node can not start execution before it get all information from its father nodes. Taking into account the precedence constraints between tasks, we can use a directed acyclic graph DAG to represents them.

Definition 1 (Parallel Tasks). Parallel tasks to be scheduled are represented by a directed acyclic graph (DAG), called a task graph G = (V, E,W, D). In general, the nodes represent tasks partitioned from an application, and the edges represent precedence constraints. An edge $e_{ij} \in E$ represents the communication from node v_i to node v_j .In other words, the output of task v_i has to be transmitted to task v_j in order for task v_j to start its execution. A task with no predecessors is called an *entry* task, v_{entry}, whereas an *exit* task, v_{exit}, is one that does not have any successors.

The weight on a task v_i, denoted as w_i, represents the computation volume of the task. The weight on an edge, denoted as $d_{ij} \in D$, represents the communication volume between two tasks, v_i and v_j. However, communication volume is only required when two tasks are assigned to different processors. In other words, the communication volume when tasks are assigned to the same processor can be ignored, i.e., 0.

A simple task graph is shown in Fig. 1 with eight nodes. Without loss of generality, it is assumed that there is one entry node to the DAG and one exit node from the DAG.

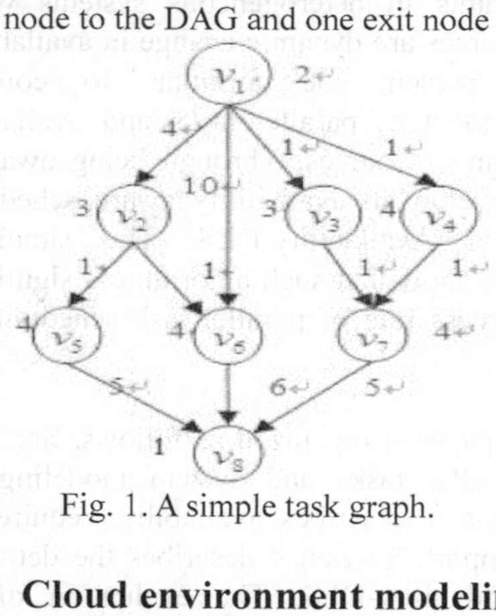

Fig. 1. A simple task graph.

2.2 Cloud environment modeling

The mode of computing nodes connection is complicated in cloud computing, which may be regular such as bus, loop, star and so on or irregular. This paper depicts cloud resources system composition by the general map.

Definition 2 (Cloud Platform). A realistic cloud system is modeled as a graph CT=(R,E,S,B),where $R = \{r_1, r_2, ..., r_m\}$ is a set of resource vertices, $C = \{c_{ij} \mid r_i, r_j \in R\}$ is a set of communication links, $S = \{s_1, s_2, ..., s_m\}$ is a set of resource calculation speed, $B = \{b_{ij} \mid r_i, r_j \in R, c_{ij} \in C\}$ is a set of communication bandwidth in C. A vertex $r \in R$ is referred to as a cloud computing resource. A edge $c_{ij} \in C$ represents a communication link from network vertex r_i to network vertex r_j, $r_i, r_j \in R$ .The nonnegative weight $b_{ij} \in B$, associated with a link $c_{ij} \in C$, represents its data communication rate. The nonnegative weight $s_i \in S$, associated with a $r_i \in R$, represents its computing speed, that is the time needed of complete unit load.

2.3 The basic hypothesis of parallel task scheduling

The task-scheduling problem in this study is the process of allocating a set V of v tasks to a set P of p processors to take into account the availability matching between availability requirement and availability support, without violating precedence constraints. Each task in this paper is atomic and not subdivided, which is non-preemptive execution. The task unified management by the center scheduler is assigned to the appropriate computing resources in accordance with a strategy for each subtask. Besides, center scheduler is independent of computing resources.

3 Availability defintion

3.1 Availability concept

The availability of the computer system refers to the proportion of normal service time in the total system run time, which can be measured by a percentage or a probability value. The popular resource availability means resources in serviceable condition and resource management system can access them. Quantitative value of resource availability can be seen as a probability of resource successful service delivery. From the perspective of the user service, resource availability describes the possibility of a resource over time in the available state.

Definition 3 (Availability). Let $F = \{F_i\}_{i=1}^{\infty}$ be a set of functionalities provided by the system. Let $I = \{I_i\}_{i=1}^{\infty}$ be a set of implementation of F, which can be used and got the service function of the service effect collection by the user, namely, $I = \{I_i\}_{i=1}^{\infty}$, $I \subset F$. System availability is defined as $A = \frac{|I|}{|F|}$.

In order to further discuss the availability concept, this paper divides availability into “availability requirement” and “availability support”.

Definition 4 (Availability Support). The availability support is relative to the computing system, i.e., the system can provide how much service function.

Definition 5 (Availability Requirement). The availability requirement is relative to the parallel tasks, i.e., the availability requirement specifying how much functional requirement a task need.

3.2 DAG tasks availability requirement

Parallel tasks may have more than one subtask and each subtask is different about the function, role and importance in parallel tasks, so we must make a difference between them to the service function demand. The degree of subtask availability needs can be defined from subtask node outdegree, the critical path and subtask execution sequence priority, etc. according to the structure of the DAG.

3.2.1 Outdegree weight

The bigger node outdegree, the greater influence on the subsequent nodes, the more it can increase the degree of concurrent execution of subsequent subtasks if the subtask is successfully completed, which has the greater availability requirements. Intuitively, subtask whose outdegree is two needs twice as much availability requirement as subtask whose outdegree is one and subtask whose outdegree is three needs triple as much availability requirement as subtask whose outdegree is one. However, one node whose outdegree is zero needs special treatment. Therefore, the weight in outdegree is defined as follows:

$$W_{Od}(v_i) = \begin{cases} \dfrac{Od(v_i)}{\max_{j=1}^{n}(Od(v_j))}, & Od(v_i) \neq 0 \\ \dfrac{\min_{j=1}^{n}(Od(v_j))}{\max_{j=1}^{n}(Od(v_j))}, & Od(v_i) = 0 \end{cases}$$

3.2.2 Critical Path Weight

The critical path, i.e. the path in the directed acyclic graph (DAG) on which the sum of the edge and node weights is maximal, denoted as Cp. Effective scheduling of critical path nodes will largely reduce the completion time of the task graph, therefore, the task node coefficient on the critical path is designated as 1 and the task node coefficient on the non-critical path is designated as 0.5. Therefore, the weight in critical path is defined as follows:

$$W_{Cp}(v_i) = \begin{cases} 1, & v_i \in Cp \\ 0.5 & v_i \notin Cp \end{cases}.$$

3.2.3 Task Execution Order Priority

DAG graph dependency exists in the execution sequence, the task whose predecessor task are completed can begin execution, therefore, we introduce task execution order priority $rank(v_i)$ to distinguish the different tasks in task graph priority scheduling sequence. The exit task node execution order priority is designated as 1, and task node v_i 's successor is expressed as $Succ(v_i)$. Therefore, task v_i execution order priority may be defined as follows:

$$rank(v_i) = \begin{cases} 1 & Succ(v_i) = \varnothing \\ \max\limits_{v \in Succ(v_i)} \{rank(v)\} + 1 & Succ(v_i) \neq \varnothing \end{cases}.$$

In this paper, task node v_i 's execution order priority weight is designated as

$$W_{rank}(v_i) = \exp\left(\frac{rank(v_i) - \max_{j=1}^{n}(rank(v_j))}{\max_{j=1}^{n}(rank(v_j))}\right).$$

3.2.4 Availability requirements of task node unified computing

In the DAG graph, the priority of a task indicates task scheduling priority level. The greater the outdegree and more the follow-up tasks of a task, which successful execution can improve the degree of parallel execution of multiple subsequent tasks.The critical path nodes effective scheduling will largely reduce task execution time of the task graph. Therefore, the availability requirements of the task node can be seen as a combined result of these three factors i.e., the greater the priority of the task node, the greater the outdegree of the task node, the task on the critical path, the greater the availability requirement of the task node.Therefore, task v_i availability requirement $A_T(v_i)$ is designated as follows:

$$A_T(v_i) = \alpha W_{od}(v_i) + \beta W_{cp}(v_i) + \gamma W_{rank}(v_i),$$

$$\alpha + \beta + \gamma = 1.$$

3.3 Cloud platform node availability support

In reality, the availability support of a computer system can be improved by means of system maintenance. System maintenance personnel repair the faulty system and the repaired system can continue to perform its function. The Markov-type repairable system is the most commonly used repairable system in practice, so this paper assumes that every computing resources is the Markov repairable.

3.3.1 Markov process definition

This paper assumes that {X(t),t ≥0} is a time-homogeneous Markov process to take values in E={0,1,...,N}. For future reference, we summarize the notation that is used throughout this paper in Table 1.

TABLE 1 Definitions of notation

Notation	Definition
$P_{ij}(t)$	Transfer probability function.($i, j \in E$)
$P(T)$	Matrix of transition probability.
$N(t)$	State transition frequency in $(0,t]$.

This paper assumes that Markov process {X(t),t ≥0} transfer probability function satisfies $\lim_{t\to 0} P_{ij}(t) = \delta_{ij} = \begin{cases} 1, for\ \ i=j \\ 0, for\ \ i\neq j \end{cases}$. Transfer probability function has the following properties: $P_{ij}(t) \geq 0$, $\sum_{j\in E} P_{ij}(t) = 1$, $\sum_{k\in E} P_{ik}(u)P_{kj}(v) = P_{ij}(u+v)$ .Let $P_j(t)$ =P{X(t)=j} be the probability of computing resource in state j at moment i, thus getting $P_j(t) = \sum_{k\in E} P_k(0)P_{kj}(t)$. Time-homogeneous Markov process has the following properties 00:

1) The time-homogeneous Markov process with limited state space has the following limit:

$$\begin{cases} \lim_{\Delta t\to 0} \dfrac{P_{ij}(\Delta t)}{\Delta t} = q_{ij}, & i\neq j,\ i,j\in E \\ \lim_{\Delta t\to 0} \dfrac{1-P_{ii}(\Delta t)}{\Delta t} = q_i, & i\in E \end{cases} \quad \text{........... (2)}$$

2) Process{X(t), t ≥0} state transition moment is expressed as $T_1, T_2, ..., T_n$. $X(T_n)$ is the state that the process visits after the nth state transition is be completed. If $X(T_n)=x$, $T_{n+1}-T_n$ is the sojourn time that process is in state i. Have the following lemma established:

Lemma 1. For $\forall i, j\in E$, we have $P\{T_{n+1}-T_n > u \mid X(T_n)=i, X(T_{n+1})=j)\} = e^{-q_i u}$ ($n=$ 0,1,...) which has nothing to do with n and state j.

Lemma 2. For sufficiently small $\Delta t > 0$, we have $P\{N(t+\Delta t) - N(t) \geq 2\} = o(\Delta t)$.

3.3.2 Markov repairable system general model

Assume that a repairable system has N + 1 state, where the state 0,1, ..., K is the system's normal operating state; the state K+1,...,N is the system's fault state. Let W={0,1,...,K} be normal operating state set and F={K+1, K+1,...,N} be fault state set. In sufficiently small time Δt, transfer probability function meet:

$$P_{ij}(\Delta t) = a_{ij}\Delta t + o(\Delta t),\ \ i,\ j\in E,\ i\neq j \text{........(3)}$$

where { $a_{ij}: i, j\in E,$ } has be given prior and state transfer probability is expressed as a_{ij}. Obviously, we have

$$P_{ii}(\Delta t) = 1 - \sum_{\substack{j\neq i\\ j\in E}} P_{ij}(\Delta t) = 1 - \sum_{\substack{j\neq i\\ j\in E}} P_{ij}(\Delta t) + o(\Delta t)$$

Let $a_{ii} = -\sum_{\substack{j\neq i\\ j\in E}} a_{ij}$, so we have

$$P_{ii}(\Delta t) = 1 + a_{ii}\Delta t + o(\Delta t) \quad \text{............ (4).}$$

we know $a_{ij} = \begin{cases} q_{ij}, & i\neq j,\ i,j\in E \\ -q, & i\neq j,\ i,j\in E \end{cases}$ from (2).

3.3.3 Resource nodes instantaneous availability support

Formally, instantaneous availability support of a system is the probability that the system is not only performing properly without failures, but also satisfying the specified performance requirements 0. The instantaneous availability support of so-called computing resource at the time *t* refers to the probability that the computing resource is in a normal state. The instantaneous availability support only relates to the computing resource and is not concerned with whether happened failure in the past.

Definition 6 (Instantaneous Availability Support). For a given initial state distribution $P_0(0)$, $P_1(0)$,... , $P_N(0)$, the computing resource r_i instantaneous availability support at the time t is designated as $A_{r_i}(t) = \sum_{j\in W} P_j(t)$, where $P_j(t)$ ($j\in W$) is the solution of following differential equations $\begin{cases} P_i'(t) = \sum_{k\in E} P_k(t)a_{ki}, & i\in E \\ \text{initial condition: } P_0(0), P_1(0), ..., P_N(0) \end{cases}$

Proof. By the total probability formula and the formula (3), (4), we obtain

$$P_i(t+\Delta t) = \sum_{k\in E} P_k(t)P_{ki}(\Delta t)$$

$$= P_i(t)P_{ii}(\Delta t) + \sum_{\substack{k\in E\\ k\neq i}} P_k(t)P_{ki}(\Delta t)$$

$$= P_i(t) + \sum_{k\in E} P_k(t)a_{ki}\Delta t + o(\Delta t) \text{ ,namely,}$$

$\frac{P_i(t+\Delta t)-P_i(t)}{\Delta t}=\sum_{k\in E}P_k(t)a_{ki}+\frac{o(\Delta t)}{\Delta t}$ whose right-hand limit exists when Δt tends to zero, so left-hand also limit exists. The proof is complete.

This paper assume that every computing resource only has two states work and fault with 0 said normal state and 1 said fault state. Computing resources lifetime X follows exponential distribution $P\{X\le t\}=1-e^{-\lambda t}$ ($t\ge 0$, $\lambda>0$). The fault repair time Y follows exponential distribution $P\{Y\le t\}=1-e^{-\mu t}$ $(t\ge 0,$ $\mu>0$). Assumes that X and Y are independent, the repaired fault computing resource's is the same as the new computing resource. For the process $\{X(t),t\ge 0\}$, which exists the following conclusion:

Conclusion: $\{X(t),t\ge 0\}$ is a continuous time time-homogeneous Markov process with limited state space.

Proof. The distribution of computing resources lifetime and repair time follow exponential distribution, so the law of computing resources development after t is entirely decided by computing resources being in work or fault at time t which has nothing to do with how long time has repaired or worked. Therefore, $\{X(t),t\ge 0\}$ is time-homogeneous Markov process.

For above Markov process, we obtain $P_{00}(\Delta t)=1-\lambda\Delta t+o(\Delta t)$,

$P_{01}(\Delta t)=\lambda\Delta t+o(\Delta t)$, $P_{10}(\Delta t)=\mu\Delta t+o(\Delta t)$, $P_{11}(\Delta t)=1-\mu\Delta t+o(\Delta t)$. Therefore, transfer matrix is $A=\begin{pmatrix}-\lambda & \lambda\\ \mu & -\mu\end{pmatrix}$.

If the computing resource r_i is in work at time t=0, we obtain r_i 's instantaneous availability support $A_R(r_i)|_t=P_0(t)=\frac{\mu}{\lambda+\mu}+\frac{\lambda}{\lambda+\mu}e^{-(\lambda+\mu)t}$ from definition 6 .

If the computing resource r_i is in fault at time t=0, we obtain r_i 's instantaneous availability support $A_R(r_i)|_t=\frac{\mu}{\lambda+\mu}-\frac{\mu}{\lambda+\mu}e^{-(\lambda+\mu)t}$ from definition 6.

4 Instantaneous availability aware dynamic level scheduling

The dynamic level scheduling (DLS) algorithm is a compile time, static list scheduling heuristic which has been developed to allocate a DAG-structure application to a set of heterogeneous computing resources to minimize the execution time of the application 0. At each scheduling step, the DLS algorithm chooses the next task to schedule and the computing resource on which that task is to be executed by finding the ready task and computing resource pair that have the highest dynamic level. The dynamic level of a task-computing resource (v_i,r_j) is defined to be

$$DL(v_i,r_j)=SL(v_i)-\max\{t^A_{i,j},t^R_j\}+\Delta(v_i,r_j) ,$$

where $SL(v_i)$ is called the static level of the task, $\max\{t^A_{i,j},t^R_j\}$ is the time when task v_i can begin execution on computing resource r_j , $t^A_{i,j}$ denotes the time when the data will be available if task v_i is scheduled on computing resource r_j , and t^R_j denotes the time when computing resource r_j will be available for the execution of task v_i . $\Delta(v_i,r_j)=t^E_i-t^E_{i,j}$ reflects the computing performance of the computing resource, t^E_i denotes the execution time of the task v_i on all the free computing resources, and $t^E_{i,j}$ denotes the execution time of task v_i on computing resource r_j .

When making a decision of scheduling, DLS algorithm considers the heterogeneous computing resources, which can adapt the heterogeneous characteristics of resources in cloud environment, but it neglects the availability support of resource nodes in the cloud system. When a task is scheduled to execute on a computing resource, the availability support of the resource reflects the availability of the service it supplies. To address this problem, the availability-dynamic level scheduling algorithm (Availability-DLS) in cloud environment is developed, and the availability dynamic level can be defined as follows: $ADL(v_i,r_j)=A_R(r_j)^{1-A_T(v_i)}(SL(v_i)-\max\{t^A_{i,j},t^R_j\}+\Delta(v_i,r_j))$ .The formula indicates that larger availability requirement task has larger availability dynamic level and larger availability support computing resource has larger availability dynamic level in the case of the same dynamic level tasks. The formula takes into consideration the dynamic level of the task, availability requirement of the task and availability support of computing resource, which is a comprehensive reflection of above three factors.

5 Simulated experiment analysis

The paper uses simulation to assess the effectiveness of the job scheduling algorithm presented in this paper. Simulation program is adapted from CloudSim platform 0. Based on CloudSim simulation environment, the node number and the link number between the nodes are given in advance and transmission speed of link is generated between 1 and 10 Megabits /sec.The initial availability support of the computing resource is randomly generated in [0,1].

5.1 Performance impact of tasks number

In this simulation experiment, CCR is set to 1, task graph with 20 to 120 subtasks is generated from the benchmark application library, and the number of computing nodes and links are both set to 200. We compared Availability-DLS with DLS and BSA in the scheduling length and the ratio of successful execution. Figs.2 and 3 show the results.

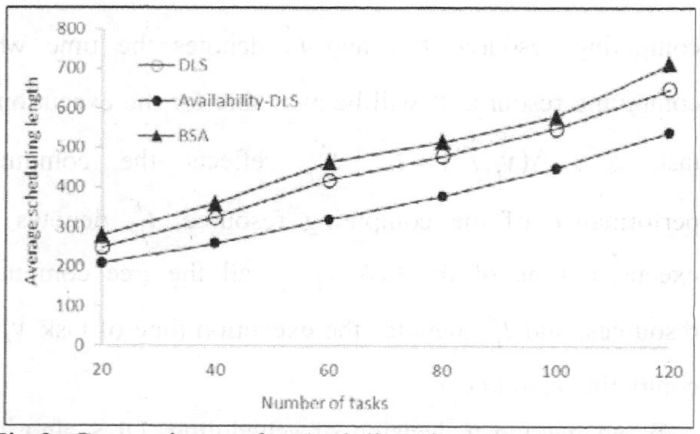

Fig.2 Comparison of scheduling length under varying number of tasks.

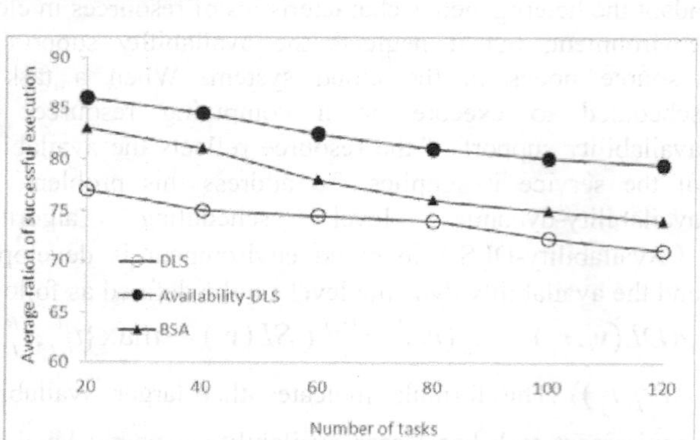

Fig.3 Comparison of successful execution ration under varying number of tasks.

In Fig.2, with the number of tasks increased, the scheduling length of the three algorithms all increased as well. The scheduling length of Availability-DLS is shorter than DLS's and BSA's. In Fig.3, with the number of tasks increased, the average ration of successful execution of the three algorithms all decreased as well. The average ration of successful execution of Availability-DLS is much higher than DLS's and BSA's. Scheduling algorithm based on the availability mechanism fully considers the availability requirement of tasks and availability support of resources, which makes the availability requirement of tasks and availability support of resources to get better matching and can reduce the number of re-scheduling. Therefor, average completion time is less and average ration of successful execution is higher by Availability-DLS algorithm.

5.2 Performance impact of nodes number

In this simulation experiment, CCR is set to 1, the number of nodes from 100 to 1500 is generated randomly, the number of links is set to 300, and the number of tasks is set to 400. We also compared DLS and BSA with Availability-DLS in the scheduling length and ratio of successful execution. The results are shown in Figs.4 and 5.

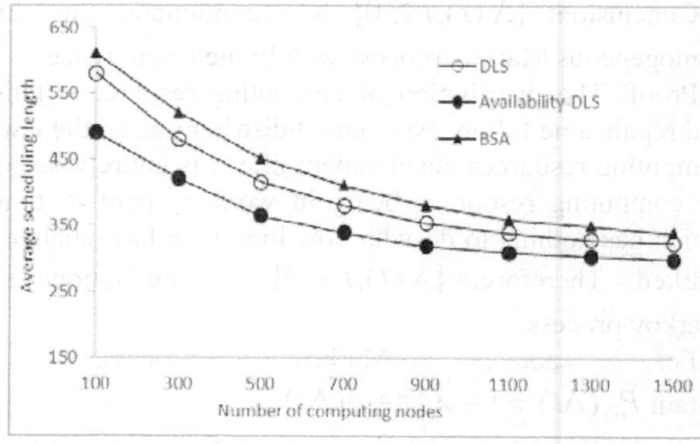

Fig.4. Comparison of scheduling length under varying number of computing nodes.

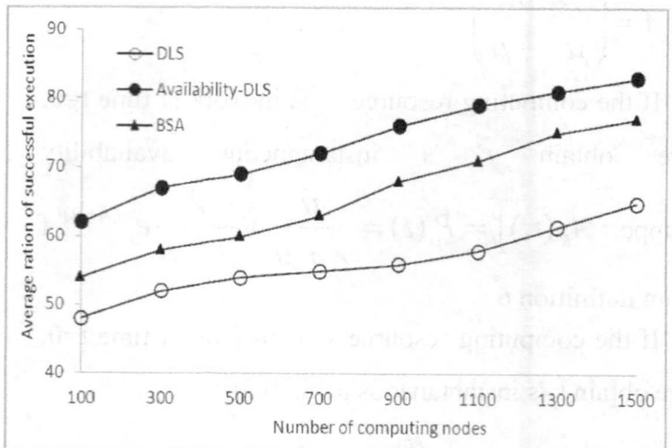

Fig.5 Comparison of successful execution ration under varying number of computing nodes.

Scheduling algorithm based on the availability mechanism fully considers the availability requirements of tasks and availability supports of resources with the increasing of computing nodes, which makes the availability requirements of tasks and availability supports of resources to get better matching and can reduce the number of rescheduling.Therefor, average completion time is less and average successful execution ration is higher by Availability-DLS algorithm.

6 Conclusions

According to the requirements of the tasks to availability, we analyze the factors that affect the subtasks availability requirements and give a measure method to compute the subtasks availability requirements based on the structural characteristics of the parallel tasks graph. According to the availability supports of the cloud platform computing resources to change over time, we give a measure method to compute availability supports of resources based on Markov-type repairable system. Quantification of the availability requirements of the tasks and availability supports of the resources provides an important reference to avoid computing resources failure, which is important to the applications that have rigid application completion time requirements under cloud computing resources performance dynamic varying. Next, we proposed Availability-DLS scheduling algorithm to enhance the availability of heterogeneous systems while maintaining good performance in response time and successful execution ration of parallel tasks.

Acknowledgments

This work was supported by the National High-Tech Research and Development Plan of China under grant No. 2009AA012201; the National Natural Science Foundation of China under grant No. 61103068 and No. 61272107; the joint of NSFC and Microsoft Asia Research under grant No. 60970155; the Program of Shanghai Subject Chief Scientist under grant No. 10XD1404400; the Ph.D. Programs Foundation of Ministry of Education under grant No. 20090072110035; the special Fund for Fast Sharing of Science Paper in Net Era by CSTD under grant No. 20110740001.

7 References

[1] S.P. Smith. An efficient method to maintain resource availability information for scheduling applications. Proceedings of the IEEE Intenational Conference on Robotics and Automation. 1992, pp 1214-1219.

[2] I. Adiri, J. Bruno, E. Frostig, A.H.G. Rinnooy Kan. Single machine flow-time scheduling with a single breakdown. Acta Informatica, 1989, 26(7): 679-696.

[3] X.Qi, T.Chen, F.Tu. Scheduling the maintenance on a single machine. Journal of the Operational Research Society, 1999, 50(10):1071-1078.

[4] I. Kacem, C. Sadfi, A. E. Kamel. Branch and bound and dynamic programming to minimize the total completion times on a single machine with availability constraints. Proceedings of the IEEE Intenational Conference on Systems, Man, and Cybernetics. 2005, pp 1657-1662.

[5] C.Y. Lee. Two-machine flowshop scheduling with availability constraints. European Journal Operational Research, 1999, 114(2): 420-429.

[6] G. Mosheiov. Minimizing the sum of job completion times on capacitated parallel machines. Math and Computer Modelling, 1994, 20(6): 91-99.

[7] X.Qin, T.Xie. An availability-aware task scheduling for hetero-geneous systems. IEEE Transaction on Computers, 2008, 57(2):188-199.

[8] Chung,K.L.,Markov Chains with Stationary Transition Probabilities, Springer, Berlin, 1960.

[9] Cinlar, E., Introduction to Stohastic Processes, Prentic-Hall. Inc.,1975.

[10] A.M. Johnson and M. Malek, "Survey of Software Tools for Evaluating Reliability, Availability, and Serviceability," ACM Computing Surveys, vol. 20, no. 4, pp. 227-269, Dec. 1988.

[11] Dogan A, Ozguner F. Reliable matching and scheduling of precedence-constrained tasks in Heterogeneous distributed computing. In Proc. of the 29th International Conference on Parallel Processing. Toronto, Canada: IEEE Computer Society, 2000. 307—314.

[12] CLOUDS Lab. A Framework for Modeling and Simulation of Cloud Computing Infrastructures and Services Introduction[EB/OL].

BLASTer: A Hub-based Tool for Bioinformatics

B. Cotton[1], **C. Thompson**[1], **and B. Raub**[1]
[1]Purdue University, West Lafayette, IN, USA

Abstract—*Basic Local Alignment Search Tool (BLAST) is a widely used sequencing tool in the bioinformatics community. BLAST searches are highly-parallelizable, lending themselves to computation on a high-throughput resource. In this paper, we describe the BLASTer tool developed by Purdue University to present an easy-to-use, web-based interface for performing BLAST searches. BLASTer uses the large HTCondor pool at Purdue University to dramatically shorten run times compared to desktop usage. Using the HUBzero platform, BLASTer can be made available for research and instruction to users worldwide. This paper describes the platform, the development process, early success stories, and efforts to grow the user community.*

Keywords: BLAST, SaaS, bioinformatics

1. Introduction

Since its initial release in 1990 [1], the Basic Local Alignment Search Tool (BLAST) has been a key part of bioinformatics research. The various programs that compose the BLAST package allow researchers to search for nucleotides or proteins in a database of known strings. The tens of thousands of citations indicate the popularity and broad utility of BLAST. It has been used in genome sequencing in a range of organisms, from e. coli [2] to humans [11].

Although the BLAST programs are freely available from the National Center for Biotechnology Information website [9], barriers to entry still exist. Long-running searches require the dedication of computing resources, often the desktop computer that a graduate student would otherwise be using for other work. Dedicated scientific computing resources alleviate this problem, but are expensive. Even if such a resource is available, it might not be approachable. Not all researchers are familiar with command line tools, presenting a challenging learning curve to those used to point-and-click interfaces. Other web-based tools, such as that offered by NCBI, alleviate this problem, but the resource pool is potentially small, large searches are often unsupported, and users generally do not have the ability to search against custom databases.

Our goal in creating the BLASTer tool was to address these issues. We wanted a tool that would easily handle large searches, both in terms of computation and storage requirements. Though powerful, the tool needed to be approachable by users. This is particularly important for use in an educational setting, where the goal is to teach the science, not the tool.

BLASTer combines existing components into a tool unique in its capability and capacity. BLASTer is powered by a large opportunistic computing resource that provides thousands of available cores. Users receive 10 gigabytes of storage, with 5 terabytes of centralized storage for NCBI databases and other common files. Future versions will incorporate visualization capabilities via Blast2Go.

Table 1: BLASTer compared to NCBI's web-based offering

	BLASTer	NCBI
Computation time	Unlimited	1 hour
Storage	10 GB default	10k characters

In addition to enabling single users, the BLASTer tool was intended to enable collaboration. Collaborators on a project should be able to share custom databases with each other. Researchers who wish to make their data publicly available should have the ability to easily publish files for use by others. Developing the user community allows mutually-beneficial knowledge sharing.

2. Computational Environment

2.1 Community Clusters

As part of its community cluster program [3], Purdue University opportunistically harvests idle cycles [10]. With millions of core hours per year available, a workflow that can make use of a high-throughput computing paradigm [6] is well-suited. Although work has been done to enable the use of MPI with BLAST [4], inter-node communication is not necessary to parallelize searches. BLAST queries can be separated and sent to individual nodes [7]. This enables BLAST searches to make ready use of opportunistic resources.

In addition to the nearly 50,000 cores provided by the community cluster program, this shared infrastructure brings additional benefits. A common application suite across the clusters ensures that the same version of the BLAST programs is on any given compute node. Shared storage allows the NCBI's standard databases to be available to all users without requiring file transfer. The BLASTer team can update BLAST binaries and NCBI databases without effecting currently-running jobs. These features mean that users only need to upload their search queries, saving effort and reducing the time to results.

2.2 HUBzero

In order to provide an easy-to-use interface for users that is accessible around the world, we decided to host BLASTer on the HUBzero Platform for Scientific Collaboration [8]. HUBzero provides a Java-based web interface for applications. The back end is a Linux server, allowing developers to make use of existing shared libraries and toolkits. The hub provides an interface to submit jobs directly into computational resources, leaving developers free to focus on application and workflow development.

The HUBzero platform also addresses other needs. Users can self-register and begin using BLASTer immediately. There is no application or allocation process that needs to be followed. Built-in feedback mechanisms allow users to quickly request help or register wishes for the application. Wishes can be commented and voted on by other users, giving developers a good way to gauge interest from the user community. Papers, data sets, and other files can be easily published by users. An in-hub user group allows the creation of wiki pages and provides a forum tool to enhance the community experience.

2.3 DiaGrid

DiaGrid is a HUBzero implementation dedicated to offering scientific applications to broad communities. Most DiaGrid applications, including BLASTer, are available for immediate use to the general public. DiaGrid applications can employ a high-throughput or high-performance paradigm by virtue of access to Purdue's HTCondor and community cluster resources. Existing applications on DiaGrid include SubmitR, a tool for submitting R jobs, and CryoEM, a tool for cryogenic electron microscopy. Tools to support molecular dynamics with GROMACS and climate modeling with the Community Earth System Model are under active development.

3. BLASTer Implementation

The HUBzero platform provides abstraction layers so that application developers do not need to be familiar with the target job scheduling system. A client-server system called "submit" receives job characteristics and files from the application and selects the appropriate venue. In the case of BLASTer, submit uses the Pegasus workflow engine [5] to submit jobs to the HTCondor resources. As jobs complete, Pegasus provides the output to submit, which sends output to the application in turn. This arrangement is presented in Figure 1.

3.1 GUI and Engine Development

To understand the design of BLASTer, one must first understand the requirements of the BLAST application suite. Instead of a single overall program, BLAST comprises a collection of independent executables, each of which uses a different search algorithm. A large portion of the BLAST community has also embraced analysis tools such as Blast2Go in production workflows. Without these additional tools, many of these users have told us they find no value in a new BLAST environment. BLASTer was designed to account for this wide range of requirements by abstracting job parameter entry, execution mechanics, and data inspection within the GUI.

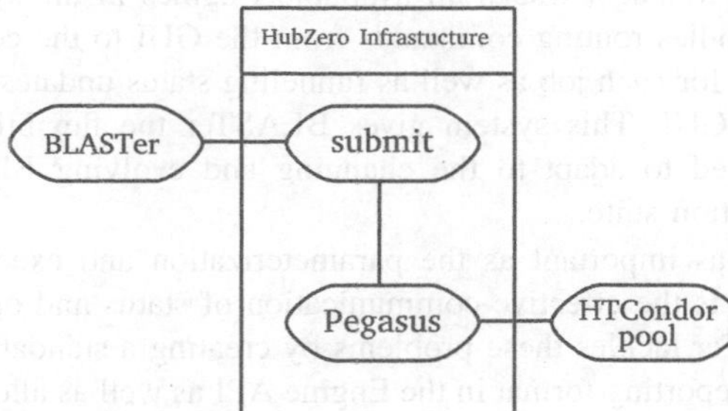

Fig. 1: The architecture of BLASTer and the HUBzero infrastructure.

The requirement of running multiple independent executables and various third-party tools makes it necessary for BLASTer to support arbitrary job descriptions. This is handled through a system of Job Profiles. Each Profile is built from a collection of Parameters organized into Parameter Groups as fits to the particular task at hand. Individual Parameter represents a particular argument of the job and has a value type. Simple value types such as integers and booleans are mapped to standard GUI widgets like text fields and checkboxes. Complex and novel value types can be added and represented with custom GUI components. At runtime, BLASTer will dynamically map a view of the Parameter list in the Profile using these widgets. Through this system any type of job can be represented to the user for option entry. Regardless of the argument format of the underlying programs, the user is presented with the same experience of an intuitive entry form customized to each job type.

To support the variety of execution needs of the many BLAST applications, an API is defined in BLASTer for common job control tasks. This abstracts all concrete details of execution away from the GUI and the user. Each type of job has a corresponding Job Engine following this API to provide access to common operations like submission, cancellation, and status retrieval. To add a new tool or even just a new execution method of an existing tool, developers only need to implement a new Engine which conforms to this API (and define a matching Job Profile for it). This allows BLASTer to hide from the user what is actually happening within the job through a set of common controls . An overall

Engine Manager tracks all available Engines in the system and handles routing commands from the GUI to the correct Engine for each job as well as funneling status updates back to the GUI. This system gives BLASTer the flexibility it will need to adapt to the changing and evolving BLAST application suite.

Just as important as the parameterization and execution of jobs is the effective communication of status and output. BLASTer tackles these problems by creating a standardized status reporting format in the Engine API as well as allowing the definition of custom GUI Job Viewer panels for each type of job performed. Just as each Profile lists which Engine to use for a job, they also list which Viewer represents a job. BLASTer uses this value at runtime to dynamically load the appropriate view for jobs a user has selected for closer inspection. With standardized status reports from the various Engines, BLASTer can also quickly communicate information to the user about any job they have created. Together, status reports and dynamic Viewers give the user both a bird's eye and ground level view of their work.

The primary mission of BLASTer is to abstract away the details of BLAST-related tools in an intuitive manner so users can focus on the science of their tasks. The design of BLASTer uses Job Profiles to dynamically support any set of arguments a task may require, Job Engines to handle any type of execution needs, and Job Viewer panels to communicate any format of data to the user. Via these three mechanisms, BLASTer can achieve its mission to execute these tasks on behalf of the user for the wide variety of BLAST applications.

3.2 Back end development

Back end development for BLASTer focused on making the best use of the computing resources available. With help from Rick Westerman, a Bioinformatics Specialist at Purdue University, we were able to gauge what a "typical" BLAST job would consist of and how the data could be parallelized. Westerman's Bioinformatics group pulls in gigabytes of raw sequence data daily and run BLAST jobs on their own servers. A typical job for this group consists of a 'fasta' file that contains biological sequences. Files are typically around 110,000 sequences, with each sequence containing between 200 and 12,215 bases, totaling about 66 million bases. A BLAST job of this size would take 8 or more hours to complete with the servers that the Bioinformatics group owns.

There are two methods of splitting data for execution. The first method splits the input file into smaller files and tests all files against a single database. The second method splits the database into parts and tests a single input file accordingly. The latter method requires MPI. With our intent to use HTCondor to harvest idle cycles, splitting the input file was clearly the most suitable option.

We assumed that a majority of the typical BLAST jobs would be roughly the size of Westerman's input file or smaller, so that was used as a baseline for splitting files. The goal was to achieve complete results within four hours of submission in order to minimize job preemption. On the community clusters, jobs arriving on a node from the primary (PBS) scheduler evict all HTCondor jobs on the node. Jobs that are evicted are automatically rescheduled by HTCondor. Although BLAST jobs respond well to rescheduling, because they must re-start from the beginning it is desirable to minimize the number of preemptions.

Testing was first done on the cluster nodes themselves to determine the optimal splits for the fastest completion times. Initial tests created jobs of 100 splits, 500 splits and 1,000 splits (1,100 sequences, 220 sequences and 110 sequences per split, respectively). With each test, the results were obtained faster and faster yet still not below the four hour threshold.

Beyond 2,000 splits, we observed a decay in completion time, suggesting we had surpassed the upper limit of file splits. This upper limit could have been for a few different reasons. When a job is submitted, all submissions are scheduled through one machine so the queue gets quite lengthy. Once all of the jobs are queued and running, each mini BLAST job compares its input file to the same database creating a bottleneck in file reads. The optimal split for such a job we determined to be about 85 sequences per file, thus equating to about 1,300 total splits.

Selecting 1500 splits per search provided us with a complete job that could run consistently within our allotted four hours. This splitting technique was further confirmed to be accurate with help from Professor Jianxin Ma and his graduate student Meixia Zhao in the College of Agriculture that had search times cut down from days to hours. Professor Andrew Dewoody and his graduate students from the Department of Biology also had similar speedups with their data analysis.

Table 2: BLAST job completion times

Sequences	Bases	Cluster wall time	HTCondor wall time
40K	15M	5:30	2:30
43K	16M	5:20	2:40
105K	49M	7:15	3:30
145K	72M	8:20	3:20

More recently, some users have used BLASTer to search against input files containing more than 700,000 sequences. The time required for each individual split to complete ran upwards of 15 hours, resulting in considerable delays as splits were repeatedly evicted from nodes. In order to accomodate these larger input files, BLASTer now splits files based on the method described in Table 3. Optimizing the balance between scheduler overhead and the node eviction rate is the primary challenge, and is the subject of ongoing testing.

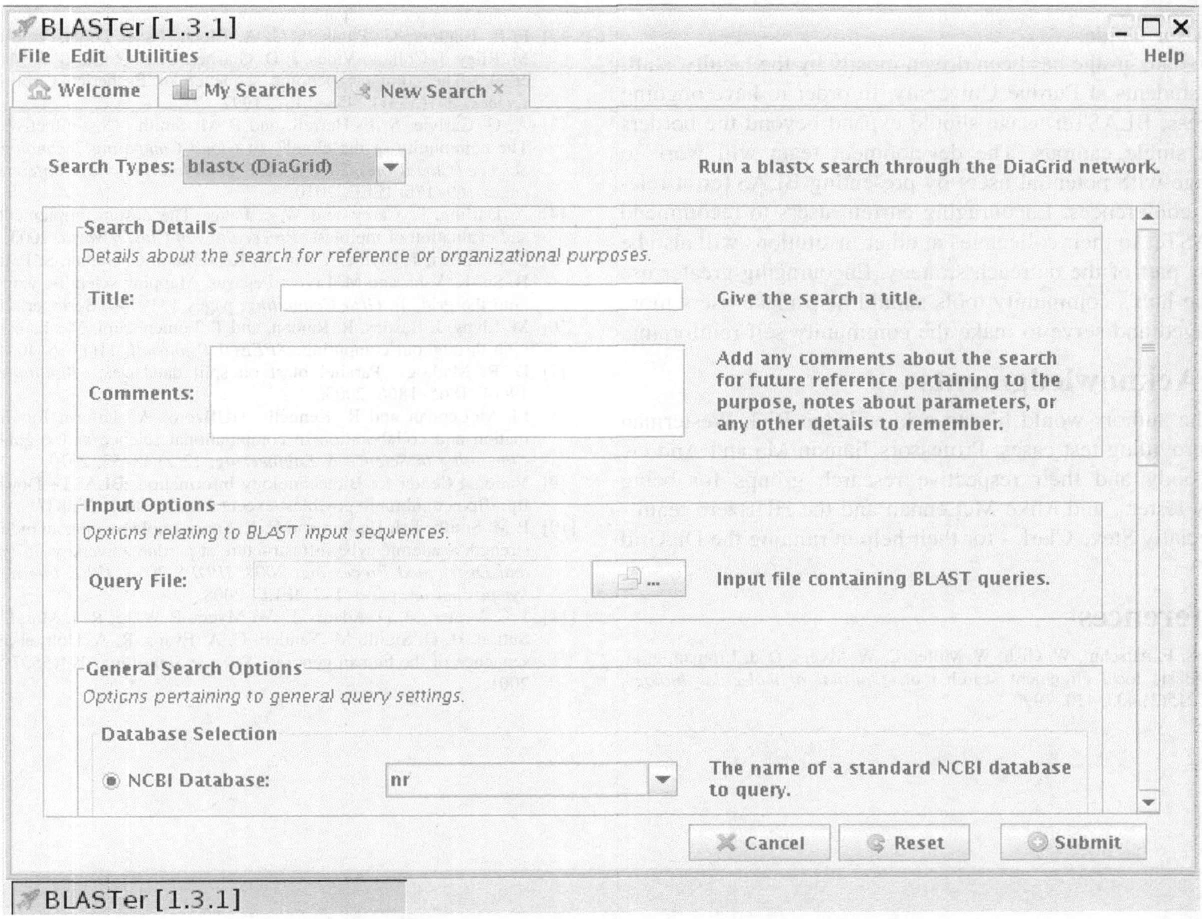

Fig. 2: BLASTer's configuration window for new searches.

Table 3: BLASTer search splitting

Sequences	Split size
<128k	85
128-750k	85 + (#sequences/750k)
>750k	160

4. Future Work

BLAST was selected as an early DiaGrid application because of the immediately-available local user base. The ability to have a core group of researchers that could help us with testing during development that we could also help by speeding up their research was key. One research group found they could complete a search in three hours that took three days on a desktop in their lab.

In BLASTer's first year, nearly 100 users have completed over a million BLAST runs. BLASTer clearly has technical merit, but much work remains to be done. Additional user-requested features are being implemented, including better management of databases and the ability to send output to the Blast2Go visualization tool. Improvements to the job splitting methodology are being investigated as well, to avoid over-splitting small jobs and ensure large jobs are not under-split.

As the BLASTer application approaches a feature-complete state, focus will shift toward engaging and growing the user community. Currently, users make light use of HUBzero's community features. Almost all wishes have been entered by DiaGrid developers in response to in-person conversations with users and wishes are rarely voted on. We expect that adding more non-Purdue users will help drive use of the community tools.

We have already created a comprehensive User Guide that focuses on walking a user through the basics of creating and managing a search. With local users, conducting periodic workshops with live demonstrations provides an easy way to reinforce the documentation and provide customized help. As the user community grows geographically, self-service training will be necessary. We plan to create short tutorial videos to provide a visual reference for the instructions in the User Guide.

To date, usage has been driven mostly by the faculty, staff, and students at Purdue University. In order to have ongoing success, BLASTer usage should expand beyond the borders of a single campus. The development team will work to engage with potential users by presenting BLASTer at relevant conferences. Encouraging current users to recommend BLASTer to their colleagues at other institutions will also be a key part of the outreach strategy. Encouraging greater use of the hub's community tools should help make users more engaged and serve to make the community self-reinforcing.

5. Acknowledgments

The authors would like to acknowledge Rick Westerman for providing test cases, Professors Jianxin Ma and Andrew Dewoody and their respective research groups for being early testers, and Mike McLennan and the HUBzero team - especially Steve Clark - for their help in running the DiaGrid hub.

References

[1] S. F. Altschul, W. Gish, W. Miller, E. W. Myers, D. J. Lipman, et al. Basic local alignment search tool. *Journal of molecular biology*, 215(3):403–410, 1990.

[2] F. R. Blattner, G. Plunkett, C. A. Bloch, N. T. Perna, V. Burland, M. Riley, J. Collado-Vides, J. D. Glasner, C. K. Rode, G. F. Mayhew, et al. The complete genome sequence of Escherichia coli K-12. *science*, 277(5331):1453–1462, 1997.

[3] A. G. Carlyle, S. L. Harrell, and P. M. Smith. Cost-effective HPC: The community or the cloud? In *Cloud Computing Technology and Science (CloudCom), 2010 IEEE Second International Conference on*, pages 169–176. IEEE, 2010.

[4] A. Darling, L. Carey, and W.-c. Feng. The design, implementation, and evaluation of mpiblast. *Proceedings of ClusterWorld*, 2003, 2003.

[5] E. Deelman, J. Blythe, Y. Gil, C. Kesselman, G. Mehta, S. Patil, M.-H. Su, K. Vahi, and M. Livny. Pegasus: Mapping scientific workflows onto the grid. In *Grid Computing*, pages 131–140. Springer, 2004.

[6] M. Livny, J. Basney, R. Raman, and T. Tannenbaum. Mechanisms for high throughput computing. *SPEEDUP journal*, 11(1):36–40, 1997.

[7] D. R. Mathog. Parallel blast on split databases. *Bioinformatics*, 19(14):1865–1866, 2003.

[8] M. McLennan and R. Kennell. HUBzero: A platform for dissemination and collaboration in computational science and engineering. *Computing in Science & Engineering*, 12(2):48–53, 2010.

[9] National Center for Biotechnology Information. BLAST+ Download. ftp://ftp.ncbi.nlm.nih.gov/blast/executables/blast+/LATEST/.

[10] P. M. Smith, T. J. Hacker, and C. X. Song. Implementing an industrial-strength academic cyberinfrastructure at purdue university. In *Parallel and Distributed Processing, 2008. IPDPS 2008. IEEE International Symposium on*, pages 1–7. IEEE, 2008.

[11] J. C. Venter, M. D. Adams, E. W. Myers, P. W. Li, R. J. Mural, G. G. Sutton, H. O. Smith, M. Yandell, C. A. Evans, R. A. Holt, et al. The sequence of the human genome. *Science Signalling*, 291(5507):1304, 2001.

An Efficient Method by Using Prediction to Reduce Times in Live Migration of Virtual Machine

Boseob Kim[1], and Sungchun Kim[1]
[1]Computer Science and Engineering Dept, Sogang Univ, Seoul, South Korea

Abstract - *Cloud system, especially IaaS has became hot issue because of its low TCO. In the field of IaaS, server virtualization has close connection due to benefits of resource sharing, fault tolerance, portability and cost efficiency. Live VM migration is one of technologies which manage virtualized server. Although live VM migration just moves virtual machine to another within few downtime, it can cause more network traffic because of longer migration time. So we suggest a method to reduce migration time through predicting iterations of pre-copy phase. Our method determines number of iterations using average dirty page rate and decides stop condition. We apply this method to Xen and demonstrate our method works efficiently.*

Keywords: Virtual machine, VM migration, Cloud systems, fault-tolerance system

1 Introduction

Nowadays, cloud system now becomes popular in field of computer science and engineering. Especially, IaaS (Infrastructure-as-a-Service) cloud computing system allows user to take resources over web platform. Subscribers can take and launch virtual machines without lacking local devices and they can lease virtual machines cheaply. In a case of data centers, these have close connections with IaaS cloud technologies because cloud system has strength of reducing TCO (Total Cost of Ownership) and it has benefits of resource sharing, fault tolerance, portability and cost efficiency. In IaaS cloud, it is important to manage virtual machine, so VMM (Virtual Machine Monitor) must provide manage function like creating, copying, and deleting virtual machine efficiently to owner. Many of VMMs like Xen[2], or VMWare[3] provide these tools. VM migration is one of managing tools that provides copying or moving virtual machine. In particular, Live VM migration [1] is a reasonable method for migrating virtual machine. The main advantage of live VM migration is possibility of low downtime. While a running source virtual machine executes its processes and sends responses to user's request, a state of destination virtual machine becomes almost ready-to-use. Because of this advantage, Live VM migration technology is used in VMMs and supported by the form of platforms. XenMotion[10] and VMotion[11] are example of platforms.

Nevertheless when source virtual machine continues to reply on user's request, network traffic continues to takes some portion of network resource because source VMM sends packet which includes dirtied pages and destination host receives those in live VM migration. If network traffic of bringing pages takes up network resource continuously, it would bring lack of response and that would cause complain of users. One way to cut down the entire traffic is guaranteeing low migration time of live VM migration. If we save the migration time, stability of network resources would be improved. Many papers try to reduce the time of migration [5,6,7,8,12] or analyze cost of it [9]. Our goal is to guarantee low migration time.

In this paper we examine stages of VM migration and key factor of reducing migration time. After that, our method would be suggested, it is applied to the real-world case (Xen) and Experimental evaluation is presented at next chapter and finally we finish the paper with conclusion and future works

2 Related factor of Live VM migration

2.1 Stages of live VM migration

Live VM migration method tries to lessen suspending time of source virtual machine by pushing and pre- copying dirty pages. The core idea of live VM migration is convergence of pre-copy. While source virtual machine is running, VMM sends dirty pages (in first round, entire memory should be transferred) to destination VMM and constructs new virtual machine. After multiple rounds of constructing there must be few dirty pages enough to halt virtual machine and bring (maybe small number of) remaining pages. Then, start copied virtual machine on destination VMM and reattach resources to it. That kind of design is guaranteed to reduce downtime.

In more details, live VM migration consists of 6 phases [1]; those are as follow.

1) *Initialization*: source virtual machine is selected for migration. Also destination host is initialized for migration.

2) *Reservation*: resources at the destination host are reserved for destination virtual machine

3) *Iterative pre-copy*: pages in source virtual machine are modified during the previous iteration are transferred to the destination. The entire RAM is sent in the first iteration.

4) *Stop-and-copy*: the source virtual machine would be suspended for last transfer.

5) *Commitment*: the destination host indicates that it has received successfully a consistent copy of virtual machine.

6) *Activation*: resources are re-attached to the VM on the destination host.

Each stage takes one step except stage 3, iterative pre-copy stage. It would continue to execute unless there is stop condition that is satisfied.

2.2 Key factors of migration time

Iterative pre-copy phase effects execution of stop-and-copy phase and time for copying pages is almost every portion of migration time, although other stages do not require much data transfer. So to achieve lower migration time, we should reduce the time of iterative pre-copy phase. So it is important to decide stop condition. Stop condition is a condition that stops iterations. In normal case, stop condition of pre-copying is 'the number of dirty pages is low enough to stop copying'. But a server environment which raises many I/O bounded events cannot stop pre-copying unless there is other stop condition in live VM migration. Because of that case, VMM is designed to limit the number of iterations or transferred capacity of memory.

The limitation could be static value. Static limitation would ensure stable migration time. At least, we can obtain maximum migration time without much measuring of scenarios. But, static limitation would have constraints of efficient migration time. So if we decide number of iterations dynamically or new stop condition ensures less number of iterations than limitation, our method can reduce the time.

3 Proposal schemes for stop condition

We propose new method which decides stop condition. Using average and changes of dirty page rate, our method decides whether to proceed next pre-copy phase. To give explanation of our model easily, we will describe how the pre-copy phase reduces downtime.

When source virtual machine reaches first pre-copy phase, entire memory is ready to copy and contents of memory (pages) are sent to destination host. During the first iteration, pages are dirtied and that might cause second iteration. Suppose dirty page rate is stable. The number of dirtied pages would be lower than that of whole entries of page. At second iteration, because transfer time of dirty page is lower than that of entire memory, transfer time is lower than earlier. Third iteration is done faster than second iteration because dirtied pages of second iteration is lower than those of first iteration. Likewise, fourth iteration is done faster than third iteration. As these iterations continue, the number of dirty pages goes to zero-value gradually. So these iterations have guaranteed satisfaction of simple stop condition, 'The number of dirty pages is little enough to go to stop-and-copy phase'. Number of shrinked pages is lower than number of whole pages. So downtime is reduced. On the other hands, if we know how many iterations are required we can make a flexible limitation. If source virtual machine requires too many rotations we can stop pre-copy phase and go to stop-and-copy phase. It can reduce migration time with small penalty of downtime.

If dirty page rate has stability for that case, we can predict limitation that satisfies stop condition. Suppose source virtual machine has fixed dirty page rate. Then required number of pages to send in (n+1)-th iteration is below.

$$D_{n+1} = R \times C \times \frac{D_n}{S} \quad (1)$$

D_{n+1} is dirtied pages while stages of live VM migration is doing n-th iteration of pre-copy, R is Dirty page rate of source virtual machine, S is transfer speed of network, and C is capacity of one page, 4 kilobytes on 32-bit computer in common case. By assumption, R is fixed value. If R is fixed, we can get dirtied pages of n-th iteration from capacity of memory by transferring recurrence relation into normal expression.

$$D_n = D_1 \times \left(\frac{R \times C}{S}\right)^{n-1} \quad (2)$$

D_1 is entire number of page, which have to be transferred in first iteration of pre-copy phase. D_1 is easily obtained from dividing memory size by C. At simple stop condition, Dn must be lower than number of pages to stop. If source VMM decides to start stop-and-copy phase, pages are transferred after (n-1)-th iteration. Basis of that, we can obtain expected number of iterations. .

$$T \geq D_1 \times \left(\frac{R \times C}{S}\right)^{N-1} \quad (3)$$

$$\frac{T}{D_1} \geq \left(\frac{R \times C}{S}\right)^{N-1} \quad (4)$$

$$\log\left(\frac{T}{D_1}\right) \geq (\mathrm{N}-1) \times \log\left(\frac{R \times C}{S}\right) \quad (5)$$

$$\frac{1}{N-1} \le \frac{\log(\frac{R \times C}{S})}{\log(\frac{T}{D_1})} \quad (6)$$

$$N-1 \ge \log_{(\frac{R \times C}{S})}(\frac{T}{D_1}) \quad (7)$$

$$N \ge \log_{(\frac{R \times C}{S})}(\frac{T}{D_1})+1 \quad (8)$$

$$N' = \left\lceil \log_{(\frac{R \times C}{S})}(\frac{T}{D_1})+1 \right\rceil \quad (9)$$

T is a threshold that decides 'little number of pages'. In expression (5), N is minimum iterations to go to stop-and-copy phase. To hold expression (6) from expression (5), it must be satisfied that $\log(T/D_1)$ is lower than 0. If T is greater than D_1, live VM migration acts like non-live because it indicates that our condition is always true and source VMM decides there is no needs for doing pre-copy iteration. So in live VM migration expression (6) holds for that assumption. Because the number of iterations is a natural value, it has to be converted. So, N' in expression (9) is actual number of iterations.

But practically, dirty page rate would not be fixed due to characteristics of virtualized server. Sometimes the server is in idle state or be in working state. Idle state would not make many dirty pages but working state would make many dirty pages. The problem is we cannot predict when the I/O event occurs and is handled. So extracting stable value of dirty page rate is too hard. Therefore, for predicting number of iterations efficiently we have to guess rate from measured dirty pages for each of iterations. In this paper, we predict dirty page rate by average value of dirty pages and pre-copying times collected on previous iterations. After first iteration is done, we obtain number of dirty pages that is dirtied and pre-copying time. Then we can obtain average dirty page rate from that parameters. Number of dirtied pages and second pre-copying time are measured after second iteration. Then parameters of obtaining average dirty page rate would increase and we can get expected value of dirty rate. In one sentence we predict expected dirty page rate of next iteration as following expression.

$$R_p = \frac{\sum_{k=2}^{n+1} DM_k}{\sum_{k=1}^{n} TM_k} \quad (10)$$

DM_k is the measured number of dirty pages and TM_k is measured pre-copying time from k-th iteration. In summary, terms of expression are described in Table I.

Table I : Terms of Expression

D_n	Number of dirtied pages that must be transferred in n-th iteration.
D_1	Number of whole pages.(number of pages that must be transferred in 1-st iteration.)
R	Dirty Page rate per unit time
C	Capacity per page(4KB in normal cases)
S	Network transfer speed per unit time
T	Threshold that is satisfying enough downtime
N	Expected number of iteration.
DM_k	Measured dirtied pages in k-th iteration.
TM_k	Measured transfer speed in k-th iteration.

With expected dirty page rate R_p, we can get expected N' (we call that N_E). If N_E is equal or lower than number of iterations that is already done we have to stop pre-copy phase because it must satisfy threshold of dirty pages. And when N_E is greater than previously obtained N_E (from first iteration to (n-1)-th iteration) we could expect there would be I/O events. Then we should stop pre-copying phase and start stop-and-copy phase because I/O events would write to pages and it may need many iterations of pre-copying.

On the other hand, N_E can be negative value because of many I/O events. In live VM migration, T/D_1 is lower than one. But when too many I/O events rise, base of logarithm is greater than one because transfer speed would be lower than dirty page rate in unit time. So, whole value of N_E cannot be positive value. We should consider that situation. When there are too many I/O events so that exceeds more than transfer speed, we would rather to stop pre-copying iteration and go to stop-and-copy phase.

Considering described situations, our algorithm is shown in algorithm I. first we start it with first iteration of pre-copying, which transfers whole pages. Transfer time and the number of dirtied pages in first iteration would be measured and using that value, we obtain average transfer speed, R_p and N_E. if N_E is equals or lower than 0 or greater than limitation L (At first it is pre-defined value), the source VMM decide to stop pre-copy phase. If value of N_E is between 0 and L, L is updated to N_E. When number of iterations is greater than L, there would be small number of pages. Then it is also the stop condition. Among all conditions, algorithm I is described below.

Algorithm I : Algorithm which controls iteration

```
T=Threshold of going next phase; // threshold must be defined
C=size of page;
D1=(memory size)/C;
TP=log(T/D1);
L=Limitation of iteration; // limitation must be defined
PRC=1; // PRC is number of iterations that is occurred.
transfer whole memory;
S=(memory size)/(transfer time in first iteration);
P[1]=(number of dirtied pages in first iteration);
T[1]=(transfer time in first iteration);
while(PRC < N)
{
  RR=0;
  TT=0;
  for(i=1;i<=PRC;i++)
  {
    RR+=P[i];
    TT+=T[i];
  }
  RR/=TT;
  NE=TP/log((RR*C)/S)+1;
  if(NE > L || NE<=0)
    break;
  else
  {
    L=NE;
    PRC++;
    transfer dirtied pages; // do next iteration
    P[PRC]=(number of dirtied pages for PRC-th iteration);
    T[PRC]=(transfer time of PRC-th iteration);
    S=(P[PRC-1] * C)/(transfer time in PRC-th iteration);
  }
}
```

Threshold and maximum number of iteration must be defined beforehand. When we define high threshold of dirtied pages, iterations would be lessened.

4 Experimental evaluation

In this paper we applied our idea to open source VMM, Xen. As we wrote it is important to define threshold and maximum number of iteration. To define those factors, we have to know stop condition of iteration applied to Xen.

In environment of Xen, stop condition of pre-copy phase is represented below.

1) Number of dirtied pages of previous iteration is less than 50.

2) Number of iterations is greater than 30.

3) Capacity of transferred page is greater than 3 times of entire memory.

First condition is considered because transfer of less pages is satisfying low downtime of live VM migration. On the other hand, second condition and third condition are considered for environment with many I/O events. Too many I/O events cause long migration time with long downtime so these conditions are to reduce migration time unless there is a risk of long downtime.

With our idea we don't want to increase downtime and migration time when source virtual machine is in that state because with that state migration time is almost equal as transfer time of entire memory while it has low I/O events. At least it ensures downtime. (Also in case of periodic I/O events that causes fixed R) So we assign T=50. On the other hands we have to consider second and third condition. We have to reduce the migration time when server is in the state with many I/O events. To prove our efficiency, we assign L=30 that is equal as static limitation of Xen.

To simulate our idea, we constructed two situations of virtual machine. First virtual machine is in idle state that few pages are modified. Automatically dirty page rate of that virtual machine is low. Second virtual machine is in environment of doing kernel compile. Kernel compile causes I/O events so that dirty page rate is higher than idle state. Both machines are generated with 512MB and 1024MB memory and set with 32-bit virtual machine. Storages are constructed with NFS [4] so we don't have to consider storage migration time. We measured migration time and downtime. And network card and router has maximum speed of 100Mbps. The version of Xen is 4.1.0. We use default value of parameters in formal Xen. We expect migration time is improved when it is in kernel compile. When migration time in idle with our method is similar to Xen.

Result of evaluation is shown below. We have compared Xen and our idea. Results of experiment when source virtual machine is in idle state is shown in Figure 1. Upper result shows memory size=512MB and lower shows case of 1024MB. There were not much significant changes of migration time and downtime. Its environment has low I/O events. So number of iterations is easily expected and that number is equal as that of Xen. Change of migration time is a little value so that is increased or decreased by changes of network traffic.

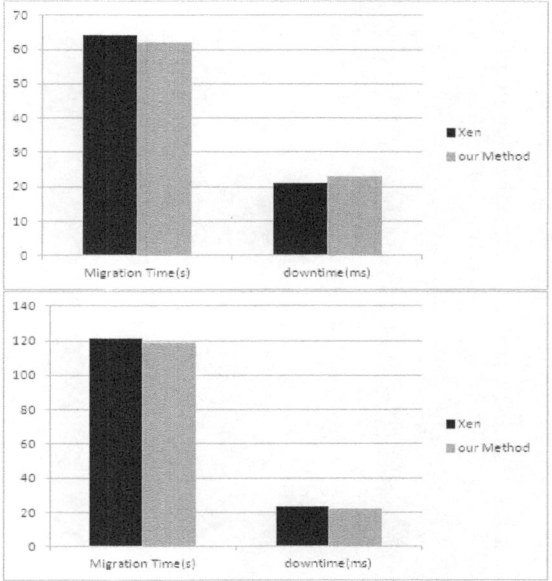

Figure 1. Results in idle state

Efficiency of our idea was evaluated when there is many I/O bounded processes. In Figure 2, migration time is improved by 17 percent in 512MB virtual machine (upper result) and 14 percent in 1024MB virtual machine. Iterations are expected and reduced when I/O events are occurred. Many I/O bounded events increases dirty page rate and once it causes increased iteration, our machine stops pre-copy. After pre-copying is stopped, VMM remains many dirtied pages. Therefore we reduced number of iterations and got lower migration time. But in trade-off, increased downtime is measured.

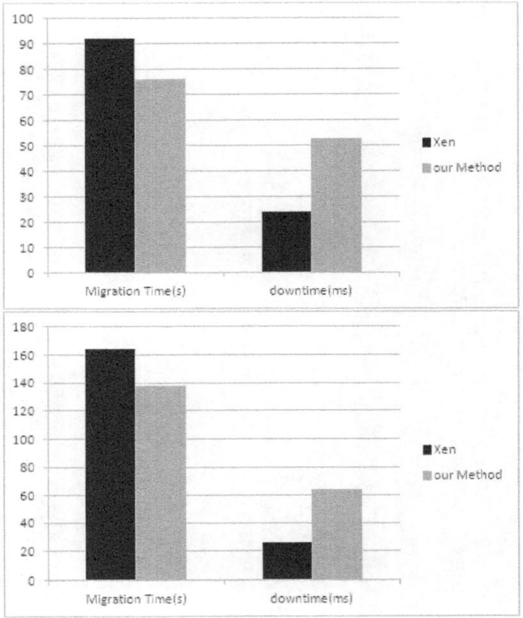

Figure 2. Results in kernel compile state

5 Conclusions

As a result of our experiment, live migration time of virtual machine is reduced by proposed scheme so that we can expect that users could have a chance to get more network resources. But as downtime is increased, response time is also increased. So we have to find efficient value of threshold and limitation. Also we did not consider network speed or other I/O speed. To ensure efficient downtime, actual network speed would be important factor of migration because more transfer speed with stable downtime causes allowance for more dirty pages. So we will add a method for threshold. This would be reduce migration time with reasonable downtime. And we had obtained average dirty page rate of source machine. If we catch all I/O bounded event, we can predict incoming event by making a model per process. It increases accuracy of iterations. We will focus on those issues and trade-off between migration time and downtime.

Acknowledgments

This research was all-supported by Basic Science Research Program through the National Research Foundation of Korea(NRF) funded by the Ministry of Education, Science and Technology(2012R1A1A2009558), and part - supported by Technology Innovation Development Program funded by Small & Medium Business Administration(S2057016)

6 References

[1] C. Clark, K. Fraser, S. Hand, J.G. Hansen, E. Jul, C. Limpach, I. Pratt, and A. Warfield. "Live migration of virtual machines", in The 2nd conference on Symposium on Networked Systems Design and Implementation - Volume 2 (NSDI'05), Vol. 2. USENIX Association, Berkeley, CA, USA, 2-5 May, 2005, pp. 273-286.

[2] P. Barham, B. Dragovic, K. Fraser, S. Hand, T. Harris, A. Ho, R. Neugebauer, I. Pratt, and A. Warfield, "Xen and the art of virtualization", in Proceedings of the Nineteenth ACM Symposium on Operating Systems Principles. ACM Press, 2003, pp. 164-177.

[3] VMWare, vmware inc, [Online]. Available : http://www.vmware.com/

[4] Sun Microsystems, "NFS: Network file system protocol specification", RFC 1094, Internet Engineering Task Force, Mar. 1989.

[5] W. Huang, Q. Gao, J. Liu, and D. K. Panda. "High Performance Virtual Machine Migration with RDMA over Modern Interconnects", in Proceedings of IEEE International Conference on Cluster Computing (Cluster'07), September 17-20, 2007, Austin, Texas, USA

[6] Li Deng, Hai Jin, Song Wu, Xuanhua Shi, and Jiangfu Zhou, "Fast Saving and Restoring Virtual Machines with Page Compression" in 2011 International Conference on Cloud and Service Computing, 2011, pp. 150-157

[7] Y. Luo, B. Zhang, X. Wang, Z. Wang, and Y. Sun, "Live and incremental whole-system migration of virtual machines using block-bitmap", in Proceedings of Cluster 2008: IEEE International Conference on Cluster Computing. IEEE Computer Society, 2008.

[8] Haikun Liu, Hai Jin, Xiaofei Liao, Liting Hu, and Chen Yu, "Live Migration of Virtual Machine Based on Full System Trace and Replay", in Proceedings of the 18th ACM international symposium on High performance distributed computing (HPDC 09), 2009, New York, NY, USA, pp.101-110

[9] Anja Strunk, "Costs of Virtual Machine Live Migration: A Survey", in 2012 IEEE 8th World Congress on Services, 2012, pp. 323-329

[10] XenMotion. Citrix Systems, Inc. [Online]. Available: http://www.citrix.com/products/xenserver/

[11] VMotion. VMware, Inc. [Online]. Available: http://www.vmware.com/products/vmotion/

[12] P. Riteau, C. Morin and T. Priol. "Shrinker: Improving Live Migration of Virtual Clusters over WANs with Distributed Data Deduplication and Content-Based Addressing", in Euro-Par 2011 Parallel Processing Lecture Notes in Computer Science, Volume 6852, 2011, pp 431-442

SESSION

CLOUD COMPUTING AND RELATED ISSUES

Chair(s)

TBA

Towards a User Deployable Service-oriented Autonomic Multi-cloud Overlay Infrastructure for Sky Computing

Courtney Powell[1], **Masaharu Munetomo**[1], **and Takashi Aizawa**[2]
[1]Information Initiative Center, Hokkaido University, Sapporo, Japan
[2]Graduate School of Information Science and Technology, Hokkaido University, Sapporo, Japan

Abstract—*Cloud computing services at the SaaS level of the cloud computing model are easy to access and utilize. In contrast, the self-service approach taken at the IaaS level results in difficulties for non-savvy users. Compounding these difficulties is the fact that for resiliency, economic, and scalability reasons, utilization of IaaS resources across multiple cloud providers in a unified manner is deemed the best strategy. In this paper, we outline our proposal for a user-centric multi-cloud autonomic overlay infrastructure that can be deployed across existing cloud systems without the need for specialized hardware or action on the part of cloud providers. We also present the results of a simple genome sequencing experiment and bandwidth measurements conducted on a crude prototype implementation of the system.*

Keywords: virtual distributed ethernet (VDE), application defined networking (ADN), virtual overlay infrastructure, simple heterogeneous inter-cloud manager (SHINCLOM), cloud federation, CloudStack.

1 Introduction

Cloud computing has rapidly advanced into the public consciousness, with software as a service (SaaS) becoming a virtually indispensable part of everyday life due to easy access and utility. In cloud computing, everything is delivered as a service [1]. However, for users who require more than the relatively simple applications offered at this uppermost layer of the cloud computing model, things are not as simple because the lower levels utilize a self-service approach, in which users are expected to provision, manage, and maintain what they need by themselves. Deploying applications at the infrastructure as a service (IaaS) level is non-trivial as the distributed applications being deployed often comprise interdependent services that form a complex hierarchy across virtual machines (VMs), and which must be configured in a particular order [2]. Thus, simply accessing and utilizing IaaS resources on any one cloud platform requires a variety of technical know-how—such as knowledge of the relevant APIs to use and how to install, launch, configure, and maintain the desired applications and services.

Adding to the difficulties outlined above is the fact that mission critical business applications require that downtime be minimized and optimum performance maintained; yet, it has become patently clear that trusting essential applications to one cloud platform or provider is not a wise strategy due to the possibility of outages and scalability, flexibility, and economic issues. Further, at present, the frightening possibility of cloud lock-in [3] awaits unwary users as dynamically migrating applications and services from one cloud to another or launching and maintaining applications across cloud systems in order to avail oneself of better prices, levels of service, etc. is still very difficult.

Cloud federation is an emerging paradigm in which resources from multiple independent cloud providers are leveraged to create a virtual cloud system that overcomes some of the limitations of single-cloud systems (such as provisioning and scalability constraints), is resilient to failures, and provides high availability. As outlined by Petcu [4], the actual clouds can be federated in a number of ways: Horizontal federation, Inter-Clouds federation, Cross-Clouds federation, and Sky Computing [5].

In this paper, we outline our user-centric approach to cloud-federation, with which we ultimately aim to spare users the tedious, time-consuming, and error-prone process of manually installing, configuring, and monitoring multi-cloud applications and services at the IaaS level. Consequently, we are currently developing a user deployable autonomic multi-cloud overlay infrastructure comprising various applications, utilities, and services that users can easily deploy and utilize. In this sense, our objective is a form of Sky Computing as our aim is to compose the *existing user-level services* offered by cloud providers into a single virtual framework (in the form of a "single-cloud like image") that is independent of any one type of cloud platform and offering new services other than those provided by each individual cloud provider (i.e., greater than the sum of its individual parts). The actual infrastructure is being developed in a holistic way with the aid of a proposed layered autonomic multi-cloud model on which existing and future technologies can be integrated in such a way that how the various elements in our framework function and interoperate can be easily understood.

The remainder of this paper is organized as follows: In Section 2, we introduce and outline our proposed layered autonomic multi-cloud model. In Section 3, we discuss our preliminary implementation of a user deployable virtual overlay infrastructure and MPI clusters. We also discuss the results of a simple genome sequencing experiment conducted on the clusters and bandwidth measurements done on the infrastructure. In Section 4, we outline future work to be done. Finally, we conclude this paper in Section 5.

2 Autonomic Multi-cloud Model

We propose that autonomic multi-cloud applications and services be developed based on the conceptual model depicted in Fig. 1. This conceptual model allows for the design and development of applications and services in a cloud-agnostic way. Our aim is to leverage the many technologies and techniques currently available and map them onto the relevant layers of our model in a transparent manner by adapting, integrating, and (where necessary) modifying and extending them in such a way that the links among the technologies are easily analyzable and optimizable. The layers and the functions they perform in the model are discussed below.

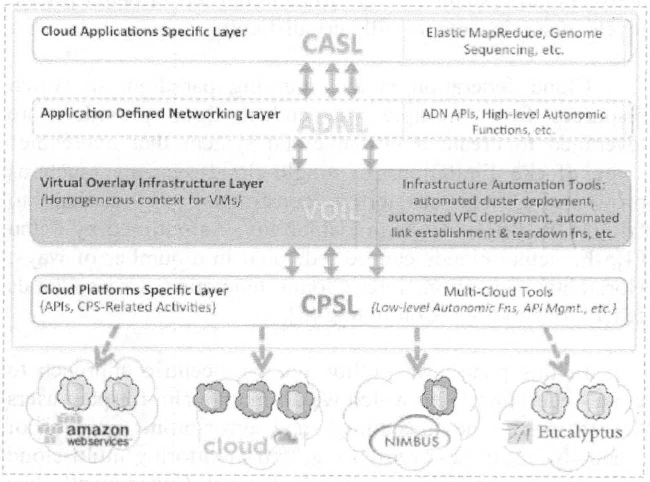

Fig. 1: Proposed layered autonomic multi-cloud model

2.1 Layer 1: Cloud Platforms Specific Layer (CPSL)

There are currently a large number of public and private cloud platforms, some better known than others. At present, these cloud platforms do not use a common set of APIs. The cloud platforms specific layer (CPSL) forms the foundation of our model as it translates the various calls from the upper layers into calls that can be initiated on the various platforms. Utilities such as LibCloud [6] and DeltaCloud [7] can be deployed at this layer to carry out these functions. Further, tools such as CloudInit.d [8] and Wrangler [9] can be extended and integrated to provide low-level autonomic functions such as monitoring and repair of VMs at this layer.

2.2 Layer 2: Virtual Overlay Infrastructure Layer (VOIL)

The virtual overlay infrastructure layer (VOIL) is a critical part of our proposed model. At this layer, the following activities and services are provided:

1. A seamless virtual overlay infrastructure that abstracts away the differences inherent in the various cloud platforms.
2. A homogeneous context for VMs from disparate clouds.
3. Infrastructure automation tools and services such as automated cluster and VPC deployment services; akin to the tool execution environment envisioned by Afgan et al. [10].

2.3 Layer 3: Application Defined Networking Layer (ADNL)

At the application defined networking layer (ADNL), the focus is on optimization and orchestration of the movement of data throughout the VOIL for each application. Application defined networking (ADN) [11] takes center stage at this layer. In contrast to software defined networking (SDN), which deals with the forwarding of individual packets throughout the network infrastructure, ADN works with data and gives applications the ability to dynamically adapt to their networking environment in order to optimize their performance. ADN is based on a feedback loop principle, which it leverages to monitor, analyze, and orchestrate infrastructure capacity and configuration in order to continuously adapt applications to facilitate optimum performance [11]. Thus, in our proposed model, ADN services monitor ADN-enabled applications in the cloud applications specific layer (CASL) and dynamically orchestrate (activate, deactivate, and tune) the services provided at the VOIL as it endeavors to achieve and maintain the performance targets of the associated application. For example, if the capacity links in the infrastructure are over-stretched and on the verge of causing imminent impairment to services and applications, ADN tools in the ADNL will be able to obviate this. At this layer, processes and agents such as those proposed in the GerNU project [12] could be modified and deployed to ensure optimum application performance and compliance with predefined service level agreements (SLAs).

2.4 Layer 4: Cloud Applications Specific Layer (CASL)

At the cloud applications specific layer (CASL), it is envisioned that applications will be able to operate without consideration for the disparate cloud platforms on which they are running. Thus, in the CASL *(pun intended)*, applications should be able to operate with impunity in pursuit of their various performance targets.

3 Prototype Implementation and Results

As a first step towards the realization of our user deployable autonomic multi-cloud overlay infrastructure based on the proposed autonomic multi-cloud model, we developed both a user-deployable virtual multi-cloud overlay infrastructure using virtual distributed Ethernet (VDE) [13] and an automated cluster deployment tool. We discuss these developments and our preliminary results below.

3.1 Overlay infrastructure implementation

We implemented the virtual infrastructure depicted in Fig. 2 using VDE as the virtual networking utility and Python Fabric [14], which provides a basic suite of operations for executing local and remote shell commands and uploading/downloading files, for system configuration. VDE has been used to implement virtual network laboratories such as Marionnet [15] and to build private networks for clusters of nodes in the Eucalyptus private cloud platform [16]. It is an open-source OSI Layer 2 virtual network software tool that can run on both virtual and physical machines and is able to forward, dispatch, and route plain Ethernet packets. VDE has the same structure as modern Ethernet networks and its main components are managed switches, wires (any tool capable of transferring a stream connection, e.g., SSH), and plugs (programs connected to a switch to convert all the traffic to a standard stream connection). A VDE cable comprises a wire with a plug at either end and is used to interconnect two VDE switches.

To implement the virtual overlay infrastructure depicted in Fig. 2, we deployed a VDE switch on the tap0 network interface of each VM (and physical computer) and connected the switches using SSH. As most cloud platforms use Class A private addressing (i.e., 10.x.x.x) on their eth0 network interfaces and small private networks use Class C private addressing (i.e., 192.168.x.x), to avoid confusion, we opted to use Class B private addressing (i.e., 172.16.x.x to 172.31.x.x) in our overlay infrastructure.

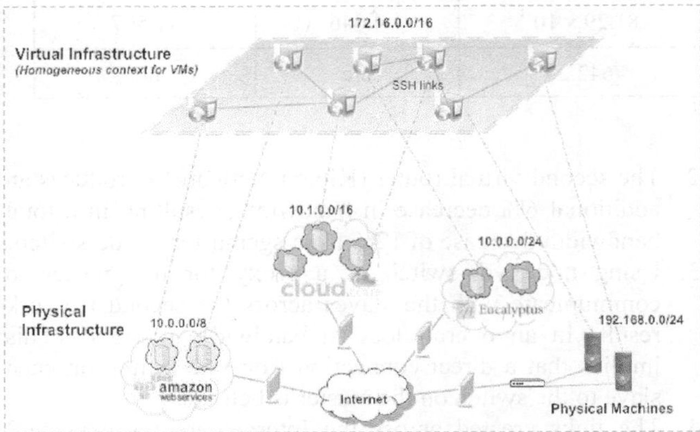

Fig. 2: Implemented virtual overlay infrastructure

3.2 Automated MPI cluster deployment

To enable automated cluster deployments on the infrastructure, we created a tool in Python that deploys and configures master and slave nodes using prebuilt CloudStack [31] templates made from Ubuntu 12.10 64-bit servers, with MPICH2 [32] installed.

3.2.1 Experimental cluster configurations

To get an idea of the performance of our multi-cloud cluster, we compared the performance of a small six-machine cluster for the three configurations illustrated in Figs. 3 to 5. For Configuration 1 (Fig. 3), the cluster was deployed on a conventional single-site CloudStack network (i.e., without the virtual overlay infrastructure). For Configuration 2 (Fig. 4), the cluster was deployed on the virtual overlay infrastructure across two CloudStack networks. For Configuration 3 (Fig. 5), the cluster was deployed on the virtual overlay infrastructure, this time comprising two CloudStack networks, two AWS [33] regions, and a physical machine.

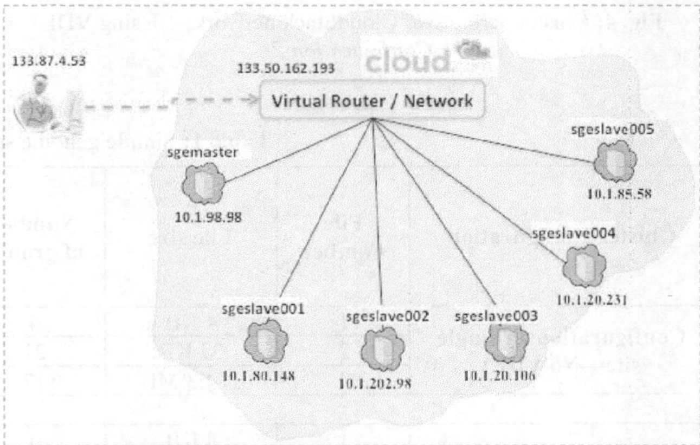

Fig. 3: Conventional single-site CloudStack cluster—No VDE *(Configuration 1)*

3.2.2 Simple genome sequencing experimental results

Executing the ClustalW-MPI alignment sequence tool [17] on three files across the cluster in each of the three configurations gave us the results shown in Table 1. For the largest file, the transfer time for Configuration 2 was almost twice that of Configuration 1, while that of Configuration 3 was almost 30 times that of Configuration 1. For the smallest file, however, Configurations 2 and 3 had very close transfer times. Large time differences between Configuration 1 and Configuration 3 were also evident in the sequence alignment times. We believe that the large time differentials are due to the fact that Configuration 3 comprised three nodes that were connected to the master via slow interconnection (Internet) links. To test the speed of the links, we conducted bandwidth measurements, which we discuss in Section 3.3.

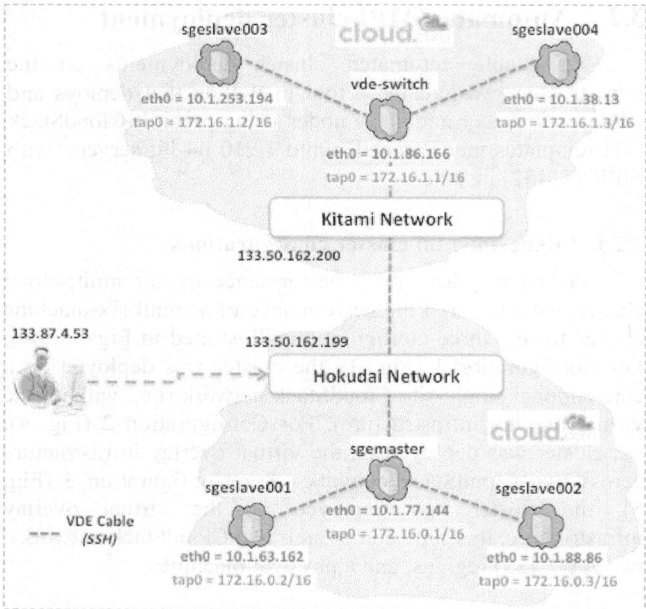

Fig. 4: Cluster across two CloudStack networks—Using VDE *(Configuration 2)*

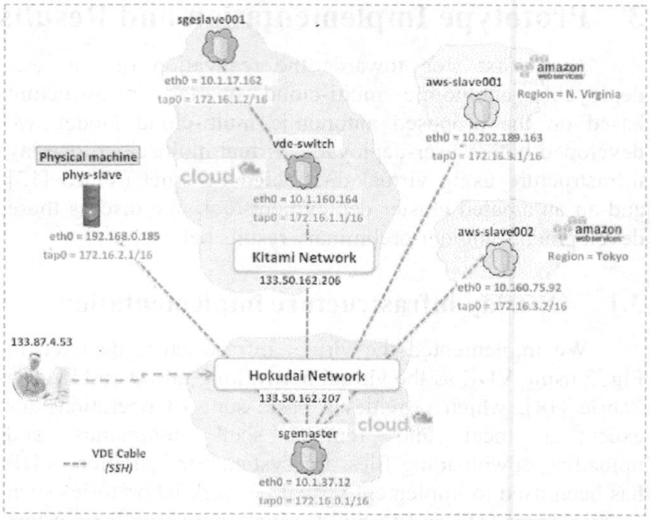

Fig. 5: Cluster across two CloudStack networks, two AWS regions, and one physical machine—Using VDE *(Configuration 3)*

Table 1: Simple genome sequencing experimental results

Cluster configuration	File number	File size	Number of groups	Time to transfer to slave nodes (s)	Time for pairwise sequence alignments (s)	Time for multiple sequence alignments (s)
Configuration 1 (Single site—No VDE)	1	4 KB	4	1.19×10^{-4}	0.011	0.077
	2	37 KB	21	3.29×10^{-4}	2.491	2.306
	3	124.3 MB	1170	23.76	n/a	n/a
Configuration 2 (Two CS networks—VDE)	1	4 KB	4	24.59×10^{-4}	0.023	0.335
	2	37 KB	21	47.65×10^{-4}	2.554	3.941
	3	124.3 MB	1170	43.23	n/a	n/a
Configuration 3 (Two CS networks, 2 AWS regions, 1 physical machine—VDE)	1	4 KB	4	21.98×10^{-4}	0.709	16.502
	2	37 KB	21	81.29×10^{-4}	4.046	71.507
	3	124.3 MB	1170	642.20	n/a	n/a

3.3 Bandwidth measurements

Using Iperf [18] with its default TCP window size of 8 KB, we conducted bandwidth tests between sgemaster and each of the slave nodes. The network configuration used is depicted in Fig. 6. The resultant bandwidth determined for the link between sgemaster and each slave node is shown in Fig. 7. Using the bandwidth obtained on eth0 as the standard (i.e., 207 Mbps), we computed the loss in bandwidth across the virtual infrastructure. The results obtained indicate the following:

1. The use of the virtual infrastructure results in a 6% decrease in bandwidth.
2. The second virtual router (Kitami Network) introduces an additional 6% decrease in bandwidth, resulting in a total bandwidth decrease of 12% from sgemaster to vde-switch.
3. Using node vde-switch as a proxy for the master to communicate with the slaves across the second network results in an overall loss in bandwidth of 43%. (This implies that a direct connection from the switch on each slave to the switch on the master is better.)
4. The links created across the Internet are (as expected) much slower than those inside the data center. This fact is reflected in the 99% and 92% bandwidth losses between sgemaster and euca-slave (in the Eucalyptus Community

Cloud (ECC) [34]) and sgemaster and aws-slave (AWS Tokyo region), respectively.

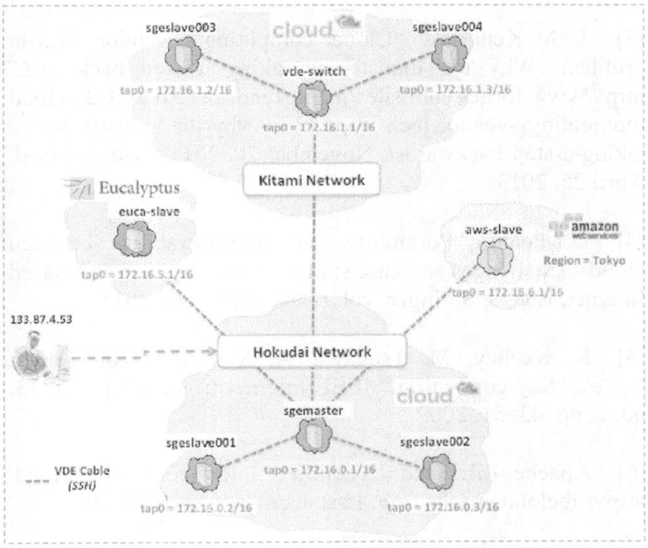

Fig. 6: Configuration used in bandwidth tests

4 Discussions and Future Work

It is obvious that in order to implement the kind of infrastructure proposed above the bandwidth disparities reported in this paper will have to be taken into account and techniques implemented to lessen their impact on the performance of the applications implemented on the virtual overlay infrastructure. The implementation of point-to-point dedicated links such as SINET [19] could be a solution for some inter-cloud links. However, as the idea is to facilitate connectivity across any available cloud system to which a user has access, other means of optimizing the user-level connections among cloud systems across the Internet are also imperative. For some applications, establishment of a primary link and the provision of a secondary link/route may be necessary. This can easily be done with VDE, as any switch on any node can be connected to a multiplicity of other nodes; thereby, providing the ability for the creation of alternate links/route. In fact, we plan to explore the performance impact of various topologies, such as star-ring hybrid and star-hypercube hybrid.

Even though our preliminary investigation indicates only a 6% fall in bandwidth due to the use of VDE, further investigations need to be done to see how the actual overlay infrastructure itself affects the performance of applications. Further, we intend to evaluate various other networking technologies to determine how well they cope with the rigors of a system such as this, and whether they can be combined and/or extended. Among these are ViNe [20], which uses user-level virtual routers (VMs on which ViNe processing software is installed and configured) to dictate overlay network communication by acting as gateways for nodes that do not run the ViNe software; VNET/U [21], which, in addition to facilitating overlay networking, may be able to provide ADN-related services such as monitoring of application communication and computation behavior [22]; and N2N [35], which uses P2P principles and the concept of edge nodes and super nodes (which relay packets across NAT boundaries for edge nodes) to facilitate overlay networks. Integration of the high-performance message passing protocol Open-MX [23] and user mode Linux related technologies such as VNX [24], Netkit [25], and Cloonix [26] also present interesting possibilities.

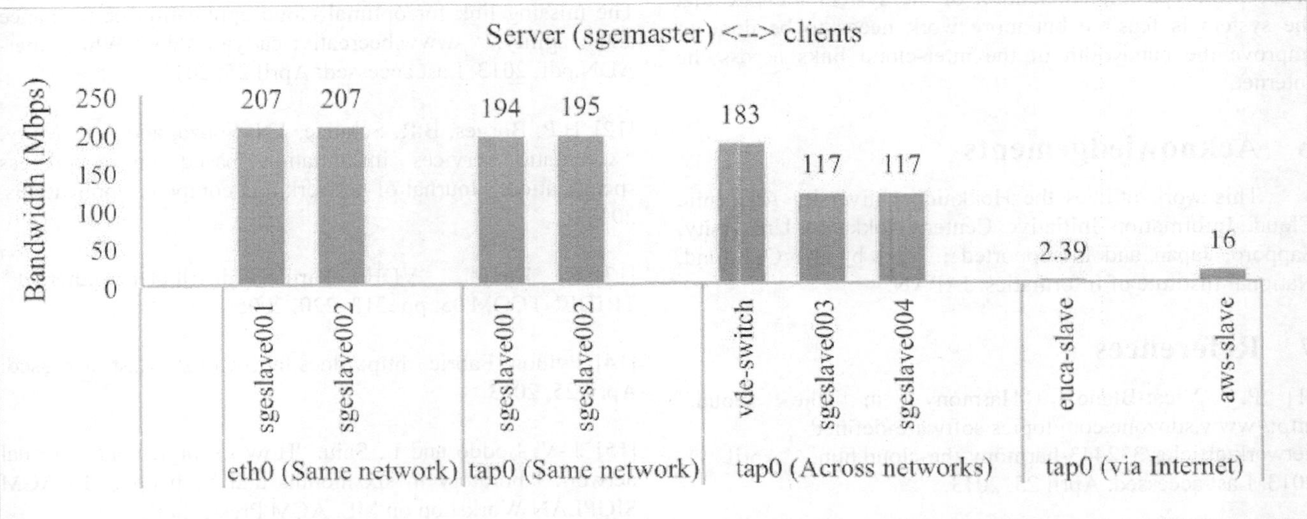

Fig. 7: Bandwidth from sgemaster to each client for the configuration in Fig. 6

Smith [27] enumerated a number of problems that may beset applications in single-site and federated clouds, such as the possibility of traffic impairment when multiple providers are utilized in order to reduce risks and difficulty avoiding network latency and bottlenecks. Our ultimate aim is to obviate such problems by applying the appropriate technology (or optimized mix of technologies) at each layer of our model. In [28], Friedman touched on the increasing trend of applications integrating across clouds, and states that *"This presents an impedance mismatch where a highly distributed and concurrent application must talk across a narrow 1-1 link with another highly distributed and concurrent application."* Some actual application challenges in the scientific arena, including the fact that application failures are prevalent in federated clouds, are also outlined by Deelman et al. [2]. We believe that the creation of an overlay infrastructure such as ours, in which applications are treated as first-class entities (i.e., ADN) and thus have the ability to autonomously act to fulfill specified requirements, can obviate this impending impedance mismatch.

The infrastructure proposed in this paper is being developed as part of the Simple Heterogeneous INter-CLoud Manager (SHINCLOM) project at Hokkaido University, Japan. In this project, we have already implemented a web interface that provides simple functions such as registration of cloud credentials in the content management system Drupal [29], which facilitates the development of the various sections of a cloud management system as modules that can be easily integrated [30].

5 Conclusion

In this paper, we outlined our proposal for the development of a user-centric multi-cloud overlay infrastructure based on a proposed layered autonomic multi-cloud model. Experimental measurements conducted on a crude prototype implementation of the system indicate that the system is feasible but more work needs to be done to improve the bandwidth of the inter-cloud links across the Internet.

6 Acknowledgements

This work utilizes the Hokkaido University Academic Cloud, Information Initiative Center, Hokkaido University, Sapporo, Japan and is supported in part by the CSI fund, National Institute of Informatics, JAPAN.

7 References

[1] P. Vicat-Blanc. "Harmony in the cloud." http://www.sdnzone.com/topics/software-defined-network/articles/332443-harmony-the-cloud.htm, April 1, 2013. Last accessed: April 25, 2013.

[2] E. Deelman, G. Juve, and G.B. Berriman. "Using clouds for science, is it just kicking the can down the road?" CLOSER 2012, pp. 127-134.

[3] J. McKendrick. "Cloud computing's vendor lock-in problem: Why the industry is taking a step backward." http://www.forbes.com/sites/joemckendrick/2011/11/20/cloud-computings-vendor-lock-in-problem-why-the-industry-is-taking-a-step-backwards/, November 20, 2011. Last accessed: April 25, 2013.

[4] D. Petcu. "Portability and interoperability between clouds: Challenges and case study." Towards a Service-Based Internet, LNCS, Springer, vol. 6994, pp. 62–74, 2011.

[5] K. Keahey, M. Tsugawa, A. Matsunaga, and J. A. Fortes. "Sky computing." IEEE Internet Computing, vol. 13, no. 5, pp. 43–51, 2009.

[6] Apache LibCloud: A unified interface to the cloud. http://libcloud.apache.org/. Last accessed: April 25, 2013.

[7] DeltaCloud. http://deltacloud.apache.org/. Last accessed: April 25, 2013.

[8] J. Bresnahan, T. Freeman, D. LaBissoniere, and K. Keahey. "Managing appliance launches in infrastructure clouds." Teragrid Conference, 2011.

[9] G. Juve and E. Deelman. "Automating application deployment in infrastructure clouds." CloudCom 2011.

[10] E. Afgan, K. Skala, D. Davidovic, T. Lipic, and I. Sovic. "CloudMan as a tool execution framework for the cloud." MIPRO 2012, pp. 437–441, May 21–25, 2012.

[11] Lyatiss whitepaper. "Application defined networking: The missing link for optimal cloud application performance and agility." www.becreative.ca/lyatiss/docs/Whitepaper-ADN.pdf, 2013. Last accessed: April 25, 2013.

[12] H.P. Borges, B.R. Schulze, J.N. Souza, and A.R. Mury. "Automatic services instantiation based on a process specification." Journal of network and computer applications, 2012

[13] R. Davoli. "VDE: Virtual distributed ethernet." TRIDENTCOM'05, pp. 213–220, 2005.

[14] Python Fabric. http://docs.fabfile.org/. Last accessed: April 25, 2013.

[15] J.-V. Loddo and L. Saiu. "How to implement a virtual network laboratory in six months and be happy." In ACM SIGPLAN Workshop on ML. ACM Press, 2007.

[16] D. Nurmi, R. Wolski, C. Grzegorczyk, G. Obertelli, S. Soman, L. Youseff, and D. Zagorodnov. "The Eucalyptus

open-source cloud-computing system." CCGRID'09, Shanghai, China, pp.124-131, May 2009.

[17] K.-B. Li. "ClustalW-MPI: ClustalW analysis using distributed and parallel computing." Bioinformatics, pp. 585-586, 2003.

[18] Iperf. http://openmaniak.com/iperf.php. Last accessed: April 25, 2013.

[19] SINET. http://www.sinet.ad.jp/index_en.html?lang=english. Last accessed: April 25, 2013.

[20] M. Tsugawa, A. Matsunaga, and J. Fortes. "User-level virtual network support for sky computing." e-Science'09, pp. 72–79, 2009.

[21] A. Sundararaj and P. Dinda. "Towards virtual networks for virtual machine grid computing." Proc. 3rd USENIX Virtual Machine Research And Technology Symposium (VM 2004), May 2004.

[22] A. Gupta and P.A. Dinda. "Inferring the topology and traffic load of parallel programs running in a virtual machine environment." Proc. 10th Workshop on Job Scheduling Strategies for Parallel Processing (JSSPP), June 2004.

[23] Open-MX: Myrinet express over generic ethernet hardware. http://open-mx.gforge.inria.fr/. Last accessed: April 25, 2013.

[24] VNX: Virtual Networks over linuX. http://web.dit.upm.es/vnxwiki/index.php/Main_Page. Last accessed: April 25, 2013.

[25] Netkit: The poor man's system to experiment computer networking. http://wiki.netkit.org/index.php/Main_Page. Last accessed: April 25, 2013.

[26] Cloonix: Dynamical topology virtual networks. http://clownix.net/. Last accessed: April 25, 2013.

[27] M. Smith. "Network and application performance in cloud." http://erpcloudnews.com/2013/04/network-and-application-performance-in-cloud/. Last accessed: April 25, 2013.

[28] J. Friedman. "Patterns for programming in the clouds." http://www.cs.york.ac.uk/library/proj_files/2010/EngDInd/julz/litreview-final-31may.pdf. Last accessed: April 25, 2013.

[29] Drupal. http://drupal.org/. Last accessed: April 25, 2013.

[30] Y. Naoi. "Clanavi: How to manage your cloud by Drupal." Bay Area Drupal Camp 2010, November 13, 2010.

[31] CloudStack open source computing. http://cloudstack.apache.org/. Last accessed: May 31, 2013.

[32] MPICH: High-performance portable MPI. http://www.mpich.org/. Last accessed: May 31, 2013.

[33] Amazon web services. http://aws.amazon.com/. Last accessed: May 31, 2013.

[34] Eucalyptus community cloud (ECC). http://www.eucalyptus.com/eucalyptus-cloud/community-cloud. Last accessed: May 31, 2013.

[35] N2N: A layer two peer-to-peer VPN. http://www.ntop.org/products/n2n/. Last accessed: May 31, 2013.

SLA-Aware Adaptive Provisioning Method for Virtualized Application Execution Environments

Seunghwan Yoo[1], **and Sungchun Kim**[1]
[1] Computer Science & Engineering Department, Sogang University, Seoul, South Korea

Abstract — *Resource provisioning is a general technique for handling the resource allocation in cloud environment. Monitoring the system performance and the user request is crucial for efficient cloud resource management. Also in cloud environments, issues such as cost and resource provisioning based on QoS constraints are yet to be addressed. In this paper, we present a SLA(Service Level Agreement) - Aware Adaptive (SAA) provisioning method for Virtualized Applications that employ a flexible determining model. We present advanced cloud infrastructure which maintain proper virtual machine numbers by optimizing resources allocation. Our experiments show that our adaptive model minimize the maintain cost of virtual machines while satisfying user average response time constraint and the request arrival rate constraint.*

Keywords: Provisioning, Service Level Agreement, Adaptive, Cloud Computing Platform

1 Introduction

Clouds computing redefine a new supplement, consumption, and delivery service model for IT web services by providing dynamically scalable and often virtualized resources as a service over the Internet[1]. Cloud computing[2,3] are provided as three kinds of services type. Such as Infrastructure as a Service(IaaS), Platform as a Service(PaaS), and Software as a Service(SaaS). We consider mainly IaaS, which provide a range of attractive features such as resource elasticity, cost efficiency, and ease of management. The main purpose of management cloud computing infrastructure is to ensure the quality and cost-effectiveness. Moreover, it also leads the reestablishment of economic relationships between the provider and the users based on cost and performance of the services. The online users can get services by sending their requests to service provider. Also, the cloud services should satisfy Service Level Agreements (SLAs). SLA is agreement about quality of cloud services signed between cloud service providers and consumers. SLA specifies concretely expected performance metric and charging model, which include response time, throughput, availability, reward and penalty, and so forth. Current cloud computing paradigms are not easily to meet users' purpose, especially facing the requirement of diverse applications from different users.

In order to satisfy SLA and provisioning existing virtualized resources optimally. Cloud computing service providers make the profits by providing high-quality services through efficiently allocating the resources on demand at the same time. We present a SLA-based framework handling resource allocation on a cloud computing platform. This would support to accomplish two goals simultaneously: minimized user response time and minimized resource usage cost.

The activities to accomplish both goals may conflict with each other. For example, user response time can be reduced by assigning more resources while the cost may be lowered by allocating less resources. Since the workload of an application service usually varies with time, this is a great challenge for resource allocation optimally. So, proposed provisioning method would need to achieve the goal.

For this reason, this paper proposes a SLA-Aware Adaptive resource provisioning method (SAA provisioning Method). SAA provisioning method provides scalable processing power with dynamic resource provisioning mechanisms, where the number of virtual machine used is dynamically adapted to the time-varying incoming request workload. To evaluate our framework and method, we applied RUBIS [19] to simulate the cloud environment. In the simulation, the workload estimation for virtualized applications is investigated comprehensively. Through, we compare it with utilized method, a dynamic resource provisioning approach proposed recently.

The remainder of the paper is organized as follows. Section 2 presents survey related to our work. Section 3 describes our SAA provisioning method on the cloud computing platform. Section 4 presents our adaptive resource provisioning algorithm and its performance evaluation. Section 5 concludes the paper and points out some future research directions.

2 Related Work

Dynamic resource provisioning [4], which has been generally used in web hosting platforms, has proven to be useful in handling multiple time-scale workloads(VMs). However, dynamic provisioning in previous research has been more focus on physical resource allocation, which is not flexible enough for the effective delivering of services. Unlike other computing resources, VMs are flexibly deployed on physical machines, which can be automatically generated for different virtualized applications. Though existing physical capacity provisioning has long been used, overprovisioning or under-provisioning has been a common difficulty for most resource IT vendors. To solve this problem it is necessary to make full use of advantages of adaptive resource provisioning. We propose the design of a virtualized resource allocation framework using the cloud platform, which allocates VMs on demand in order to provide services, as well as minimizing the cost of using those virtual resources.

Nowadays, some researches have focused on the issue of resource management and performance control in cloud computing platform[5,6]. However, new challenges are introduced while service providers benefit from the planning flexibility in technical and economic aspects. Some challenges and opportunities of automated control in cloud computing is discussed in [7]. And other researchers work to improve the resource utilization, such as resource virtualization [8,16], on-demand resource provisioning management based on virtual machines [9, 10], and QoS management of virtual machine [11].

Also, many researchers [12, 13] focus on improving resource utilization as well as guaranteeing quality of the hosted services via on-demand local resource scheduling models or algorithms within a physical server. However, most of them could not be good solutions to tradeoff between resource utilization and SLA. For example, [12] present a novel system-level application resource demand phase analysis and prediction prototype to support on-demand resource provisioning. The process takes into consideration application's resource consumption patterns, pricing schedules defined by the resource provider, and penalties associated with SLA violations. The authors in [13] improve resource utilization and performance of some services by hugely reducing performance of others. How to improve resource utilization, as well as guarantee SLA, is a challenge in a VM-based cloud data center

In the context of the dynamic resource provisioning, the author in [16] introduce three mechanisms for web clusters. The first mechanism, QuID [14], optimizes the performance within a cluster by dynamically allocating servers on-demand. The second, WARD [15], is a request redirection mechanism across the clusters. The third one is a cluster decision algorithm that selects QuID or WARD under different workload conditions.

For multi-tier internet applications, the modeling is proposed that a provisioning technique which employs two methods that operate at two different time scales : predictive provisioning at the time-scale of hours or days, and reactive provisioning at time scales of minutes to respond to a peak load[17].

In this section, we first discuss the service level agreements (SLAs) that we use in the paper. Then we give a highlevel description of the test bed and three types of workload generators for our experimental studies. Finally, we describe the control system architecture that we use throughout the paper.

2.1 Service Level Agreements

Service level agreements (SLAs) are firm contracts between a service provider (IT Bender) and its clients (Users). SLAs in general depend on certain chosen criteria, such as latency, reliability, availability, throughput and security, and so on. In this paper, we focus on end-to-end latency, or maintain cost. Although SLA cost function may have various forms, we believe that a staircase function is a natural choice used in the real-world contracts as it is easy to describe in natural language [18]. We use a single step function for SLA in our paper as a reasonable approximation. We assume that if response time is shorter than arranged time, then the service provider will earn some revenue. Otherwise, the service provider will pay a penalty back to the client. As a result, in order to minimize the SLA penalty cost, our method should keep the response time right below arranged time

3 Proposed Scheme

3.1 SAA Framework

This section presents a scalable framework for virtualized applications on the cloud computing platform. The framework deals with the scenario that hosted on a cloud computing platform, handle many virtual machines simultaneously according to the incoming user requests. Since the amount of incoming requests changes with time and the cloud platform is a pay-per use service, the application has to dynamically assign the resources it uses to maintain guaranteed response time and reduce the total owner cost under various workloads. In the framework, server pool, combining a distinct computing server, is capable of processing multiple hybrid workload requests.

To efficiently utilize resources, there are two main issues considered in the cloud computing platforms. The first is finding the least loaded resource for dispatching incoming requests. The second issue deals with SAA provisioning for adaptively handling dynamic user's requests. With resource state monitoring, each workflow enactment request will be sent to the least loaded resource for service. The effectiveness of least load dispatching largely depends on how to accurately capture the computing load on each resource.

Fig. 1 shows an overview of the framework in handling user requests for virtualized application execution environments (VAEEs). The architecture consists of four main components that Monitor, Analyzer, Resource scheduler, and Virtualized Application Executor (VAE) control loops architecture. The goal is to meet the user requirements while adapting cloud architecture to workload variations. Usually, each request requires the execution of virtualized application allocated on the VM of each physical server. A cloud computing resource amount enables multiple virtualized applications may be increased when request increases and reduced when request reduces. This dynamic resource provisioning allows flexible response time in a VAEE where peak workload is much greater than the normal steady state.

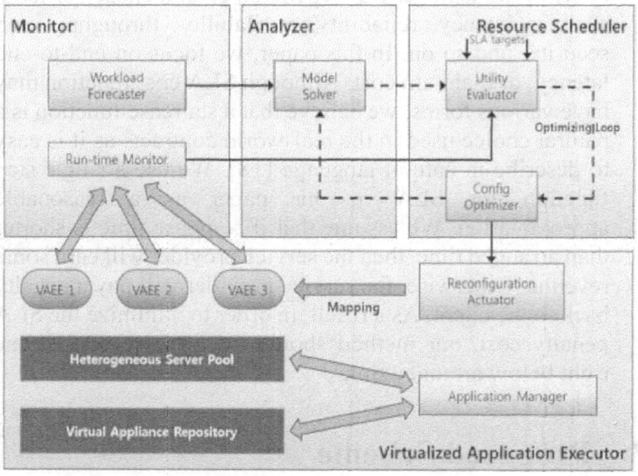

Fig. 1 Proposed SAA-Provisioning Framework

Fig 1 provides a high-level dynamic resource provision architecture for cloud computing platform, which shows relationships between heterogeneous server resources pool and self-management function. Server pool contains physical resources and virtualized resources. A lot of VMs hold several VAEEs sharing the capacity of physical resources and can isolate multiple applications from the underlying hardware. VMs of a virtualized application may correspond to a physical machine.

Self-management function means mechanisms to automate the VMs of configuring and tuning the virtualized application so as to maintain the guaranteed response time for requirements of the diverse users. As previously stated, four main components more detail explanation are as follows:

① Monitor: Collects the workload and the performance metric of all running VAEEs, such as the response time, the request arrival rate, the average service time, and the CPU utilization, etc.

② Analyzer: Receives and analyzes the logged parameter from the monitor to estimate next state workload. It also receives the response times of different users

③ Resource Scheduler: Sets up updated configuration metric for each VAEE, and uses its optimizer with the optimization model to determine resource provisioning according to these workload estimates and response time constrains of different users such that the resource requirements of the overall VAEE is minimized.

④ Virtualized Application Executor: Assigns the virtual machine configuration, and then runs the VAEEs to satisfy the resource requirements of the different customers according to the optimized decision.

In conclusion, Fig. 1 is presented the dynamic resource provisioning method. Our research is a great help of on the improved design of resource scheduler for requested workload. The goal is to minimize the using of resources for request workload while satisfying different users for the guaranteed response time.

3.2 Proposed SAA provisioning Algorithms

In this section, we propose an auto-control algorithm denoted as SAA provisioning method (SLA Aware Adaptive) to dynamically provide an adequate amount of resources to virtualized application. To maintain acceptable response time and cost efficiency, it would find the configuration value which the Sum of each VAEEs profits is maximized. Considering all of virtual machine system parameters observed by monitor, especially response time and usage cost, we compute the profit value of each VAEEs. Through equation (1), our method calculates the optimized next step setting value. Resource scheduler receives the modified configuration parameter. Then it reflects the value next schedule period.

Table.1 List of Notations

Symbol	Definition
r(RA)	Rate of Arrival Request
r(SLAS)	Rate of SLA Satisfied
r(VMF)	Rate of VM Failed
c(VMA)	Active VM maintain Cost
c(VMI)	Idle VM maintain Cost
α	Created Value (per Application)
β	Weight Value (per Application)

$$\text{Profit}(P_i) = \alpha \times \{r(R_{Ai}) \times r(SLA_{Si}) - r(VM_{fi})\} - \beta \times \{c(VM_{Ai}) + c(VM_{Ii})\} \quad (1)$$

After each VAEE Profit(Pi) is calculated, Periodically it is updated and check SLA-requirements. After the specific point which variability is minimized, Our Scheme elect optimized parameter for Global Profit.

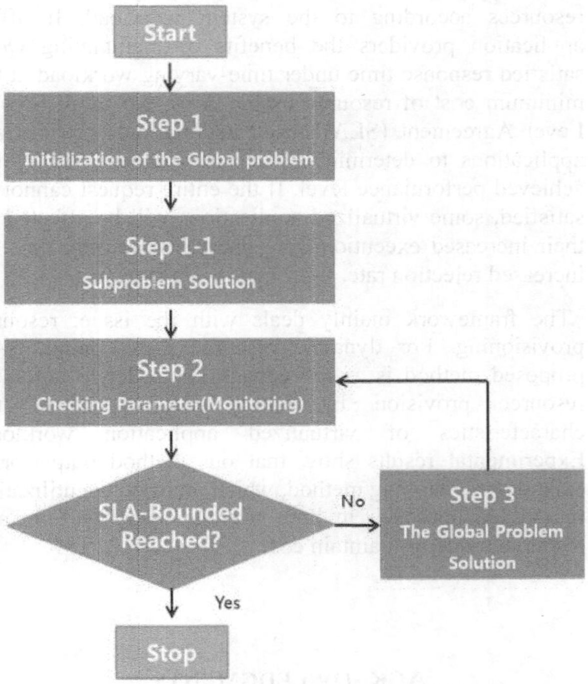

Fig. 2 Flowchart Calculate Optimized Profit

$$\max\{\, Profit_{global} = \textstyle\sum_{i=1}^{n} p_i \,\} \qquad (2)$$

After all, our mechanism collect local profit and calculate Global profit as shown in (2). It would find the optimal value for certain period. Also it is adaptively perform in the course of time. Since it has sufficient information about virtualized application. For example, there are a little difference between current parameter and next-step parameter. It check prefixed threshold. If it is not exceed, retain the system current parameter. Finally, Our SAA provisioning algorithms would find SLA- guaranteed response time and low maintenance cost.

4 Performance Analysis

4.1 Experiment

In the following experiments, we evaluate our dynamic resource provisioning technique for virtualized applications. We establish a prototype system of cloud environment such that each of the server nodes was run on Intel Xeon 3.2GHz processors with 8GB RAM. Processing capacity of each VM server is equal in cloud platform. VAEE Host ran the open-source version of the Xen 3.0.3 to build the virtualization environment. All machines were conducted on a Linux kernel 2.6.16.29.

The RUBiS online auction benchmark [19], running on VMs hosted on different VM servers. RUBiS implements the core functionality of an auction site similar to eBay, can be performed from a client's Web browser. We perform the three-different kind of applications. The first kind of application was based on the Apache 2.2 Web server. The second was based on Java servlets that implement the application logic with an embedded Tomcat 5.0.28. And Third application was based on MySQL 4.0. Because our tested application is CPU-intensive, the only computing resource we currently regard is CPU resource allocation and we assume that all VM resources are identical. Table 2 shows the values for various RUBiS parameters in our simulation experiments.

Table.2 Workload Setting Parameter for RUBiS

	Web Service	App Service	DB Service
End–End Response Time	0.15 sec	0.45 sec	0.40 sec
Service Rate	350 req/s	200 req/s	150 req/s
Request Probability	-	0.85	0.85
Guaranteed Response time	1 sec		

4.2 Experiment result

Existing method, focus on maximizing resource utilization is approximately demonstrated 87% SLA-satisfied rate. We give consideration to improve SLA-satisfied ratio. Our mechanism indicate settlement for content better SLA-satisfied rate and diminish maintain cost.

Our method conducts initiation and removal of VMs before each interval while considering the utilization of the previous interval. It is noticeably cost-aware. And the results of response times and costs are shown in Fig. 3 and Fig. 4.

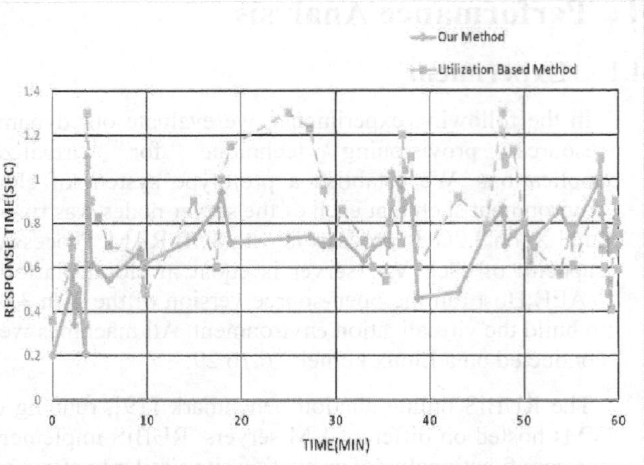

Fig. 3 Comparative results of response times between our method and utilization-based method

The benefit of our proposed method is appeared in Fig 3 and 4. Response time is faster 8.46% than existing method. And on average, maintain cost is reduced 14.35%. Through comparative results, we can notice that utilization-based methods can also handle the workload variations. However, it is not rapid enough to supply the proper number of VMs in order to meet the response based on time restricted. In respect of cost, this method occasionally uses fewer resources than our proposed method, sometimes at the cost of violating the SLA. In conclusion, the minimized number of VMs as well as the maximized CPU resource utilization can be achieved with our method by dynamic resource provisioning mechanism, and then we can keep the high global utility.

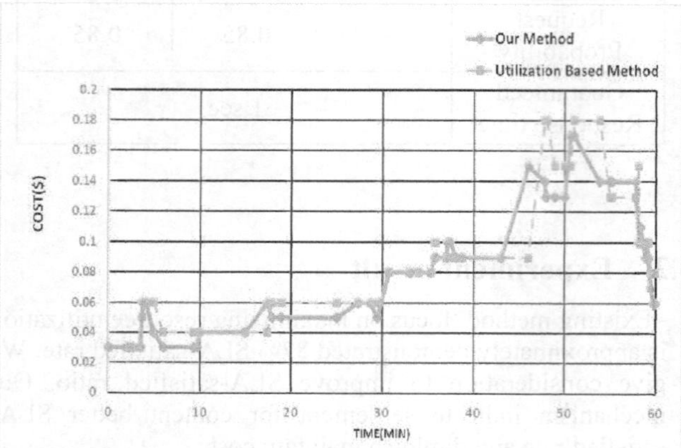

Fig. 4 Comparative results of costs between our method and utilization based method

5 Conclusions

In this paper, it is argued that dynamic provisioning of virtualized applications environment raises new challenges not addressed by prior work on provisioning technique for cloud computing platform. We presented an optimal autonomic virtual machine provisioning architecture. We proposed a novel dynamic provisioning technique, which was algorithms for virtualized applications in cloud computing platform. Hence the efficiency and flexibility for resource provisioning were improved in cloud environment.

Currently many server applications adjust the amount of resources at runtime manually. The framework in this paper allows applications to automatically manage the amount of resources according to the system workload. It offers application providers the benefits of maintaining QoS-satisfied response time under time-varying workload at the minimum cost of resource usage. Also, we adopt Service Level Agreement (SLA) based negotiation of prioritized applications to determine the costs and penalties by the achieved performance level. If the entire request cannot be satisfied, some virtualized applications will be affected by their increased execution time, increased waiting time, or increased rejection rate.

The framework mainly deals with the issue: resource provisioning. For dynamic resource provisioning, SAA proposed method is as a feedback controller to automate resource provision by taking information of the characteristics of virtualized application workload. Experimental results show that our method outperforms existing provisioning method, which focus on the utilization rate based approach in both average response time and resource usage or maintain cost.

ACKNOWLEDGMENTS

This work was supported by the National Research Foundation of Korea (NRF) grant funded by the Korea government(MSIP) (No. 2012R1A1A2009558)

6 References

[1] R. Nathuji, A. Kansal, and A. Ghaffarkhah, "Q-clouds: managing performance interference effects for qos-aware clouds," in Proc. of EuroSys, 2010.

[2] M. Armbrust, A. Fox, and R. Griffith, et al, "Above the clouds: A Berkeley view of cloud computing", Technical Report No. UCB/EECS-2009-28, University of California Berkley, USA, Feb. 10, 2009.

[3] R. Buyya, C.S. Yeo, and S. Venugopal, et al, "Cloud computing and emerging IT platforms: Vision, hype, and reality for delivering computing as the 5th utility", Future generation computer systems, Elsevier science, Amsterdam, the Netherlands, 2009, 25(6), pp. 599- 616.

[4] S. Li, and D. Tirupati. Technology choice with stochastic demands and dynamic capacity allocation: A two-product analysis. *Journal of Operations Management*, Vol. 12, no 3-4, pp. 239-258, 1995.

[5] E. Kalyvianaki, T. Charalambous, and S. Hand, "Self-adaptive and self-configured CPU resource provisioning for virtualized servers using kalman filters", Proceedings of the 6th international conference on Autonomic computing, Barcelona, Spain, June 15-19, 2009.

[6] W. E. Walsh, G. Tesauro, and J. O. Kephart, "Utility functions in autonomic systems", Proceedings of the First IEEE International Conference on Autonomic Computing, New York, NY, USA, May 17-18, 2004

[7] E. H. Miller Lim, H., Babu, S., Chase, J., Parekh, S.: Automated Control in Cloud Computing: Challenges and Opportunities. In: 1st Workshop on Automated Control for Datacenters and Clouds, 2009.

[8] P. Barham, B. Dragovic, and K. Fraser, et al, "Xen and the art of virtualization", Proceedings of the 19th ACM Symposium on Operating Systems Principles, Bolton Landing, NY, USA, 2003, pp. 164-177.

[9] Y. Song, Y. Li, and H. Wang, et al, "A service-oriented priority based resource scheduling scheme for virtualized utility computing", Proceedings of the 9th IEEE International Symposium on Cluster Computing and the Grid, 2009, pp. 148-155.

[10] J. Zhang, M. Yousif, and R. Carpenter, et al, "Application resource demand phase analysis and prediction in support of dynamic resource provisioning", Proceedings of the 4th International Conference on Autonomic Computing, 2007.

[11] X.Y. Wang, Z.H. Du, and Y.N. Chen, et al, "Virtualization based autonomic resource management for multi-tier Web applications in shared data center", The Journal of Systems and Software, 2008, 81(9), pp. 1591-1608

[12] J. Zhang, M. Yousif, and R. Carpenter, et al, "Application resource demand phase analysis and prediction in support of dynamic resource provisioning", Proceedings of the 4th International Conference on Autonomic Computing, 2007, pp. 12-12.

[13] P. Padala, X. Y. Zhu, M. Uysal, et al, "Adaptive control of virtualized resources in utility computing environments", EuroSys, 2007, pp. 289-302.

[14] Ranjan, S., Rolia, J., Fu, H., Knightly, R.: QoS-Driven Server Migration for Internet Data Centers. In: The Tenth International Workshop on Quality of Service, Miami, FL, 2002

[15] Ranjan, S., Karrer, R., Knightly, E.: Wide Area Redirection of Dynamic Content in Internet Data Centers. In: The IEEE INFOCOM, HongKong, 2004

[16] Ranjan, S., Knightly, E.: High-Performance Resource Allocation and Request Redirection Algorithms for Web Clusters. IEEE Transactions on Parallel And Distributed Systems 19(9), 2008.

[17] Urgaonkar, B., Shenoy, P., Chandra, A., Goyal, P., Agile, T.W.: Dynamic Provisioning of Multi-Tier Internet Applications. ACM Transactions on Autonomous and Adaptive Systems 3(1), 2008.

[18] S. Malkowski, M. Hedwig, D. Jayasinghe, C. Pu, and D. Neumann, "Cloudxplor: A tool for configuration planning in clouds based on empirical data," in Proc. of SAC, 2010.

[19] http://rubis.ow2.org/

Harnessing the Benefits of Big Data in the Cloud

Felix Njeh and Dr. Bo Yang
Department of Computer Science
Bowie State University, Bowie, Maryland 20715

Abstract *- In recent years, data has gained more visibility and importance to organizations and governments worldwide. Innovative technologies have emerged to more efficiently collect, process and disseminate data or information, bringing transformational value to these organizations. In the current information age, the transformation of data to useful information is playing a vital role in driving effectiveness and efficiency. Innovation in social computing, the proliferation of mobile devices, and the emergence of cloud computing have magnified data availability and accessibility. These changes have caused a shift from traditional data management systems and processes to an emerging paradigm of Big Data. In this paper we present a Cloud based Big Data platform for collecting and transforming distributed data into knowledge or insightful information.*

Keywords: Big Data, Analytics, Cloud, Grid, Computing, Distributed Computing

Submitted as a full paper for consideration to The 2013 International Conference on Grid & Cloud Computing and Applications (GCA'13).

1 Introduction

The definition of Big Data has yet to be formalized. During a recent workshop at the National Institute of Standards and Technology (NIST), there were discussions on collaborating to define Big Data. So far, several definitions are being used with no general consensus on the definition. The most popular one defines Big Data as "a massive volume of both structured and unstructured data that is complex and of diverse data types that traditional database and software techniques cannot be used for efficient processing." Gartner defines Big Data as "high volume, velocity and/or variety information assets that demand cost-effective, innovative forms of information processing that enable enhanced insight, decision-making, and process automation." This definition uses the three Vs (Volume, Velocity, and Variety) to define Big Data (see Figure 1). Other definitions include value or veracity to make it the forth V.

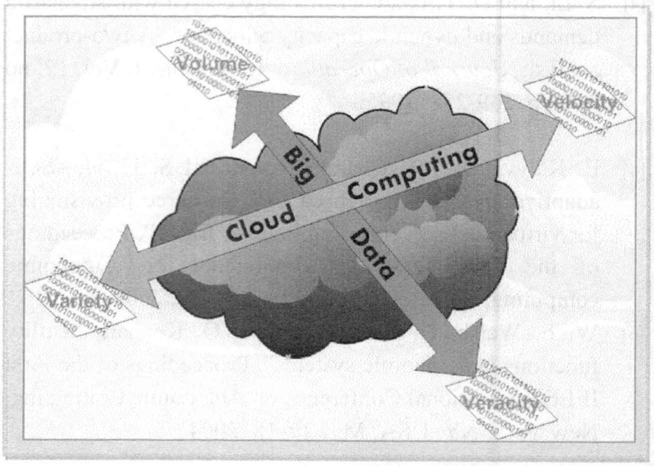

Fig. 1.: Big Data in the Cloud

Big Data sources include machine-to-machine (M2M), web and social media, transaction data, biometrics, and human-generated. Due to the increase in data sources and the corresponding exponential increase in the amount of data generated, the processing capacity of conventional database systems has become inadequate. Data set sizes have become too big, the data creation rates too high, and existing database structures do not fit the varied data types. Without the right tools, it becomes impossible to collect, store, and analyze this data to reveal practical insights [9].

Technologies such as Hadoop and Cloud Computing offer a lot of promise to solve some of the problems emanating from Big Data. When these technologies are applied correctly, useful information, hidden patterns and unknown correlations in the data, will be discovered.

2 Background

In this section we discuss Big Data standards efforts, trends and platform.

2.1. Big Data Standards

Some of the challenges facing Big Data are invoked by its distributed nature (multiple data sources and destinations), data governance (reliability and integrity of data) and interoperability (different data sources with various data types).

Though there has been a broad and growing consensus on the challenges posed by big data, there is however no consensus on standardization. Many in the IT industry are advocating the need for a standardization body, such as the

NIST, to spearhead an effort towards standardizing Big Data. Some suggested areas needing standardization include but are not limited to interoperability, security, and privacy. These standards will result in commonly accepted best practices for Big Data solutions.

A few, however, reject the idea of standardization arguing that standardization may stifle development. This is countered by the majority that finds huge benefits in standardizing Big Data.

2.2. Big Data Trends

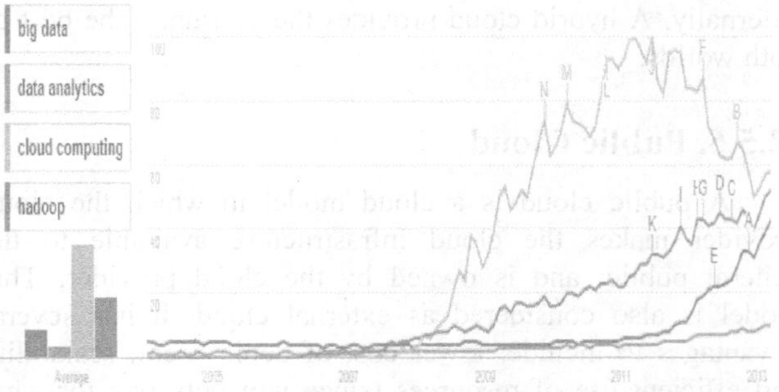

Fig. 2. Search trends on Big Data, data analytics, Cloud Computing. Source: Google trends

There confusion as to when the term Big Data originated; some literature suggests that the term originated in the 1990s during conversations at Silicon Graphics.

From Fig. 2 above, we realize that the terms big data, data analytics, cloud computing and Hadoop were all used on a limited basis before 2009. It was until after this time that the search for information relating to these key technologies became very popular. At this time the interest in Cloud Computing had an exponential growth, seconded by Hadoop and then big data. Data analytics is termed the "killer app" of Big Data since it provides the resultant insight from Big Data. The interest in data analytics started to peak after 2011 and we predict this trend to grow much faster in the near future.

Big Data, Hadoop, Cloud Computing and data analytics are key components of our proposed Cloud based Big Data platform.

2.3. Hadoop as a platform for Big Data

Hadoop is a framework comprising of a parallel computing system and a parallel database. It is highly scalable and well suited for the distributed processing of large data sets across clusters of computers. Hadoop is based on a simple data model, in which any data (structured or unstructured) will fit. This contrasts the relational data model in which there must exist a schema for the data before any input .

The Hadoop framework comprises of two key components or systems: MapReduce implementation and Hadoop Distributed File System (HDFS).

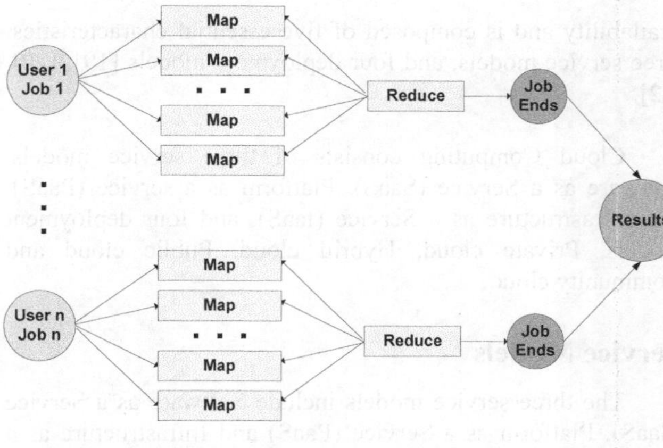

Fig. 3.: Hadoop MapReduce Model

During the execution of a Hadoop service each task is either a map or reduce job.

2.3.1. MapReduce

MapReduce is a framework introduced by Google for processing parallelizable problems across large datasets in a distributed computing environment. MapReduce is considered the execution engine.

2.3.2. Hadoop Distributed File System

HDFS is a scalable and distributed file system designed to store large amounts of data. It is a block-structured file system in which a file is broken into blocks of a fixed size and stored across a cluster of one or more data storage systems. A HDFS cluster primarily consists of a NameNode that manages the file system metadata and DataNodes that store the actual data. HDFS is a master-slave architecture with the master being considered the namenode while the slaves are considered datanodes.

2.4. NoSQL (Not Only SQL)

A NoSQL database provides a simple, lightweight and scalable mechanism for storing and retrieving data. In the Big Data arena, it is preferred over traditional relational databases especially when working with a huge quantity of data when the data's nature does not require a relational model. NoSQL systems allow the use of a SQL-like query language. Hbase, for example is a NoSQL database and part of the Hadoop ecosystem modeled from Google's BigTable system [6].

2.5. Cloud Computing

Cloud Computing is a model for enabling ubiquitous, convenient, on-demand network access to a shared pool of configurable computing resources (e.g., networks, servers, storage, applications, and services) that can be rapidly provisioned and released with minimal management effort or service provider interaction. This cloud model promotes availability and is composed of five essential characteristics, three service models, and four deployment models [19], [20], [22].

Cloud Computing consists of three service models, Software as a Service (SaaS), Platform as a service (PaaS), and Infrastructure as a Service (IaaS); and four deployment models, Private cloud, Hybrid cloud, Public cloud and Community cloud.

Service Models

The three service models include Software as a Service (SaaS), Platform as a Service (PaaS) and Infrastructure as a Service (IaaS).

2.5.1. Software as a Service (SaaS)

This is a software delivery model in which the provider gives customers on-demand access to the applications hosted in a cloud infrastructure. The infrastructure is managed by the provider while the consumer has only limited user-specific application configuration settings. SaaS is increasingly becoming a common delivery model for most business applications. The consumer usually pays a subscription fee instead of a licensing fee.

2.5.2. Platform as a service (PaaS)

This service delivery model allows the customer to rent the cloud infrastructure (virtualized servers and associated services) to run consumer-created or acquired applications or to develop and test new ones. The infrastructure is managed and controlled by the provider; the consumer has some control over the deployed applications and possibly application hosting environment configurations.

2.5.3. Infrastructure as a Service (IaaS)

IaaS is a delivery capability in which the consumer provisions processing, storage, networks, and other fundamental computing resources. The consumer can deploy and run arbitrary software (operating systems and applications) but does not manage or control the underlying cloud infrastructure.

Deployment Models

The deployment models include Private cloud, Hybrid cloud, Public cloud and Community cloud.

2.5.4. Private Cloud

With this model, the internal or corporate cloud infrastructure (systems and services) is operated solely for an organization. This gives the organization better management and control over their data and systems. It is also considered a proprietary network or a data center that supplies hosted services to a limited number of people.

2.5.5. Hybrid Cloud

A Hybrid Cloud is made up of at least one private cloud and at least one public cloud. An example is when a vendor has a private cloud and forms a partnership with a public cloud provider, or a public cloud provider forms a partnership with a vendor that provides private cloud platforms. In other instances, the organization owns and manages some of the cloud resources internally while others are made available externally. A hybrid cloud provides the consumer the best of both worlds.

2.5.6. Public Cloud

A public cloud is a cloud model in which the cloud provider makes the cloud infrastructure available to the general public; and is owned by the cloud provider. This model is also considered as external cloud. It has several advantages to include: lower cost of deployment, scalability and efficient use of resources (since you only pay for what you use).

2.5.7. Community Cloud

A Community Cloud allows the cloud infrastructure to be shared by several organizations and supports a specific community that has shared concerns. This model can be managed by the organizations involved or a third party, and may exist on premise or off premise.

3 Motivation

With the multitude and ever increasing data sources nowadays, we are challenged with a wealth of data coming from scientific and medical instruments, geospatial sources, and sensor data from other sources.

In order to reap the benefits of Big Data, we have to be capable of examining large amounts of data of various data types to uncover hidden patterns, unknown correlations and derive useful information.

The rapid expansion and availability of data necessitates a corresponding development of tools that will efficiently collect, process, analyze and derive useful information from this plethora of data.

Several tools have been developed and available on the commercial market to solve some of the problems posed by Big Data. Big Data analytics is of prime importance as it provides users with tools needed to perform advanced analytics [3]. We have attempted to identify some of these tools and will examine how they can be used in combination.

3.1. At the crossroads of Big Data and the Cloud

Our objective is to define and study a combined platform to leverage the beneficial features of the combination. Cloud Computing has come a long way and has now attained a reasonable level of maturity that makes it a viable platform for multiple applications. In this work, we adopt a Cloud based platform as the underlying technology on which Big Data tools reside.

In Fig. 4, we depict the collage of Big Data, Hadoop, Cloud Computing and NoSQL. This platform provides a very solid infrastructure for collecting, storing, analyzing and producing insightful information.

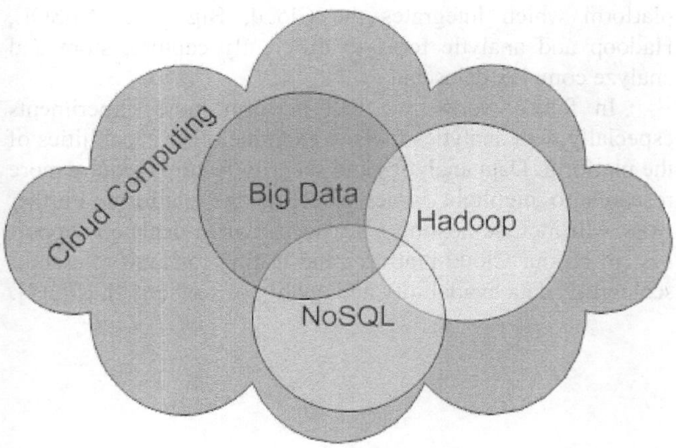

Fig. 4.: The integrated Big Data Cloud

3.1.1. Big Data Platform as a Service (PaaS)

The Big Data PaaS is a Cloud platform that leverages the Cloud provider's distributed capabilities, compute power, analytical tools, storage capacity, elasticity and others.

Our experiment demonstrates how conventional systems are insufficient to solve the Big Data problem. It further shows some of the benefits of adopting a Cloud solution.

4 Experimental Setup

In this experiment, we use simulation to demonstrate resource utilization in a traditional computing environment.

We define a resource request function f of a real variable t (time) and an interval [a, b] of the real line. The definite integral f(t) can be defined as follows:

$$\int_a^b c * f(t)dt, \qquad where\ f(t) = \cos(t)\ and\ c\ is\ a\ constant$$

The total amount of a given resource requested and/or consumed by a user is defined by the area of the region in the xy-plane bounded by the graph of f, the x-axis, and the vertical lines x = a and x = b.

We examine different scenarios in the conventional computing environments and assess the utilization of resources with respect to a Cloud Computing platform. The example under study considers that resources such as memory, storage, bandwidth, CPU, etc. are provisioned and utilize over a certain period of time.

Fig. 5a represents the use of a given resource over a period of 17 days. This scenario was provisioned for peak load which leads to the underutilization of the resources. The shaded area represents the quantity of excess wasted.

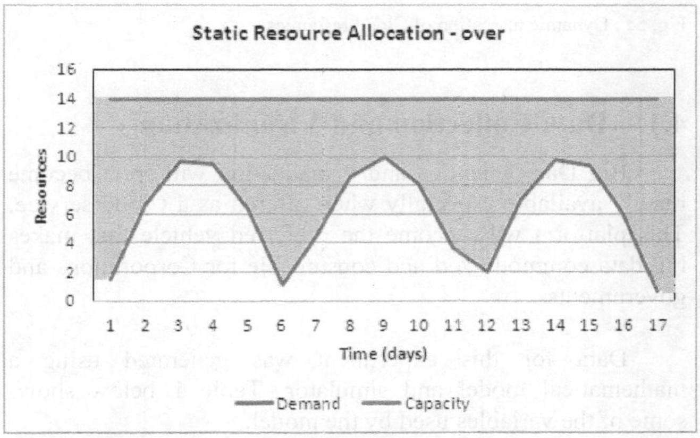

Fig. 5a.: Allocation of resources over user demands

In Fig. 5b, illustrates a situation where the resource allocated does not accommodate spikes in user demands. The shortage during the peak periods is represented by the shaded sections of the chart. These shortages could result in applications crashing or systems delays.

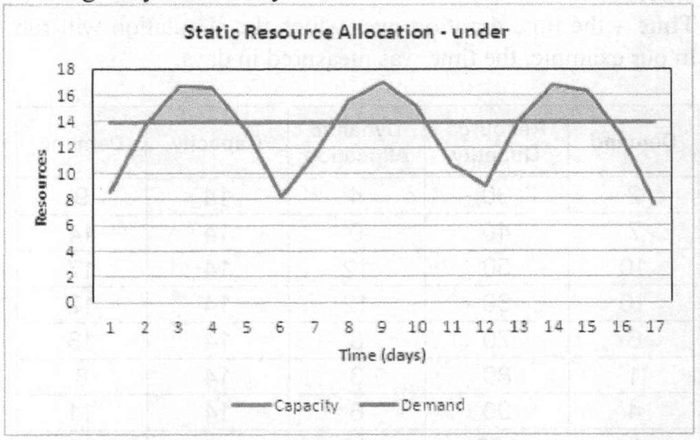

Fig. 5b.: Allocation of resources under user demands

Fig. 5c below demonstrates the dynamic allocation of resources (pay-as-you-go or pay per use) in a Cloud Computing environment. Compared to Fig. 5a and 5b, we realize the benefits in Fig. 5c where the amount of resources wasted is minimized.

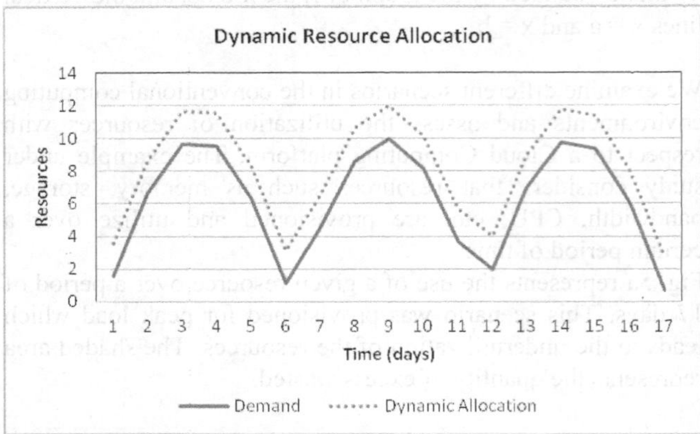

Fig. 5c.: Dynamic allocation of Cloud resources

4.1. Data Collection and Visualization

Big Data analytics and visualization will soon become readily available especially when offered as a Cloud service. This platform will become the preferred vehicle that makes big data commoditized and consumable for Corporations and governments.

Data for this experiment was generated using a mathematical model and simulator. Table 1 below shows some of the variables used by the model.

Demand – user demand for a specific resource over a given time frame.

Resource Quantity – total amount of the datacenter resource available.

Dynamic Allocation - the quantity of the of the specified datacenter resource dynamically allocated by the Cloud.

Capacity – the maximum quantity of the datacenter resource provisioned.

Time – the time duration over which the simulation will run. In our example, the time was measured in days.

Demand	Resource Quantity	Dynamic Allocation	Capacity	Demand
2	30	4	14	9
7	40	9	14	14
10	50	12	14	17
10	60	12	14	17
6	70	8	14	13
1	80	3	14	8
4	90	6	14	11
9	100	11	14	16
10	110	12	14	17
8	120	10	14	15
4	130	6	14	11
2	140	4	14	9
7	150	9	14	14
10	160	12	14	17
9	170	11	14	16
6	180	8	14	13
1	190	3	14	8

Table 1: Resource Allocation

The input data generated by our model was processed by the simulation system and the results displayed in Table 1 above. The data are displayed as graphs as shown in Fig 5a-c.

Our experimental setup was limited to the Cloud layer of our platform. This is still sufficient to illustrate the concept as the Cloud is the underlying foundation of the platform.

5 Conclusions

In this paper we discuss Big Data and propose a platform which integrates the Cloud, Big Data, NoSQL, Hadoop and analytic tools to efficiently capture, store and analyze complex datasets.

In future works, we will perform more experiments especially with analytics tools to examine other capabilities of the platform. Data analytics and security features require more research to highlight issues affecting the platform. Further work will include hosting a service-oriented decision support system on our Cloud platform and testing for fault tolerance, scalability, data availability and quality of service [8], [5], [8].

6 References

[1] Abbadi, A. El. (2011). Big Data and Cloud Computing : Current State and Future Opportunities, 530–533.

[2] Chaudhuri, S. (2012). What Next ? A Half-Dozen Data Management Research Goals for Big Data and the Cloud. Proceedings of the 31st symposium on Principles of Database Systems, 1–4. doi:10.1145/2213556.2213558

[3] Cohen, J., Dolan, B., & Dunlap, M. (2009). MAD skills: new analysis practices for big data. Proceedings of the …. Retrieved from http://dl.acm.org/citation.cfm?id=1687576

[4] Dean, J., & Ghemawat, S. (2004). MapReduce: Simplified Data Processing on Large Clusters. Operating Systems Design and Implementation (OSDI ', 04.

[5] Demirkan, H., & Delen, D. (2012). Leveraging the capabilities of service-oriented decision support systems: Putting analytics and big data in cloud. Decision Support Systems, in press(0), 1–10. doi:10.1016/j.dss.2012.05.048

[6] Ghemawat, S., Gobioff, H., & Leung, S.-T. (2003). The Google file system. ACM SIGOPS Operating Systems Review, 37(5), 29. doi:10.1145/1165389.945450

[7] Greenberg, A., Hamilton, J., Maltz, D. A., & Patel, P. (2009). The Cost of a Cloud : Research Problems in Data Center Networks, 39(1), 68–73.

[8] Herodotou, H., Lim, H., Luo, G., Borisov, N., & Dong, L. (2011). Starfish : A Self-tuning System for Big Data Analytics. Systems Research, (1862), 261–272. Retrieved from http://www.cs.duke.edu/~hero/files/cidr11_starfish.pdf

[9] LaValle, S., Lesser, E., & Shockley, R. (2011). Big data, analytics and the path from insights to value. MIT sloan management …, 52(2), 21–31. Retrieved from http://sloanreview.mit.edu/the-magazine/2011-winter/52205/big-data-analytics-and-the-path-from-insights-to-value/

[10] Long, P., & Siemens, G. (2011). Penetrating the Fog: Analytics in Learning and Education.

[11] Manyika, J., Chui, M., Brown, B., & Bughin, J. (2011). Big data: The next frontier for innovation, competition, and productivity. McKinsey Global Institute, (June). Retrieved from http://scholar.google.com/scholar?hl=en&btnG=Search&q=intitle:Big+data+:+The+next+frontier+for+innovation+,+competition+,+and+productivity#0

[12] McGuire, T., Chui, M., & Manyika, J. (2012). Why Big Data Is The New Competitive Advantage. Ivey Business Journal, 76(4), 1–4. Retrieved from http://web.ebscohost.com/ehost/pdfviewer/pdfviewer?sid=370d66cc-740c-4531-a268-28955083c818@sessionmgr11&vid=2&hid=14

[13] Padhy, R. P. (2013). Big Data Processing with Hadoop-MapReduce in Cloud Systems, 2(1), 16–27.

[14] Prekopcsk, Z., Makrai, G., & Henk, T. (2011). Radoop : Analyzing Big Data with RapidMiner and Hadoop. Technology. Retrieved from http://www.prekopcsak.hu/papers/preko-2011-rcomm.pdf

[15] Rajaraman, A., & Ullman, J. D. (2010). Mining of Massive Datasets.

[16] Russom, P. (2011). Big data analytics. October, 19(September) 2011, 40. Retrieved from http://faculty.ucmerced.edu/frusu/Papers/Conference/2012-sigmod-glade-demo.pdf

[17] Tsuchiya, S., & Lee, V. (n.d.). Big Data Processing in Cloud Environments, 159–168.

[18] Begoli, E., & Horey, J. (2012). Design Principles for Effective Knowledge Discovery from Big Data. 2012 Joint Working IEEE/IFIP Conference on Software Architecture and European Conference on Software Architecture, 215–218. doi:10.1109/WICSA-ECSA.212.32

[19] Peter Mell, Tim Grance. "Effectively and Securely Using the Cloud Computing Paradigm", NIST, Information Technology Laboratory.

[20] NIST Cloud Computing Standards Roadmap. "NIST CCSRWG – 070 Eleventh Working Draft". May 2, 2011

[21] Madoka Yuriyama, Takayuki Kushida, "Sensor-Cloud Infrastructure - Physical Sensor Management with Virtualized Sensors on Cloud Computing", IBM Research - Tokyo, March 17, 2010

[22] Peter Mell and Tim Grance. "The NIST Definition of Cloud Computing". 10-7-09

[23] Cloud Computing, 227-234. Ieee. doi:10.1109/CLOUD.2011.20

[24] Benson, K., Dowsley, R., & Shacham, H. (2011). Do you know where your cloud files are? Proceedings of the 3rd ACM workshop on Cloud computing security workshop - CCSW '11, 73. New York, New York, USA: ACM Press. doi:10.1145/2046660.2046677

[25] Hauswirth, M., & Decker, S. (2007). Semantic Reality – Connecting the Real and the Virtual World Position Paper, 1-4.

A Stream Symmetric Homomorphic Encryption Scheme with Finite Automata

Alejandro Llamas[1] **and Raúl González**[1]
[1]Computer Sciences, CINVESTAV, Guadalajara, Jalisco, México

Abstract— *This paper presents a new homomorphic encryption scheme which uses sequential machines as a basis to produce a stream-symmetric encryption, which can be expanded to a homomorphic encryption with the help of the operation over automata called serial composition, allowing the application of any operation that can be represented by means of a finite automaton, on the set which contains the cipher-text. Unlike conventional cryptographic schemes this is not aimed at sharing information securely, so key distribution is not necessary and a symmetrical or asymmetrical cryptosystem makes no difference. With regard to safety, the intruder can only design cryptanalytic algorithms having as input a set of encrypted text and a composite automaton, constructed with the keys and an operation automaton. To illustrate the correct operation of the cryptographic scheme, we include the implementation of the greatest common divisor of two numbers.*

Keywords: Homomorphic Encryption, Finite Automata, Cloud Computing.

1. Introduction

Stream-symmetric cryptography comes perhaps from the old VigenÃlre code, in which one character is exchanged for another according to a key or pad, many studies and developments have been made in this field, perhaps one of the most important is shown by Shannon in his article [1], where under certain conditions proved that the one time pad can be perfectly safe, being the basis of stream-symmetric encryption. One of these conditions is to generate a random string, such that the cipher-text is calculated using as parameters the plain-text and the random string, for this reason the designers of stream-symmetric cryptosystems, use sequential machines to generate pseudo-random strings called key-streams, in order that these chains may be repeated if it is introduced to the sequential machine, the initialization vector (IV) and the key. However we use sequential machines, for they have the characteristic of being invertible and not due to the ability to generate pseudo random repeatable chains. One of the first to talk about invertible circuits and their inverses was James L. Massey in [2].

Returning to symmetric encryption, an important feature is that its keys must be kept secret. If we want to send data securely, keys have to be transmitted through a secure channel, this is the problem of key distribution, solved by Rivest, Shamir and Adleman with RSA in 1978 [3] (note that, in the scheme that we show here is not necessary key distribution). Also Rivest et al. were the first to propose, in [4], a homomorphic encryption, a problem that many have tried to solve (e. g. [5], [6]), but for some time could only design a partial homomorphic encryption, until 2009 when C. Gentry showed, using lattice-based cryptography, the first fully homomorphic encryption scheme. His scheme supports evaluations of arbitrary depth circuits by effectively refreshing the cipher-text, thereby reducing its associated noise and hence solving the problem of indecipherable cipher-text. However, this scheme is still impractical. For this reason, we attack the open problem of designing a cryptographic scheme which has an algebraic homomorphic ring, i.e. the two basic operations (addition and multiplication) can be performed on the cipher-text, this calculation must be done in a practical time for the implementation of more complex programs that use these basic operations in the cipher-text.

The rest of the paper is organized as follows. In section II we review elements of automata theory that requires the cryptographic scheme. Section III shows the design of a stream-symmetric encryption with the automata defined in section II. In section IV we extend the encryption designed in section III, to a full homomorphic encryption and we show the operations that can be performed on the cipher-text. Section V shows the implementation of the greatest common divisor of two integers, that can be executed by a third party without the data or the process is known by him. Section VI provides a new safety factor (covert operations) for homomorphic encryption schemes and the analysis of a possible attack to the encryption scheme shown here. Finally, in section VII we speak of work performed, current and future on this research.

1.1 Working in a parallel world

It all starts with "Alex", a researcher who discovers how to get access to parallel worlds, unfortunately send a person by the wormhole was impossible, he can only send data into a sequence of bits, Alex sends a string of bits and then receives a different string of the same length, seems that some kind of transformation is performed on the chain but is unknown. Days later he discovers that each different world responds differently to the same strings, definitely something amazing was happening. Eventually Alex discovers a tool that helps to communicate with these strange worlds, something called invertible finite automata and inverse finite automata, encoder and decoder respectively, one pair for each different world. He then meets "Ragde" an entity that works in something like a computer in that world. That gives Alex an idea: "What if I send some data to be processed on his computer". Soon he realized that the capacity of Ragde's computer is somewhat limited. Ragde can only perform operations that can be represented by finite automata, so for really significant computations Alex would have to intervene in some way, but even this can take a long time running on Alex's old computer, so he needed someone with a lot of computing power and that person was "Bugsy" a rich guy who was known to sniff the data of people and make them known. Due to this Alex needed to think of a way for Bugsy doing the remaining process that Ragde's computer could not perform, keeping in secret most of the information. His solution was to give Bugsy access to the wormhole and instructions on how use it.

Without the encoder and decoder Bugsy could never communicate with Ragde to find out what calculation is done. The tasks of Bugsy are: store data and feed the wormhole, in this way the data and the calculation remain unknown. Once that Bugsy has completed the sequence of instructions with the "data" that was initially sent by Alex (data that were transformed with the encoder used to communicate with Ragde), he sends the results to Alex. Finally, Alex gets the results generated with the decoder. Results that he wouldn't be able to obtain from his computer or that would simply take a long time to be useful. Summarizing, Alex managed to create a tool in order to use the services of supercomputers (such as Ragde's computer), without the data used and the operations performed are known.

2. Finite Automata

Definition 1. A *finite automaton* is a quintuple $M = (\Sigma, A, Q, \delta, \lambda)$, where Σ, A and Q are non empty finite sets, δ is a function from $Q \times \Sigma$ to Q and λ is a function from $Q \times \Sigma$ to A. Σ, A and Q are called the input alphabet, the output alphabet and the state set of M, respectively. δ and λ are called the next state function and the output function of M, respectively. We can extend the domain of the function δ to $Q \times \Sigma^*$ as follows:

$$\boldsymbol{\delta} : Q \times \Sigma^* \to Q$$

Let $q \in Q$, $w \in \Sigma^n$, $\nu \in \Sigma^{n-1}$, $a \in \Sigma$ and $w = \nu a$

$$\boldsymbol{\delta}(q, \varepsilon) := q$$
$$\boldsymbol{\delta}(q, w) := \delta(\boldsymbol{\delta}(q, \nu), a)$$

Similarly, we can extend the domain of the function λ

$$\boldsymbol{\lambda} : Q \times \Sigma^* \to Q$$

Let $q \in Q$, $w \in \Sigma^n$, $\nu \in \Sigma^{n-1}$, $a \in \Sigma$ and $w = \nu a$

$$\boldsymbol{\lambda}(q, \varepsilon) := q$$
$$\boldsymbol{\lambda}(q, w) := \boldsymbol{\lambda}(q, \nu)\lambda(\boldsymbol{\delta}(q, \nu), a).$$

This kind of automata is also known as "Mealy machine" or "finite automata with outputs" for this paper is just "finite automata".

2.1 Finite automata with memory defined by a function

Definition 2. Let $f_M : A^t \times \Sigma^{r+1} \to A$, be a function and x_0, $x = x_{-1}, \ldots, x_{-r}$, $x' = x_{-1}, \ldots, x_{-r+1} \in \Sigma$, y_0, $y = y_{-1}, \ldots, y_{-t}$, $y' = y_{-1}, \ldots, y_{-t+1} \in A$. The (r, t)-*order memory finite automaton* defined by f_M is formed as follows:

$$M = (\Sigma, A, A^t \times \Sigma^r, \delta, \lambda)$$
$$\lambda(\langle y, x\rangle, x_0) = y_0 = f_M(y, x_0, x)$$
$$\delta(\langle y, x\rangle, x_0) = \langle y_0, y', x_0, x'\rangle.$$

In the case of $t = 0$ then we have a r-order input memory finite automaton, if $r = 0$ then we have a t-order output memory finite automaton.

2.2 Linear finite automata

The study of linear automata has been carried out for a long time and many advances have been made in their understanding, the references [7], [8], [9], [10] contain more information on this and other types of finite automata. Here we show only the necessary concepts.

Definition 3. Let M be a finite automaton defined by the function f_M. If f_M is a linear transformation then M is a *linear finite automaton.*

Let us show the following as the canonical form of the function of any linear finite automaton with memory:

$$f_M(x_i, \ldots, x_{i-r}, y_{i-1}, \ldots, y_{i-t}) = y_i = \sum_{j=0}^{j \le r} A_j x_{i-j} + \sum_{h=1}^{h \le t} B_h y_{i-h} \quad (1)$$

where the A_j are matrices of $m \times l$, the B_j are matrices of $m \times m$, the x_j are vectors of dimension l and the y_j are vectors of dimension m, all over a Galois field of q elements denoted by $GF(q)$. We define the next as the transformation matrix of the finite automaton M:

$$G = [A_0 A_1 \ldots A_r B_0 B_1 \ldots B_t] \quad (2)$$

where the matrices are accommodated horizontally to form a matrix of $m \times [(l * r + 1) + (m * t)]$, we also define

$$E(i) = [x_i \ldots x_{i-r} y_{i-1} \ldots y_{i-t}]^T \quad (3)$$

where vectors are vertically arranged to form a new vector of dimension $[(l*r)+(m*t)]$, with this we can define the function f_M as follows:

$$f_M(x_i,\ldots,x_{i-r},y_{i-1},\ldots,y_{i-t}) = G*E(i) = y_i. \quad (4)$$

2.3 Inverse of a linear finite automaton

Consequent to the study of linear automata, it was found the property of this to be invertible, this implies to calculate the input from the output and an initial state, there are many ways to invert a finite automaton, either from the definition function or the finite automaton itself, each of these techniques requires the automaton or definition function meets certain conditions, references [8], [10] and [2] show some types. In this paper we will show how to invert the linear automata that we have defined. We will focus on finding the inverse from the values of the matrix G. In the article [11] Shimon showed how to get the inverse of a finite invertible automaton through the states of the machine. We begin the process of invert the given automata, verifying if it is invertible.

Proposition Let M be a finite automata and G its transformation matrix. If A_0 has left inverse then M is invertible.

Definition 4. Let M be an invertible finite automaton defined by f_M. *The inverse automaton* of M is M' and is defined by:

$$f_{M'}(y_i,\ldots,y_{i-t},x_{i-1},\ldots,x_{i-r}) =$$

$$x_i = A_0^{-1}y_i - \sum_{h=1}^{h\leq t} A_0^{-1}B_h y_{i-h} - \sum_{j=1}^{j\leq r} A_0^{-1}A_j x_{i-j} \quad (5)$$

2.4 Serial composition of finite automata

Definition 5. Let M=$(\Sigma, A, Q_1, \delta_1, \lambda_1)$ and M'=$(A, \Gamma, Q_2, \delta_2, \lambda_2)$ be two finite automata. We define the *composite finite automaton* as follows:

$$C(M_1, M_2) = (\Sigma, \Gamma, Q_1\times Q_2, \delta, \lambda)$$
$$\delta(\langle q_1,q_2\rangle, x) = \langle \delta_1(q_1,x), \delta_2(q_2,\lambda_1(q_1,x))\rangle$$
$$\lambda(\langle q_1,q_2\rangle, x) = \lambda_2(q_2,\lambda_1(q_1,x))$$
$$q_1\in Q_1, q_2\in Q_2, x\in\Sigma.$$

This kind of composition produces a finite automaton that output, the result of introducing the exit of the first automaton into the second, however is only half the time it would take execute separately, as shown in the figure 1 where $X = x_0,\ldots,x_t$, $Y = y_0,\ldots,y_t$ and $Z = z_0,\ldots,z_t$, $t\in\mathbb{N}$.

2.5 Operations with finite automata

Our scheme is limited to those operations that we can represent by a finite automaton but even if is not as powerful as a Turing machine it capacity is large, indeed

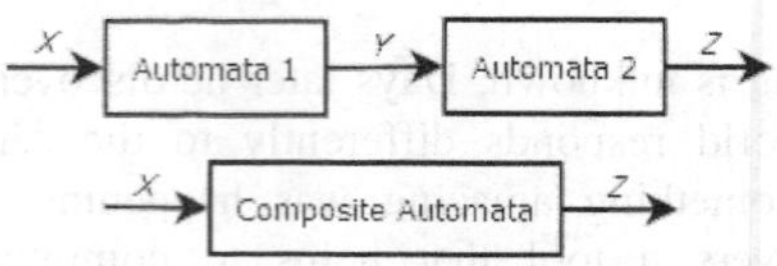

Fig. 1: Finite Automata Composition

any operation that we can design with a linear sequential circuit can be represent by a finite automaton, Kohavi [8] shows a method to transform any finite automaton in a linear sequential circuit and biseversa. Now even if we have an infinite number of operations that can be represented with finite automata, we are only interested in two in order to declare our scheme fully homomorphic encryption, these are the addition and multiplication in binary. The addition is simple, the problem is that a multiplication of two undefined numbers can not be represented by an automaton, however we can limit the size of the input, as it does with digital circuits and generate finite automata that multiply n-bit strings.

Definition 6. We call an *operation automaton*, to any transformation that is represented by a finite automaton.

3. Stream-symmetric Encryption

The traditional stream-symmetric encryption is based on the idea of the one time pads, an encryption scheme that Shannon proved to be perfectly safe in [1], for this stream encryption designers, focus on algorithms that generate pseudo random strings called key-streams, these generators have the property that the same seed (the key and initialization vector IV) can repeat the key-stream, as with the one time pads, perform a simple XOR between the plain-text and the key-stream generates the cipher-text, for decoding is necessary to repeat the key-stream with the generator and operate along with the cipher-text to obtain the plain-text. The security of these systems is mainly based on the following:

- The difficulty of estimating the initial state of the sequential machine that generates the key-stream.
- The chain length of the repeating pattern e.g. the chain 132132 has a pattern of length 3, ideally it is a very large number.
- The distribution of generated key-stream, ideally the distribution is uniform.

For more information about the types of stream cipher see [12], also are many stream-symmetric ciphers available, in [13] shown the algorithms selected as the best.

3.1 Stream-symmetric encryption with finite automata

The Stream-symmetric encryption with finite automata requires, a key generator algorithm $KeyGen$, which in our case is a generator of invertible finite automata and their inverses, an encryption algorithm $Encrypt$ and one for decryption $Decrypt$.

$KeyGen$. To generate the keys we have to define the following: the value of q, i.e. the number of elements in the field, normally we handle bit sequences to represent the data so q is usually 2, the space vector of input elements l, these depend on the size of the character being used as input, normally 8 bit, the space vector of output elements m which must be equal or greater that l because if is less, there is a loss of information and retrieve the plain-text is impossible, the larger the value m, more secure is the encryption but beware because this value increases exponentially the number of states in the finite automaton. Finally select the values for the input memory r and output memory t, as before higher safer but more states in the automaton. Just to get an idea of how involved the selected memory are, the number of states that have the finite automata is defined by the following rule:

$$q^{(r*l)+(t+m)} \tag{6}$$

while the key space of our encryption scheme is greater than:

$$\prod_{j=1}^{j\leq r} q^{m*l} * \prod_{h=1}^{h\leq t} q^{m*m}. \tag{7}$$

Once you choose those parameters, select random numbers from the field $GF(q)$ to form the transformation matrix G, before continuing, we verified that the matrix A_0 from G is invertible, if it is then G is the transformation matrix for our invertible finite automaton, otherwise select new values for A_0 until find a matrix that has left inverse. Once we have selected the matrix G, form f_M as shown in equation (1) and using the technique of the section II, generate its corresponding finite automaton, then generate its inverse. All that remains is to select the corresponding initial states, to do this arbitrarily select a state $s_0 = \langle x_{i-1}, \dots, x_{i-r}, y_{i-1}, \dots, y_{i-t} \rangle$ from M as initial state, then the initial state of M' is $s_0^* = \langle y_{i-1}, \dots, y_{i-t}, x_{i-1}, \dots, x_{i-r} \rangle$. Summarizing M is our finite automaton for encryption with initial state s_0 and M' is our finite automaton for decryption with initial state s_0^* i.e. the private keys for the stream-symmetric scheme. Must take into account that the encryption key can be any invertible finite automaton, need not be linear, the linear automata is used to show a basic technique of inversion, we can use nonlinear finite automata or invertible finite automata with delay as shown Tao in [7].

$Encrypt$. Let $p_1, \dots, p_n \in \Sigma^n$ be the plain-text and $M = (\Sigma, A, Q, \delta, \lambda)$ our invertible automaton used to encrypt, we calculate the cipher-text $c_1, \dots, c_{2*n} \in A^{2*n}$ as follows:

$$\lambda(s_0, d_1 p_1 d_2 p_2, \dots, d_n p_n) = c_1, \dots, c_{2*n} \tag{8}$$

where $d_1, \dots, d_n \in \Sigma^n$ is a string selected at random with a uniform distribution.

$Decrypt$. Let $c_1, \dots, c_{2*n} \in A^{2*n}$ be the cipher-text and $M' = (A, \Sigma, Q', \delta', \lambda')$ our inverse automaton used to decrypt, we recover the plain-text by computing:

$$\lambda'(s_0^*, c_1, \dots, c_{2*n}) = d_1 p_1 d_2 p_2, \dots, d_n p_n \tag{9}$$

finally remove all $d_j, 1 \leq j \leq n$ and we get $p_1, \dots, p_n$ i.e. the plain-text.

4. Homomorphic Encryption

This form of encryption allows specific types of calculations are conducted in the cipher-text and obtain an encrypted result, which corresponds to the encryption result of the operations performed on the plain-text. When we speak of homomorphic encryption, we can refer to partial homomorphic encryption or fully homomorphic encryption, the first has the characteristic that we can find over elements encrypted a binary operation resulting in an algebraic group, homomorphic to the group we have in the plain-text, these operations are called homomorphic operations e.g. RSA is multiplicative homomorphic, we can multiply two encrypted numbers and the result after decoding, is the multiplication of the two corresponding plain-texts.

If we have a fully homomorphic encryption, then we can find over elements encrypted, two binary operation leading to an algebraic ring, homomorphic to the ring we have in the plain-text, such operations as in the previous case are called homomorphic operations, in other words, let P be the set of plain-texts, $+$ and $\times$ binary operations over P and $+_c$ and $\times_c$ binary operation over the set of cipher-texts then for all $p_1, p_2 \in P$:

$$Encrypt(p_1 + p_2) = Encrypt(p_1) +_c Encrypt(p_2), \tag{10}$$

$$Encrypt(p_1 \times p_2) = Encrypt(p_1) \times_c Encrypt(p_2), \tag{11}$$

normally $+$ and $\times$ are modular addition and multiplication. In recent years this type of scheme has been largely worked, however most of the schemes are based on the same blueprint, using as basis an asymmetric cipher, then find an adaptation that allows get operations over the cipher-text that lead to a fully homomorphic scheme, some are RSA and "El Gamal", this and other examples are described by Fontaine in [14]. Gentry shows in his PhD thesis [15] the generation of a homomorphic scheme with latices, however its outline as many more, presents the noise problem i.e. after a finite number of operations, plain-text can not be obtained from the cipher-text, which Gentry resolves by encrypting the cipher-text again, however this makes the scheme impractical. Unlike regular schemes, ours is based on stream-symmetric encryption with sequential machines,

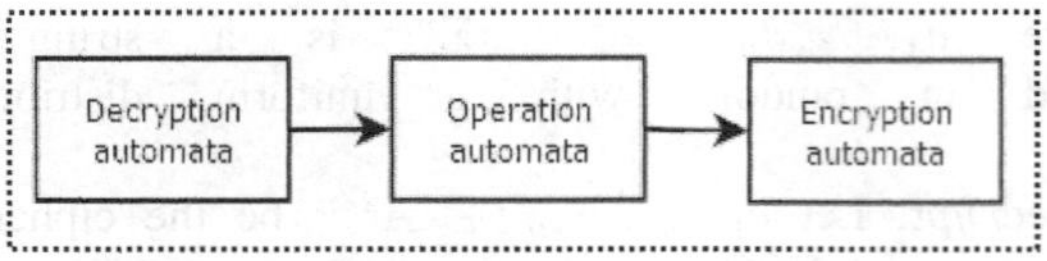

Fig. 2: $Transform$

which does not have the noise problem, as consequence operations are unlimited.

4.1 Stream-Symmetric-Homomorphic Encryption (SSHE)

A symmetric-homomorphic encryption scheme has four algorithms, $KeyGen$, $Encrypt$, $Decrypt$ and an additional algorithm that differs in the definition given by Gentry in [16], for our case the algorithm $Transform$, that takes as input the encryption key (the invertible finite automaton), the decryption key (the inverse finite automaton) and an operation $C \in \Omega$ = the set of finite automata, (i.e. the operation can be represented by a finite automaton), it outputs an automaton C^c that can process encrypted data. C^c take as input a set of cipher-texts $\Psi = \langle \psi_1, \ldots, \psi_t \rangle$, it outputs a cipher-text ψ. in other words, Let $\psi_j = Encrypt(\pi_j), 1 \leq j \leq t$.

If $\psi = C^c(\Psi)$ Then $C(\pi_1, \ldots, \pi_t) = Decrypt(\psi)$.

$Transform$. The other 3 algorithms needed for the homomorphic encryption are the same that we show in section III, we now describe the last. The algorithm $Transform$ has the function of composing three finite automata that receives as input, these are the decryption, the operation and the encryption automata, as shown in the figure 2. The result is an automaton that can perform the operation realized by the operation automaton, but receives as input a cipher-text and outputs an encryption of the result given by the operation automata.

4.2 SSHE operations

What operations can we apply on the cipher-text? As discussed in section II, any operation performed by a sequential linear circuit can be represented by a finite automaton and with the algorithm $Transform$ we can convert any operation automaton, to a SSHE operation, so unlike other schemes here we can design an infinite number of SSHE operations, even if we only need addition and multiplication to declare our scheme fully homomorphic, the point of this difference is that with an infinite number of possible homomorphic operations (SSHE operations), we introduce the new security parameter *covert operations*, if it is required not only the host unknown the data but also the operations performed in the cipher-text, more on this in the security section.

5. A worked example

The following example shows an implementation that calculates, the greatest common divisor of two encrypted numbers.

Definition 7. Let x, y, c and c' be positive integers, then the *greatest common divisor* is c, if $c|x$ and $c|y$ also their not exist $c' > c$ such that $c'|x$ and $c'|y$. Where $c|x$ means that c exactly divides x.

For this we use the technique of successive subtraction so we only need three basic operation automata, the "subtraction automaton", the "comparison automaton" and the "equal automaton". Once these have been designed, we use the algorithm $Transform$ to operate on the cipher-text and we get to host.

5.1 Basic operations

The following subsection shows the designed operation automata, noting that all consecutive automata have been composed, whereby the keys (here encryption and decryption automata) remain safe, even we can make that the host does not know which operation has being performed. Furthermore the operation automata are designed to ignore the values corresponding to the random input embedded in the plain-text. The following three automata form the basis of the implementation:

- SubC. This automaton subtracts two bit strings that have been encrypted.
- CMC. This lets us know, given two encrypted strings two things, if the output is 0, the first component is greater than or equal to the second, if the output is 1, the first component is less than the second. Basically do a subtraction and observe the value of the most significant bit, attempting to destroy the value of the decoded data.
- EqualC. Here we have a finite automaton that checks bitwise if the input data are equal, leaving the most significant bit in 1 if they are, zero otherwise, again all possible traces of data that could be used in cryptanalysis is destroyed.

5.2 How the GCD works

Figure 3 shows how the host will use the basic operation automata to calculate the greatest common divisor, as mentioned at the beginning of the section, SSHE operations hide the operation actually applied on the plain-text, however not all the process is performed with a finite automata, storage and decisions on program flow are still taken by the host freely, however the final goal remains unknown. The host has a general structure of the software as shown

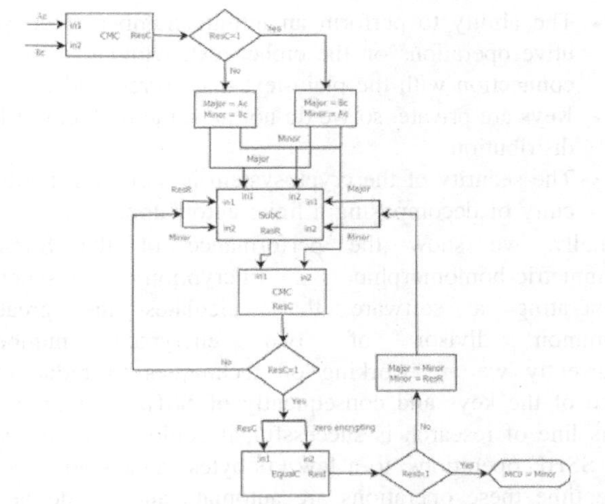

Fig. 3: Flow diagram of the GCD

in figure 3, for the response of a user "A" the host use the SSHE operations that corresponds to the user without modify the software structure. Each one of the SSHE operations, functions like a black box, responding after receiving inputs. Once built the software on the host's machine steps are:

1) The user A, which generated the SSHE operations with their encryption and decryption keys, select any two positive integers x, y, computes its binary representation, separately encrypts and sends to the host.
2) The host introduces the two encrypted data into the software and using the SSHE operations of the user A, calculates the answer and sends it to the user.
3) Finally the user A, using its decryption key, calculates the plain-text corresponding to the greatest common divisor of x and y, not forgetting eliminate random elements embedded in the string at the beginning.

5.3 How the software works

When we implement the software, the host was ignore, however the calculation is performed as described in the previous section, the software takes as input two integers greater than 0 and when we press "Encrypt data", using an invertible finite automaton, encrypts the data and once we press "calculate" takes the encrypted data and calculates the cipher-text that correspond to the greatest common divisor, finally decrypts the value to verify that the algorithm works. One program screen shown in figure 4.

6. Security

The safety analysis of an encryption scheme is very complicated, because the actions that the intruder can perform are vast, which is why to know how safe it is an encryption

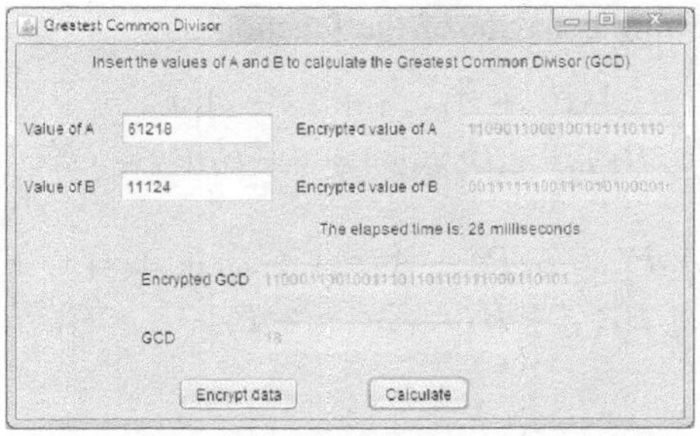

Fig. 4: GCD software view

scheme, are designed some possible attacks and is observed the complexity of implement them.

6.1 A new security approach (covert operations)

The idea can be implemented in two ways, one where software is designed by the host and another where the user designs, being designed by the host, security level covert operations, can not be reached. In case that the software is designed for the user, given that the SSHE operations are the operation automata compounds with encryption and decryption keys, it can achieve new security approach where not only the host unknown the data but also the calculation being made by the SSHE operations, to know the operations performed on the plain-text, the intruder must decompose the basic operation in its components automata and do this is considered a complicated task, as shown in [17] and [8], besides that the resulting automata from the decomposition are not unique, there is a very large number of automatons which can be the answer of the decomposition.

6.2 Algebraic attack

In most of the attacks, we has to suppose that parts of the data that should be kept in secret have been discovered, in the following we will analyze a case where the functions defining the encryption and decryption automata have been discovered by the intruder and also is able to obtain the corresponding cipher-text from a selected plain-text, the attack is carried out as follows: let Σ be a l-dimensional vector space over $GF(q)$, A be a m-dimensional vector space over $GF(q)$, $x_j \in \Sigma, y_j \in A$ where $j \in \mathbb{Z}$ and the equation (1) is the definition function of the encryption automata.

Suppose we know A_j and B_h, $0 \leq j \leq r, 1 \leq h \leq t$. The goal now is to get the initial state formed by $x\_1, \ldots, x_{-r}, y_{-1}, \ldots, y_{-t}$. To achieve this we need to create a system of $(r+t)$ equations with $r+t$ unknowns, to generate them do the following, assume that P_i^x corresponds to a known value of x_i and C_i^y corresponds to a known value of y_i. Introduced a sequence of length r to observe the following behavior of the function:

$$A_0P_0^x + A_1x_{-1} + \ldots + A_rx_{-r} + B_1y_{-1} + B_2y_{-2} + \ldots + B_ty_{-t} = C_0^y$$

$$A_0P_1^x + A_1P_0^x + A_2x_{-1} + \ldots + A_rx_{1-r} + B_1C_0^y + B_2y_{-1} + \ldots + B_ty_{1-t} = C_1^y \quad (12)$$

$$\vdots$$

$$A_0P_{r-1}^x + A_1P_{r-2}^x + \ldots + A_{r-1}P_0^x + A_rx_{-1} + B_1C_{r-2}^y + \ldots + B_{r-1}C_0^y + \ldots + B_t(y_{(r-1)-t}||C_{(r-1)-t}^y) = C_{r-1}^y$$

where $(y_{(r-1)-t}||C_{(r-1)-t}^y)$ indicates that there may be a known variable (C_i^y) or unknown (y_i), to find out we have to verify, if $(r-1)-t$ is negative then is $y_{(r-1)-t}$, if it is zero or positive then is $C_{(r-1)-t}^y$. After we introduce a sequence of length t to observe the following behavior of the function:

$$A_0P_0^x + A_1x_{-1} + \ldots + A_rx_{-r} + B_1y_{-1} + B_2y_{-2} + \ldots + B_ty_{-t} = C_0^y$$

$$A_0P_1^x + A_1P_0^x + A_2x_{-1} + \ldots + A_rx_{1-r} + B_1C_0^y + B_2y_{-1} + \ldots + B_ty_{1-t} = C_1^y \quad (13)$$

$$\vdots$$

$$A_0P_{t-1}^x + \ldots + A_{t-1}P_0^x + \ldots + A_r(x_{(t-1)-r}||P_{(t-1)-r}) + B_1C_{t-2}^y + \ldots + B_{t-1}C_0^y + B_ty_{-1} = C_{t-1}^y$$

where $(x_{(t-1)-r}||P_{(t-1)-r})$ indicates that there may be a known variable (P_i^x) or unknown (x_i), to find out we have to verify, if $(t-1)-r$ is negative then is $x_{(t-1)-r}$, if it is zero or positive then is $P_{(t-1)-r}^x$. Finally we solve the system of equations for $x\_1, \ldots, x_{-r}, y_{-1}, \ldots, y_{-t}$. Note that Solving systems of multivariate equations is known as a complex task. The complexity of this attack is defined by the memory of the automata.

7. Conclusion

In this paper, we create a new fully homomorphic encryption scheme, using as a base stream-symmetric encryption and finite automata theory. We show that our cryptographic scheme has the following characteristics:

- Is defined by the following algorithms: $KeyGen$, $Encrypt$, $Decrypt$ and $Transform$.
- By using finite automata to encrypt and decrypt, bitwise or character by character, we have a stream cipher, so is faster that any other know homomorphic encryption.
- We can define on the cipher-text, any operation that can be represented with a finite automaton, not only addition and multiplication.
- The ability to perform an infinite number of consecutive operations on the cipher-text, without losing the connection with the plain-text that corresponds.
- Keys are private, so we do not have the problem of key distribution.
- The security of the cryptosystem is based on the difficulty of decomposing a finite automaton.

Finally, we show the performance of the Stream-symmetric-homomorphic Encryption scheme, generating a software that calculates the greatest common divisor of two encrypted numbers. Currently we are working on techniques to reduce the size of the keys and consequently of SSHE operations, If this line of research is successful, it could reduce the size of SSHE operations, to a few kilobytes, remember, that by the time these operations are automata and for define an automaton $M = (\Sigma, A, Q, \delta, \lambda)$, we can use a matrix of size $Q \times \Sigma$, having as elements, pairs of the form: (Q, A).

References

[1] C. Shannon, "Communication theory of secrecy systems," *Bell System Technical Journal, Vol 28, pp. 656âĂŞ715*, Oktober 1949.
[2] J. L. Massey and M. K. Sain, "Inverses of linear sequential circuits," *IEEE Trans. Comput.*, vol. 17, no. 4, pp. 330–337, Apr. 1968.
[3] R. Rivest, A. Shamir, and L. Adleman, "A method for obtaining digital signatures and public-key cryptosystems," *Communications of the ACM*, vol. 21, pp. 120–126, 1978.
[4] R. L. Rivest, L. Adleman, and M. L. Dertouzos, "On data banks and privacy homomorphisms," *Foundations of Secure Computation, Academia Press*, pp. 169–179, 1978.
[5] R. Cramer, R. Gennaro, and B. Schoenmakers, "A secure and optimally efficient multi-authority election scheme." Springer-Verlag, 1997, pp. 103–118.
[6] M. Kuribayashi and H. Tanaka, "Fingerprinting protocol for images based on additive homomorphic property," *IEEE Transactions on Image Processing*, vol. 14, p. 2005.
[7] R. Tao, *Finite Automata and Application to Cryptography*. Springer Publishing Company, Incorporated, 2009.
[8] Z. Kohavi, *Switching and Finite Automata Theory: Computer Science Series*, 2nd ed., R. W. Hamming and E. A. Feigenbaum, Eds. McGraw-Hill Higher Education, 1990.
[9] A. Gill and C. U. B. E. R. LAB., *Analysis of Linear Sequential Circuits by Confluence Sets*. Defense Technical Information Center, 1964.
[10] I. Amorim, A. Machiavelo, and R. Reis, *On Linear Finite Automata and Cryptography*, 2011.
[11] S. Even, "On information lossless automata of finite order," *Electronic Computers, IEEE Transactions on*, vol. EC-14, no. 4, pp. 561–569, Aug.
[12] A. Maximov, "Some words on cryptanalysis of stream ciphers," Ph.D. dissertation, Lund University, 2006.
[13] S. Babbage, C. De Canniere, A. Canteaut, C. Cid, H. Gilbert, T. Johansson, M. Parker, B. Preneel, V. Rijmen, and M. Robshaw, *The eSTREAM Portfolio*, 2008.
[14] C. Fontaine and F. Galand, "A survey of homomorphic encryption for nonspecialists," *EURASIP J. Inf. Secur.*, vol. 2007, pp. 15:1–15:15, Jan. 2007.
[15] C. Gentry, "A fully homomorphic encryption scheme," Ph.D. dissertation, Stanford University, 2009.
[16] Gentry, "Fully homomorphic encryption using ideal lattices," in *Proceedings of the 41st annual ACM symposium on Theory of computing*, ser. STOC '09. New York, NY, USA: ACM, 2009, pp. 169–178.
[17] C. Halatsis, M. Sigala, and G. Philokyprou, "Polylinear decomposition of synchronous sequential machines," *IEEE Transactions on Computers*, vol. 27, no. 12, pp. 1144–1152, 1978.

Energy Efficiency Models Implemented in a Cloud Computing Environment.

Thusoyaone Joseph Moemi and Obeten Obi Ekabua

(Department of Computer Science, North-West University, Mafikeng Campus, Private Bag X2046, Mmabatho, 2735, South Africa)

Email: 17071100@nwu.ac.za; obeten.ekabua@nwu.ac.za

Abstract: Cloud computing is a paradigm of computing that shifts the way computing has been done in the past. In cloud computing, recourses are rented. For example cloud computing provides flexible services to cloud users services such as software, platform and infrastructure as services. The goal behind this is to provide computing resources on-demand to cloud users efficiently, through making data centers as green as possible, by reducing data center energy consumption and carbon emissions. To solve this problem, we came up with a power model and an efficient energy usage metric to calculate power consumption. We also developed a Load Balancing Virtual Machine Aware (LBVMA) model that conforms to reduction of energy consumption and proposed a defragmentation algorithm to help improve quality of service. The simulation tool used is cloud analyst. The results show that the LBVMA model and throttled load balancing algorithm consumed less energy. Also, the quality of service in terms of response time is much better for data centers that have more physical machines, but memory configurations at higher frequencies consume more energy. The results show that using the LBVMA model together with the throttled load balancing algorithm, less energy is used meaning less carbon is produced by the data center.

Keywords: Cloud Computing, Energy Efficiency, Models, Algorithms, Data Center, Service Delivery.

1. Introduction and Background

People around the world today are using computers, computer networks and applications to do most of their business processes, communication and social networking [1]. As a result, the popularity of web-based applications is on the increase. Most of the companies rendering these web based applications use cloud computing services to host their applications. One can only imagine how much data processing power is needed to process this world wide work load. Well, this work load is distributed across data centers within a cloud computing environment [1] [2].

The goal of cloud computing is to provide computing resources as utilities [3], just like today electricity, clean water and telephoning services are rendered as utilities. The services provided by cloud computing are software as a service (SaaS), infrastructure as a sersice (IaaS) and platform as a service [2]. The new aspects about cloud computing are its acquisition model which is based on purchasing of services; its business model which is based on pay for use, its access model which is over the Internet to any device and its technical model which is scalable, elastic, dynamic, multi-tenant, and sharable [4]. There are different types of cloud computing environments and these are: Public cloud, where services are available from a third party service provider; Private cloud, which is very similar to public cloud, the only difference is that in private cloud all the services are managed within one organization; Community cloud, which is controlled by a group of organizations that have a common goal or concern, like security; Hybrid cloud, which is a mix of any of the other cloud environments [2]. Figure 1 shows the relationship between some of the services in a cloud computing environment.

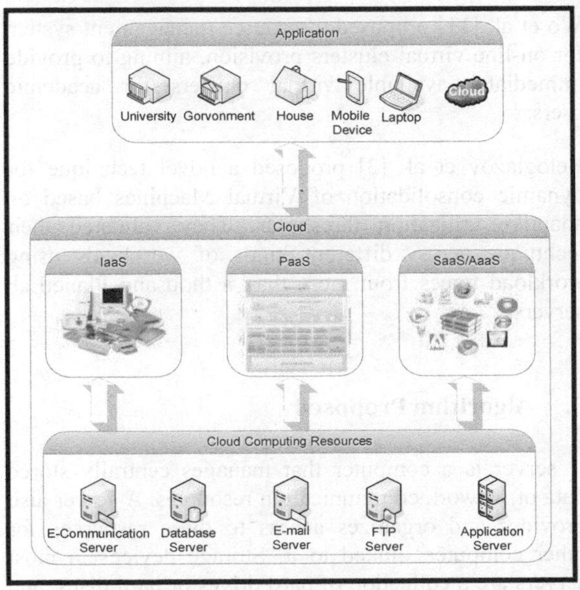

Figure 1: Cloud Computing Environment

Global warming combined with more affordable computing technologies are some of the main reasons for coming up with cloud computing [4]. Paying for services such as infrastructure, platform and applications has been a big challenge for organizations in the past. Cloud computing with its new models helps companies improve their business models, communication and relationship with their customers.

The models and algorithms existing in cloud computing have been implemented for one common goal of improving efficiency and optimizing energy consumption in cloud data centers [5] [6] [7]. Evidently the cloud is growing and will continue to evolve. Hence, there is a need to provide more efficient models and algorithms to optimize quality of service and energy consumption in a cloud computing environment [8].

2. Related Works

Li B. et al. [6] proposed EnaCloud, a novel approach that enables dynamic application live placement with the consideration of energy efficiency in a cloud platform. They use a Virtual Machine to encapsulate the application and since this application is abstracted as a bin packing problem, they also proposed an energy-aware heuristic algorithm to get better results.

Daim et al. [10] explored important issues on reasons why energy savings in data centers are significant. Part of their work examines twodata center metrics (PUE and DCP) from the point of strength and weakness. The authors also created a model that measures the component of the data center and provide a framework that supports metrics result organization and communication in a data center.

Wo et al. [11] proposed a resource management system for on-line virtual clusters provision, aiming to provide immediately-available virtual clusters for academic users.

Beloglazov et al. [3] proposed a novel technique for dynamic consolidation of Virtual Machines based on adaptive utilization thresholds. They validated their technique across different kinds of workloads using workload traces from more than a thousand PlanetLab servers.

3. Algorithm Proposed

A server is a computer that manages centrally stored data or network communication resources. A server also provides and organizes access to these resources for other computers linked to it. Storage devices in most servers are a collection of hard drives or hard discs, and as people or nodes connected to the server in the network insert and delete into the server, the hard drives get fragmented. This fragmentation causes processing speed to be slow because the Central Processing Unit (CPU) collects and stores its data and information in the hard drive or Random Access Memory (RAM). The reason for that is that the hard drive after fragmentation has variable distance between data or information stored in it in terms of space in bytes. Defragmentation is a process of removing this distance and bringing information in the hard drive closer together, and in so doing making processing time faster because searching time is reduced. Virtual machine migration is when virtual machines are moved from one physical machine to another. This migration also causes fragmentation. So to solve this problem we propose a defragmentation algorithm, figure 2, which should be active after virtual machine migration, just before the server turns off, to optimize processing time and energy consumption.

```
Quicksort(HD,p,t) {
 if (p < t) {
  q <- Partition(HD,p,t)
  Quicksort(HD,p,q)
  Quicksort(HD,q+1,t)
 }
}

Partition(HD,p,t)
  x <- HD [p]
  i <- p-1
  j <- r+1
 while (True) {
  repeat
      j <- j-1
   until (HD [j] <= x)
   repeat
      i <- i+1
   until (HD [i] >= x)
  if (i<-=""> A[j]
   else
     return(j)
 }
}
```

Figure 2: Defragmentation Algorithm

The algorithm is based on the assumption that the hard drives found in servers of the data centers are designed liked an array.

Input: HD fragmented array HD, a pivot element p and a traversing element t.
Output: HD defragmented array HD.

4. The Power Model

A linear relationship between CPU utilization and electrical power is assumed for our model. For example, for a given job say j1, information of the processing time and the processor utilization is enough to calculate its power consumption. We define the consumption of a resource r_i at any given time as:

$$C_i = \sum_{j=1}^{n} c_{i,j} \quad (1)$$

Where n = number of task running at that time and $c_{i,j}$ is the resource usage of job j_j.

We also define energy usage, Pi, of a resource at any time as:

$$P_i = (P_{max} - P_{min}) * C_i + P_{min} \qquad (2)$$

Where P_{max} refers to the peak load consumed and P_{min} refers to active mode minimum power consumption usually as low as one (1%) percent.

5. Efficient Energy Usage (EEU)

The total energy consumed in cloud data center together with other necessary resources needed for service in a cloud data center are what we referred to as EEU.

$$EEU = \frac{\sum_{n=1}^{\infty} \text{Yearly Consumption}}{\text{Yearly Consumption}} \qquad (3)$$

$$1 <= \text{EEU} <= \infty \qquad (4)$$

EEU can be varied from 1 to ∞ as seen in (4). Meaning that every data center with a EEU value of 2 or more shows that for every kWh consumed by the server, one kWh is consumed by the supplementary services like the cooling system of the data center, the lighting system, etc.

6. Load Balancing

Load balancing is the process of taking complex or large work load that needs a lot of processing power to be processed and dividing it into modules and distributing it to different machines or notes for processing. In so doing, the processing time and processing power are reduced. For example, taking a large mathematical equation and using a distributed system to compute it just like in Grid computing. In cloud computing the process is the same. The only difference is that the process is done on a virtual plain, which is at virtual machine management or hypervisor level.

In this work we determine which load balancing algorithm is more energy efficient in a virtual machine management level. Virtual machine management level is referd to as vitual machine queues in our designed model as can be seen in Figure 3 (Load Balancing Virtual Machine Aware) LBVMA Model.

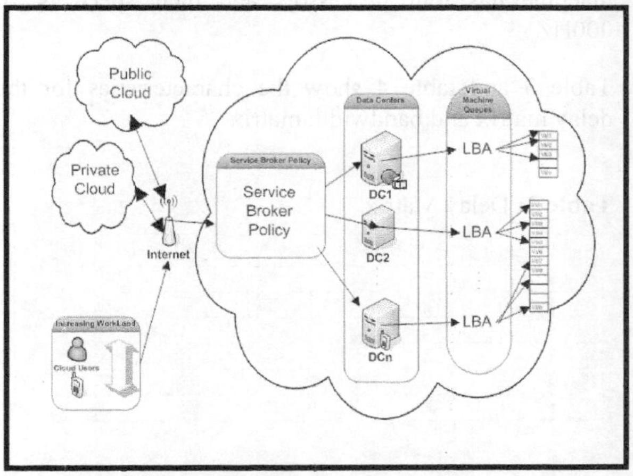

Figure 3: LBVMA Model

7. Simulation Tool - Cloud Analyst

Cloud Analyst is a simulation tool designed to simulate real cloud environments and scenarios. It is built on top of CloudSim which is based on java programming language and iText 2.1.5. On the other hand cloud analyst has all the capabilities of CloudSim and it has a user friendly Graphic User Interface (GUI). For the purpose of our experiments as reported in this paper, we use CloudAnalyst to simulate our data [9] [12].

8. Experimental Setup

The experiment was run on a machine having core *i5* intel processor and 4Gig RAM. The simulation tool used was Cloud Analyst. Six geographically located user bases were created and two data centers as shown in table 1 and table 2 respectfully.

Table 1: User Bases

Name	Region	Requests per User per Hr	Data Size per Request (bytes)	Peak Hours Start (GMT)	Peak Hours End (GMT)	Avg Peak Users	Avg Off-Peak Users
Ifeoma	4	20	150	15	20	300000	80000
Mike	2	20	150	12	24	450000	300000
Nnnenna	0	20	150	14	18	250000	20000
Nosipho	1	20	150	16	20	500000	60000
Thuso	3	20	150	13	22	350000	5000

Table 2: Data Centers

Data Center	#VMs	Image Size	Memory	BW
DC1	5	10000	512	1000
DC2	5	10000	512	1000

Also, for each data center, the physical machines uses x86 architecture while running in a Linux operating system and Xen virtual machine manager. Each physical machine has four processors and their speed is 10 000Hz.

Table 3 and table 4 show the characteristics for the delay matrix and bandwidth matrix

Table 3: Delay Matrix

Region\Region	0	1	2	3	4	5
0	25	100	150	250	250	100
1	100	25	250	500	350	200
2	150	250	25	150	150	200
3	250	500	150	25	500	500
4	250	350	150	500	25	500
5	100	200	200	500	500	25

Table 4: Bandwidth Matrix

Region\Region	0	1	2	3	4	5
0	2,000	1,000	1,000	1,000	1,000	1,000
1	1,000	800	1,000	1,000	1,000	1,000
2	1,000	1,000	2,500	1,000	1,000	1,000
3	1,000	1,000	1,000	1,500	1,000	1,000
4	1,000	1,000	1,000	1,000	500	1,000
5	1,000	1,000	1,000	1,000	1,000	2,000

The following Internet characteristics were defined between regions on the map. Figure 4 shows the regions as created by the simulation tool.

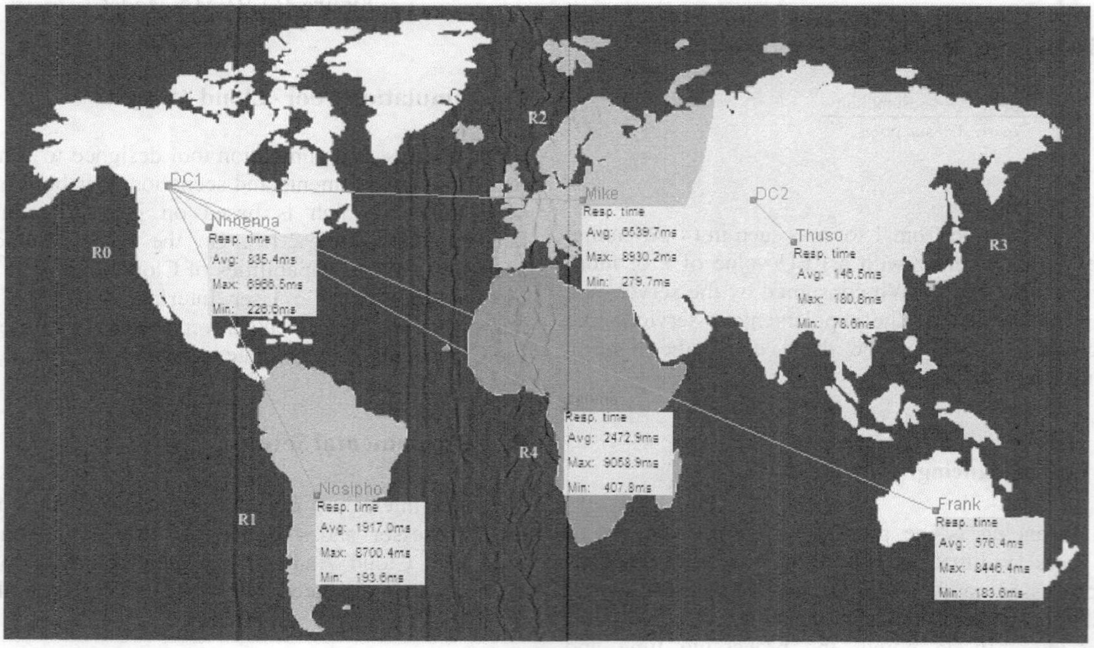

Figure 4: Region Showing Map

9. Results and discussions

When the amount of data processed at user base level as shown in table 1 is compared to the amount of user base response time shown in table 5, it is evident that quality of service in terms of response time is much better for data centers that have more physical machines.

Figure 5 shows a correlation of user bases and their corresponding response time, which is used to determine the min, max and avg response time for the two (DC1, DC2) data centers reported in table 6 with the results obtained, it was possible to graphically show the min, max and avg response time for the data centers as shown in figure 6.

Table 5: User Base Response Time

User Bases	Min (ms)	Max (ms)	Avg (ms)
Frank	172.83	1718.89	461.95
Ifeoma	401.4	7688.57	1526.57
Mike	254.16	7304.98	2464.76
Nnnenna	49.23	736.05	292.74
Nosipho	160.75	2453.54	848.1
Thuso	50.43	5461.83	370.14

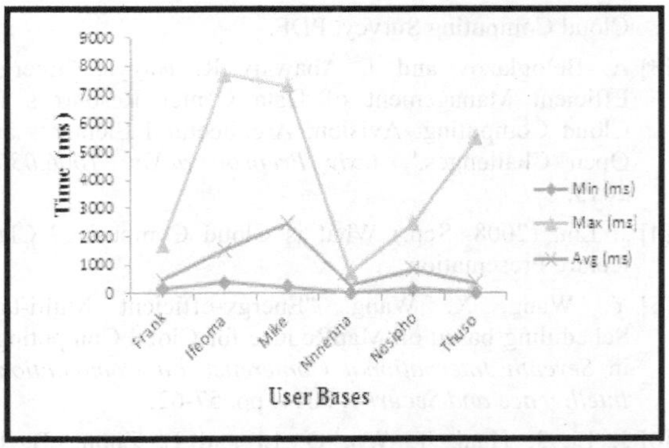

Figure 5: User Base Response Times

Table 6: Data Center Response Time

Data Centers	Min (ms)	Max (ms)	Avg (ms)
DC1	0.11	7076.86	1831.7
DC2	8.71	3295.29	1106.04

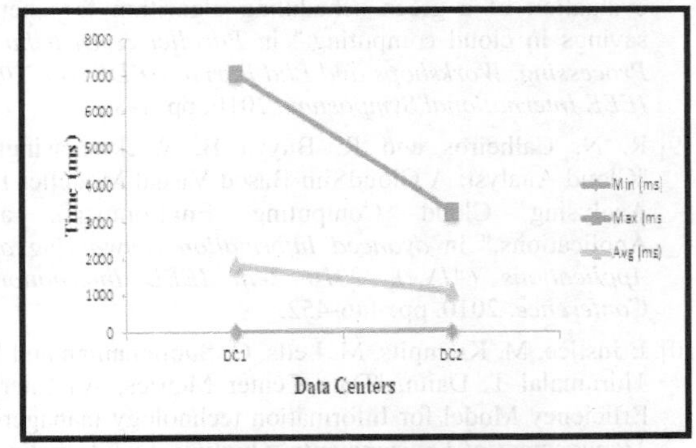

Figure 6: Data Center Response Time

Figure 7 shows a comparison of energy consumed by a data center facility using the LBVMA Model, where the load balancing policy is throttled and service broker policy is set to optimal time response. Therefore figure 7 shows a correlation between execution time and the energy consumed. From LBVMA model and the chosen parameters, it can be seen that energy consumption is less.

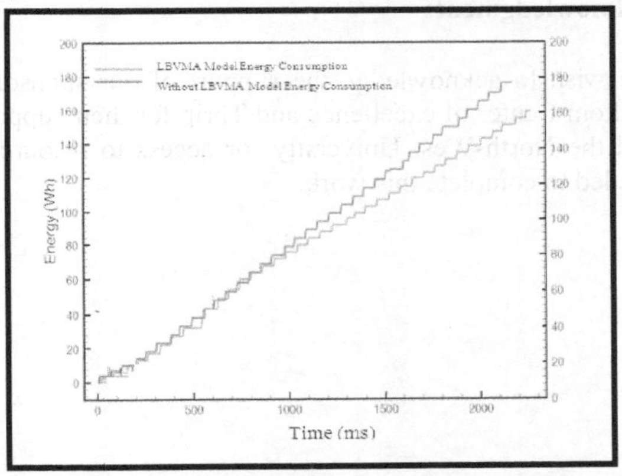

Figure 7: Consumed Energy for Power Model

Figure 8 shows power consumption due to deferent memory configurations. The memory configurations are 1000 MHz, 1200 MHz and 1500 MHz respectfully. The x-axis shows time in mille seconds and the y-axis shows the power in kilo Watts. From the figure it is clear to see that memory configuration at higher frequencies consume more power.

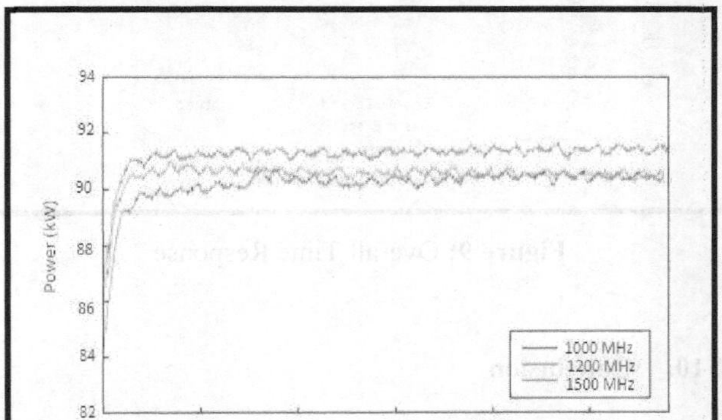

Figure 8: Power Consumed by Memory

Recall that, in section 6 we mentioned we were going to determine which load balancing algorithm is more energy efficient in a virtual machine management level. This next experiment shows exactly that. We used the same configuration in section 8 for all algorithms.

Table 7: Overall Time Response

	Round Robin	Equally Spread Current Execution Load	Throttled
Avg (ms)	3739.52	3613.4	1996.66
Min (ms)	75.28	72.77	49.23
Max (ms)	7673.36	7721.21	7688.57

Table 7 shows overall response time of requests processed from user bases to data centers and vice versa. Figure 9 shows a graphical representation of the data in table 7 and represent a correlation of the load balancing algorithm with respect to response time represented in mille seconds. From figure 8 it is clear that the throttled load balancing algorithm performs better in terms of response time.

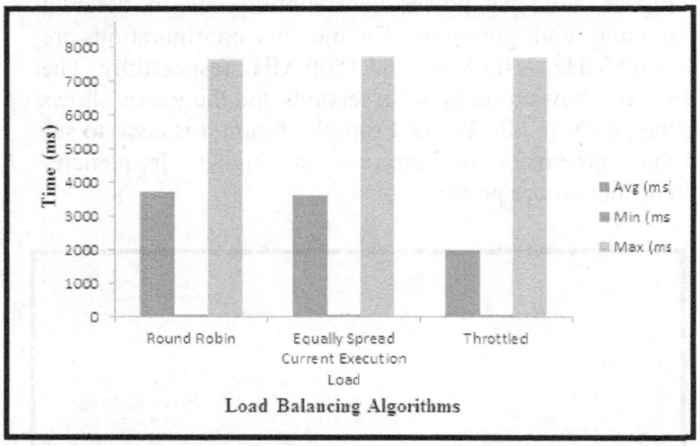

Figure 9: Overall Time Response

10. Conclusion

In conclusion, reported in this research paper is a comparison of three load balancing algorithms (Round Robin, Equally Spread Current Execution Load and Throtled) to determine which load balancing algorithm is more efficient in a virtual machine management level. Therefore, we conclude that using the LBVMA model and the throttled load balancing algorithm, less energy is consumed. From obtained results, we conclude that in terms of quality of service, the response time is much better for data centers having more physical machines than for those with less machines, but there was an observable higher energy consumption for memory configurations with higher frequencies.

More so, in this paper, we implemented a power model to calculate the power consumption of a data center, using a Load Balancing Virtual Machine Aware (LBVMA) Model, an Efficient Energy Usage (EEU) matric that determines whether or not the energy used in a cloud data center is used effectively. We also implemented a defragmentation algorithm to optimize processing time in cloud data centers after virtual machine migration.

References

[1] Y. Zhao, I. Raicu, L. Shiyong, I. Foster, "Cloud Computing and Grid Computing 360-Degree Compared," , Chicago, IL, USA, 2008, pp. 1-10.

[2] J. Hermans and M. Chung. (2012, Mar.) KPMG's 2010 Cloud Computing Survey. PDF.

[3] A. Beloglazov and J. Abawajy R. Buyya, "Energy-Efficient Management of Data Center Resources for Cloud Computing: Avision, Architectural Elements and Open Challenges," *Arxiv Preprint arXiv: 1006.0308*, 2010.

[4] J. Lin. (2008, Sep.) What is Cloud Computing? Class lecture Presentation.

[5] Y. Wang, X. Wang, "Energy-efficient Multi-task Scheduling based on MapReduce for Cloud Computing," in *Seventh International Conference on Computational Intelligence and Security*, 2011, pp. 57-62.

[6] J. Li, J. Huai, T. Wo, Q. Li and L. Zhong B. Li, "Enacloud: An energy-saving application live placement approach for cloud computing environments," in *CLOUD'09. IEEE International Conferenc*, 2009, pp. 17-24.

[7] A. Beloglazov and R. Buyya, "Adaptive Threshold-Based Approach for Energy-Efficient Consolidation of Vertual Machines in Cloud Data Centers," in *8th International Workshop on Middleware for Grids, Cloud and e-Science*, 2010, p. 4.

[8] Y. Sato and Y. Inoguchi T. V. T. Duy, "Performance evaluation of a green scheduling algorithm for energy savings in cloud computing," in *Parallel & Distributed Processing, Workshops and Phd Forum (IPDPSW), 2010 IEEE International Symposium*, 2010, pp. 1-8.

[9] R. N. Calheiros and R. Buyya B. Wickremasinghe, "Cloud Analyst: A CloudSim-Based Visual Modeller For Analysing Cloud Computing Environments and Applications," in *dvanced Information Networking and Applications (AINA), 2010 24th IEEE International Conference*, 2010, pp. 446-452.

[10] J. Justice, M. Krampits, M. Letts, G. Subramanian and M. Thirumalai T. Daim, "Data Center Metrics: An Energy Efficiency Model for Information technology managers," *Management of Environmental Quality: An International Journal*, vol. 20, pp. 712-731, 2009.

[11] T. Wo and J.Li Y. Chen, "An Efficient Resource Management System for On-Line Virtual Cluster Provision," in *IEEE International Conference* , 2009, pp. 72-79.

[12] University of Melbourne. (2012, May) Melbourne Clouds Lab. [Online]. http://www.cloudbus.org/cloudsim/

Acknowledgments

We wish to acknowledge the support of our sponsors, Telkom Center of excellence and Thrip for their support and the North-West University for access to resources needed to complete this work.

A system of Cloud Services and SOA to improve Health Care Organizations

Katiuscia Mannaro[1], Luisanna Cocco[1], Manola D'Onofrio[2], Marco Di Francesco[2]
[1]Department of Electrics and Electronics Engineering, University of Cagliari, Piazza d'Armi Cagliari, Italy
[2] ExperTeam Srl, Viale Elmas 142, Cagliari, Italy

Abstract - *The interoperability among different systems in healthcare is an historical problem. The development of interoperability standards, the interest for an approach based on Personal Health Record (PHR) and Electronic Health Record (HER) led a significant evolution in the field of the e-health. In the meanwhile, Cloud Computing (CC) is a very interesting solution for IT Applications. This paradigm presents many advantages for management. CC is still in its early stage; for this reason we think that it is very important to study and assess its impact on e-health solutions. In this paper we present a model which takes advantages of the features of the software infrastructure, known as Enterprise Service Bus, and of the Cloud services. This model makes interactions possible among different and heterogeneous entities in a generic health information system.*

Keywords: Enterprise Service Bus, Cloud, SOA, Software Engineering, Open Source

1 Introduction

The Health Information Systems were already developed at the beginning of Computer Science history. Hospitals have always been equipped with Hospital Information Systems; also, practitioners have often used instruments for supporting their own activities and storing medical data on Information Systems. Concepts such as Electronic Health Record (EHR) were born to represent the semantic feature of electronic health information about individual patients or populations.[1] A particular focus has been put on information about individual patients, which have been defined as Personal Health Record (PHR) [2].

Meanwhile, the need to exchange medical data among different subjects operating in this field grew. This brought to the demand of defining specific standards to manage such exchange of data. In the last years, this process has been quickened by the development of communication technologies. HL7 and its members provide a framework (and related standards) for the exchange, integration, sharing and retrieval of electronic health information. Many ot these standards have been adopted by ISO. The HL7 Clinical Document Architecture (CDA) - ISO/HL7 27932 - is an XML-based markup standard intended to specify the encoding, structure and semantics of clinical documents for the exchange.

Nowadays, the recent, rapid development of a health information policy to improve data complexity management, the volumes of patients served and the common understanding among workforce are the basis to have efficient health information systems. The standardization of data and the format and interchange protocols have been developed to support these needs. All the benefits of Electronic Health Records (EHRs), which focus on the total health of the patient, stemmed to shared information among healthcare organizations, such as laboratories, hospitals, general practitioners and specialists. Service-Oriented Architecture (SOA) is the model of choice for developing complex information services within highly integrated systems, because PHRs contain information from all the subjects involved in patient's care [3][4]. The evolution of all these concept is the basis of e-health.

Cloud Computing is a new paradigm to manage services in the world of services. This standard offers many opportunities for the development of e-health. The new e-health is based on data, infrastructure, services and things (in the sense of Internet of Things).

Our research work is part of an industrial project in conjunction with a private company to develop a Virtual Organization (VO) to manage patients. The organization is based on the role of general practitioners as reference points for the patients as well as real coordinators of activities and repositories of medical data on a Cloud infrastructure. This Virtual Organization must consult laboratories, hospitals and PHR's repositories to obtain the complete case of the patient. The goal of our work is to ensure the manageability of this interchange of data among all the organizations and individuals involved in the process. Thus, we designed a model for the management of data interchange based on interoperability; we also developed a middleware subsystem to manage interfaces among subjects and infrastructures.

The paper is organized as follows: in Section II we present a brief description of some key concepts related to Cloud

Computing and Service Oriented Architecture, and in Section III we present the project. Section IV specifies our ESB infrastructure, and we will focus on the ESB functional specifications. Finally, Section V summarizes the conclusions of our research and ends the study with recommendations for future works.

2 Cloud Computing and Service Oriented Architecture

Cloud computing is an interesting way of delivering and using services. It is an emerging technology of primary importance to business competitiveness. There are many definitions of cloud computing. According to the definition developed in 2009 by the US National Institute of Standards and Technology (NIST) Information Technology Laboratory, Cloud computing is a model for enabling a convenient access to a shared pool of configurable computing resources (e.g., networks, servers, storages, applications, and services). These resources are accessible via the Internet, paying a subscription based on a pay as you go model. In addition, they can be rapidly provisioned and released with the lowest management effort ant the minimal service provider interaction.

Cloud Computing contains three different paradigms, i) Software as a Service (SaaS), ii) Platform as a Service (PaaS), iii) Infrastructure as a Service (IaaS).

The first one is a cloud hosting model where providers offer a complete end-user application. The second one is a model which provides a full or partial application development environment. The providers offer, apart from the hardware, a platform including OS, middleware and runtime environment. Finally the last, IaaS, is a model providing a full computer infrastructure, server, router, storage, hardware and virtualization software.

Therefore, a more service-oriented approach is often found in SaaS – this delivery of applications over the internet offers significant cost savings because resources in massive warehouse-sized data centres are pooled at scale.

Services Oriented Architecture (SOA) is an architectural style that supports the service-orientation. It is a way of thinking in terms of services and service-based development and the outcomes of services. SOA is an architecture pattern for designing and managing a software portfolio made up from loosely coupled, well-encapsulated, reusable services. [5]

In general, business services delivered in a Cloud form are SOA services. What do these two things have in common? The success of the Cloud is possible only with a proper architecture, which applies the most relevant SOA principles such as loose-coupling, governance and manageability.

3 Project description

The purpose of the project is the creation of a VO based on knowledge for Dermatological Telemedicine aiming at giving a combined and synergic set of services for the clinical management optimization of dermatological patient.

A VO is composed by a set of individuals and organizations cooperating for a common interest and sharing a set of resources, based on prearranged policites. The VO in this project wants to make the relationship among general practitioners and specialists in Dermatology more efficient and effective, defining models, methodologies and techniques for the management of a knowledge base related to diagnostic-therapeutic guidelines which, as for therapies, has to include complementary, alternative, non-conventional and supplementary medicine, with a particular focus on the use of phytotherapy products in dermatology, directed to: i) the screening of subjects in need of specialist care, ii) the direct management of subjects with minor pathologies by the general practitioner.

Another purpose of Virtual Organization is the development of advanced services for supporting diagnosis and teleconsultation through the creation of many diagnostic supports (online consulting of an "historical" dermatologic atlas; an image analysis software for the semi-automatic classification of dermatologic pathologies; a flow chart of diagnostic procedures, etc.).

These cross-features are strongly interconnected: the final result of the research will be the design of a VO model able to gather different Competence Centres which, in turn, will offer the aforementioned innovative services. In order to maximize the effectiveness of the services offered, models and methodologies will be studied and applied for the explicit representation, the sharing, the retrieval and the connection of spread knowledge in VO.

Therefore, the subject of the reaserch will not be the recognition of already-existing solutions to re-adopt for the problem we are examining, but the identification of a substantially new system solution able to support Telemedicine services. The quite low amount of time and the development of the research activity on a modular basis will allow for the portability of each single result of the research in restricted time, with respect to the start of activities.

The final results of industrial research, fundamental research and experimental development activities will be able to be used at international level for the creation of a functioning and useful Telemedicine system.

The project puts at its core the solution of the diagnostic problem of patients, going through their paths, and taking advantage of the potentialities of teleconsultation as main instrument.

As for what has been declared in the guidelines by the Ministry of Health (www.salute.gov.it), the 'path' is a pre-defined, well-structured and coordinated sequence of health services involving the integrated participation of different specialists and professionals, with the aim of achieving a diagnosis and the most adequate therapy for a specific pathology.

For some time, there has been a research for coordination among different specialists and professionals, even belonging to different structures, often using high-cost technologies. This led to many difficulties in management, causing health organizations' ability to react to be stretched to the limit. This makes the optimization of the resources necessary to guarantee efficiency, effectiveness, pertinence and promptness. The system too has been developed with the Global Software Development (GSD) paradigm on Cloud [7].

4 Managing information

An Enterprise Service Bus (ESB), sometimes called "messaging middleware", is a platform for data exchange among different and heterogeneous applications. Data is carried to and from a series of endpoints which must be defined for each application. The implementation of an ESB includes routing mechanisms that drive specific data from source point A to destination point B [12].

The ESB model is popular because it helps organizations to manage multiple connections to services through a central bus that provides the level of abstraction above the details of the underlying messaging. Once a service is located on the bus, any element on the bus can connect. In other words, ESB is a logical channel that spans each endpoint and allows data to be sent or received from various applications over the bus. Data is transferred using a particular protocol, for instance HTTP. However, the ESB is more than just protocols or communication channels: it is a messaging framework.

The adopted ESB architectural solution has been designed as a natural evolution of the Service Oriented Architecture, in order to reduce the coupling among architectural elements characterized by specific and heterogeneous technologies and systems. A SOA architecture allows for a deep integration among application components, reducing the adjustment inside every single organization's information systems [13].

The Enterprise Service Bus (ESB) approach is based on a Centralized approach and uses a Bus Architecture and Open standards [14]. ESBs are represented as an abstract layer based on a message driven architecture under the applications that are integrated. The ESB tries to abstract the connections between applications by using a neutral transportation layer with respect to all nodes that have to be connected. ESBs are based on open standards like HTTP, XML, XSLT [6]. and the applications communicate using message-driven or event-driven paradigms, allowing for the implementation of complex systems with low efforts [15]. This model has a level of communication in a roundabout way among the various services on the bus and among composite applications and services they use.

Thanks to the ESB software infrastructure, the different organizations involved can easily communicate and when possible and necessary they may use complete Cloud services and applications on the Web, simply paying to use. The ESB infrastructure helps companies to manage different service connections without entering in detail of the underlying messaging aspects. On the other hand, Cloud Computing allows healthcare organizations to avoid costs and difficulties associated with building or managing software applications that would require high costs for their design, development and maintenance. In this way, healthcare organizations can remotely access software applications hosted by other companies with experience for example in storage data, email and so on.

The created model is similar to ESB in terms of functionality, but it is more similar to the SaaS model in terms of the standard and scalability. In this way it is easier to adopt ESB infrastructure.

The integration between architectural elements are implemented as a centralized strategy where the middleware is the actor that links services, letting them talk properly, helping them understand messages and eventually providing a secure communication channel. The infrastructure can be easily extended by adding new entry points that will enrich the palette of services offered by the platform. In practice, the complete architecture will be a complex system able to provide a huge list of services to every single entry point of the platform; in other words, the services will derive from every single entry point of the User Plane, the Medical Plane or the Statistical Plane.

5 Conclusions

Cloud computing market in the health care sector has been growing recently. Cloud services may offer new opportunities for the storage and communication of patient data to help physicians and clinicians make better their work. Moreover, the healthcare organizations may save money avoiding redundancy and high operational costs.

We designed and developed a middleware subsystem acting as a communication interface among organizations, by ensuring interoperability among heterogeneous data and services, as well as a reliable and secure PHR.

In order to support these subjects, as further works we will evaluate [17], [18] this model by using a simulation modeling approach, useful to better understand the process and to evaluate its effectiveness [8][9][10][11].

The proposed solution is an evolution of the Service Oriented Architecture proposed. Indeed, our architecture takes advantage from the software infrastructure ESB, and from the Cloud services. We offer a solution to the needs of health industry that enables the interoperability among data and applications from several and remote health organizations. In our opinion, the model could enable more effective collaboration, and facilitate the compliance with standards, in order to manage different service connections.

Nowadays, healthcare data need to be shared among several health organizations, even very distant ones; this burdens the health industry and the patients, causing delay and loss of time.

Cloud can help improve the sharing of the EHR data reducing delay and loss of time. It offers the health industry an incredible opportunity to improve services for their customers, sharing information more easily with respect to the traditional SOA architecture, and improving the efficiency of the whole health care system. The main advantages that Cloud offers to health's Virtual Organizations are collaboration, speed, mobility, security and privacy, and finally lower costs.

It has arrived the moment for health care organizations to capitalize on the Cloud advantages; the Virtual Organization will find significant benefits such as quick access to computing and large storage facilities which are not provided in traditional settings.

6 References

[1] Hoerbst, A., and E. Ammenwerth. "Electronic Health Records." Methods Inf Med 49.4 (2010): 320-336.

[2] Tang, Paul C., et al. "Personal health records: definitions, benefits, and strategies for overcoming barriers to adoption."*Journal of the American Medical Informatics Association*13.2 (2006): 121-126.

[3] Jan Walker, Eric Pan, Douglas Johnston, Julia Adler-Milstein, David W. Bates, Blackford Middleton , The Value Of Health Care Information Exchange And Interoperability, Health Affairs, 2005.

[4] Arthur L. Kellermann, Spencer S. Jones, What It Will Take to Achieve the As-Yet-Unfulfilled Promises of Health Information Technology, Health Affairs, v. 32, no. 1, Jan. 2013, p. 63-68, 2013.

[5] Chi Po Cheong, C. Chatwin, R. Young, "An SOA-based diseases notification system", ICICS Information, Communications and Signal Processing, 2009.

[6] M. Eichelberg, T. Aden, J. Riemsmeier, A. Dogac, G. B. Laleci, "A Survey and Analysis of Electronic Healthcare Record Standards", Journal ACM Computing Surveys (CSUR), Volume 37 Issue 4, December 2005

[7] Cocco L., Mannaro K., Concas G., "A Model for Global Software Development with Cloud Platforms". EUROMICRO-SEAA 2012, pp. 446-452, 2012.

[8] Turnu, I., Concas, G., Marchesi, M., Tonelli, R.Entropy of some CK metrics to assess object-oriented software quality, 2013 International Journal of Software Engineering and Knowledge Engineering 23 (2) , pp. 173-188.

[9] Turnu, I., Concas, G., Marchesi, M., Pinna, S., & Tonelli, R. A modified Yule process to model the evolution of some object-oriented system properties. Information Sciences, 181(4), 883-902.2011.

[10] Concas, G., Marchesi, M., Murgia, A., Tonelli, R., & Turnu, I.. On the distribution of bugs in the eclipse system. Software Engineering, IEEE Transactions on, 37(6), 872-877. 2011.

[11] Turnu, I., Melis, M., Cau, A., Setzu, A., Concas, G., Mannaro, K., "Modeling and simulation of open source development using an agile practice", 2006, Journal of Systems Architecture 52 (11), pp. 610-618

[12] Min Luo, B. Goldshlager, Liang-Jie Zhang, "Designing and implementing Enterprise Service Bus (ESB) and SOA solutions", IEEE International Conference on Services Computing, 2005.

[13] The Open Source ESB for SOA & Integration, available on :https://open-esb.dev.java.net, 2010

[14] Open-ESB: The Open Enterprise Service Bus, http://Java.net, 2008.

[15] dM. Schmidt, B. Hutchison, P. Lambros. R. Phippen, "The Enterprise Service Bus: Making service-oriented architecture real", IBM Software Group, 2005.

[16] B. Van Den Bossche, S. Van Hoecke, C. Danneels, J. Decruyenaere, B. Dhoedt, F. De Turck, "Design of a JAIN SLEE/ESB-based platform for routing medical data in the ICU", Computer Methods and Programs in Biomedicine archive, 2008

[17] Turnu, I., Marchesi, M., Tonelli, R., Entropy of the degree distribution and object-oriented software, quality 3rd International Workshop on Emerging Trends in Software Metrics, WETSoM 2012 - Proceedings , art. no. 6226997 , pp. 77-82, 2012

[18] Turnu, I., Concas, G., Marchesi, M., Tonelli, R., The fractal dimension of software networks as a global quality metric, 2013 Information Sciences, http://dx.doi.org/10.1016/j.ins.2013.05.014, (Article in Press)

Essential Cloud Security Features in Windows Azure

Ramya Dharam[1], **and Sajjan G. Shiva**[2]
[1]Department of Computer Science, University of Memphis, Memphis, TN, USA
[2]Department of Computer Science, University of Memphis, Memphis, TN, USA

Abstract - *Cloud computing technology is recently gaining widespread popularity among business owners and consumers/users for hosting and delivering services over the Internet. This technology offers users on-demand access to shared resources, services, and applications with the Internet access by eliminating the need for tedious installation procedures. Security and privacy issues in cloud computing is one of the major barriers for the wide adoption of this emerging technology. In this paper, we first discuss the security and privacy guidelines pertinent to the public cloud computing environment as described by NIST. We then investigate different security features of the Microsoft Azure cloud computing platform and analyze how the security and privacy guidelines described by NIST are implemented in this cloud platform.*

Keywords: Cloud Computing; NIST; Cloud Security; Privacy Issues; Microsoft Azure Cloud Platform; Public Cloud.

1 Introduction

Over the last few years, cloud computing technology has become an evolving paradigm with lots of benefits to its users and providers. Cloud computing is an integration of different traditional computing technologies and network technologies such as distributed computing, parallel computing, grid computing, virtualization, etc.

Various definitions exist explaining the concept of cloud computing, but the most widely accepted comprehensive definition about cloud computing was made by National Institute of Standards and Technology (NSIT) [1] and in this paper we adopt the same. It describes cloud computing as a model for enabling ubiquitous, convenient, on-demand network access to a shared pool of configurable computing resources (e.g., networks, servers, storage, applications, and services) that can be rapidly provisioned and released with minimal management effort or service provider interaction.

The essential characteristics provided by cloud computing makes it different from traditional service computing. Following are the five essential characteristics of cloud computing as discussed in [1] that has currently made an impact on the Information Technology industry:

1) On-demand self-service: Services such as applications, storage, etc., can be provisioned by users based on their demand.

2) Broad network access: A variety of cloud services is available over the network and heterogeneous thin or thick client platforms (e.g., mobile phones, tablets, laptops, and workstations) can be used to gain access to them.

3) Resource pooling: Computing resources such as storage, processing, memory, and network bandwidth are pooled to serve multiple consumers according to consumer demand.

4) Rapid elasticity: Capabilities can be elastically provisioned and released to meet the rapidly increasing demand of users.

5) Measured service: Metering capabilities are employed to automatically control and optimize resource usage and to charge the users accordingly. Resource usage can be monitored, controlled, and reported, providing transparency for both the provider and consumer of the utilized service.

Service driven business models are employed by cloud computing. In this model software, platform, and hardware level resources are provided as services to users/consumers from the cloud service providers. Three major cloud computing models as discussed in [1] have evolved, which include: 1) Software as a Service (SaaS), which provides consumers the capability to use provider's applications running on cloud infrastructure. 2) Platform as a Service (PaaS), which provides consumers the capability to deploy the application developed by them onto the cloud infrastructure. 3) Infrastructure as a Service (IaaS), which provides consumers the capability to provision processing, storage, networks, and other computing resources.

Private, Public, Community, and Hybrid clouds are the four cloud deployment models currently available. Private cloud is used by a single organization. Community cloud is provisioned for use by a specific community of users from different organizations that have shared concerns. Public cloud can be used by any general public. Hybrid cloud is formed by the combination of two or more distinct cloud infrastructures (private, public, or community).

With cloud computing becoming more and more popular because of its many benefits and characteristics it possesses as discussed above, security and privacy issues in cloud computing have also raised major concerns due to the unique architectural features and characteristics of the cloud. Hence security and privacy issues existing in cloud computing need to be addressed for this technology to be more widely adopted.

In this paper, we first discuss the different security and privacy issues that exist in the cloud computing technology and also the NIST guidelines to achieve security and privacy in public cloud computing. We then study in detail security features of one of the most popular cloud platforms i.e. the Microsoft Windows Azure, and analyze how the NIST guidelines on security and privacy in public cloud computing are accomplished in this platform.

The rest of the paper is organized as follows. In Section 2, we discuss the common security issues in cloud computing. In Section 3, we discuss the NIST guidelines to accomplish security and privacy in public cloud computing. Section 4 discusses about the features of Microsoft Windows Azure cloud platform and Section 5 discusses security features established in the Microsoft Windows Azure platform. Section 6 provides an analysis by helping us understand how the security and privacy guidelines mentioned by NIST are implemented in the Microsoft Windows Azure platform, and Section 7 concludes the paper.

2 Security Issues in Cloud Computing

In cloud computing, security is one of the prominent concerns. Security issues in cloud computing hinder the process of it being widely adopted. So in this section, we discuss in detail the different security issues that exist at different levels in this technology, which includes cloud data, cloud access, and cloud platform.

2.1 Security Issues related to Cloud Data

Data stored in cloud belongs to different users, enterprises, etc., and is an important asset. Maintaining the confidentiality, integrity, and availability of cloud data is currently the foremost concern to be addressed for this new technology. The inherent nature of cloud computing architecture itself raises several questions about the security of the data stored in the cloud. Some of the issues as discussed in [3] include the following: 1) What ensures integrity and prevents loss of data in cloud? 2) How is the confidentiality of the data maintained? 3) Is the data available to users in case the cloud services are down? 4) Will the data be completely deleted from the cloud storage if the user decides to withdraw the services from the cloud? 5) How do we know that the updates to the data are done periodically and the user gets access to the most updated version? Addressing these issues about cloud data is essential.

2.2 Security Issues related to Cloud Access

User authentication, authorization, and access control (AAA) is one of the important security concern related to cloud access. Multitenancy is one of the major features of the cloud computing where a single instance of software running on a server is utilized to serve multiple clients. This feature is known to cause interoperability, authentication, and identification problems because of the usage of distinct negotiation protocols by different clients. A management interface is essential so that the cloud services can be accessed by users. The probability that unauthorized access to this management interface could occur is much higher than for traditional systems where the management functionality is accessible only to a few administrators as discussed in [4].

Some of the issues related to cloud access as discussed in [3] consist of the following: 1) Different users access their data stored in the cloud and in such situations, how can it be ensured that authentication is provided at different levels to access cloud services? 2) How does one ensure that there is no unauthorized access to the cloud by an employee who has left the organization?

2.3 Security Issues related to Cloud Platform

This comprises of the security issues related to the cloud platform which include virtualization, networking, etc. Virtualization is the key technology for the success of cloud computing. It results in the creation of multiple VMs out a single physical layer. Each VM is itself a virtual server compromising a guest OS, middleware, application, and data. A Hypervisor/Virtual Machine Manager is a piece of software that allows multiple OSs to share a single hardware host and a computer on which a hypervisor is running one or more virtual machines is defined as a host machine. Each virtual machine is called a guest machine and the hypervisor presents the guest OSs with a virtual operating platform and manages the execution of the guest operating systems. Some of the virtualization induced cloud security issues as discussed in [5] consist of the following: 1) VM hijacking: In case of multitenancy, a single server would host several VMs on it and thus would have respective configuration files of all VMs stored on the host. Since each VM is separated by a virtual boundary, an attacker gaining access to one such files could be able to predict the actual hardware configuration of another VM residing on the same host. The primary configuration files contain all necessary information of a VM. Gaining access to these files and breaking into a VM is termed as "VM hijacking." A malicious user having control of a VM can try to gain control over the other VMs' resources or utilize all system resources leading to denial of service (DoS) attack over other VM users. A malicious user can also try to steal the data of other users located on the same server. 2) VM hopping: This is the process of hopping from one VM to another VM. An attacker on one VM can gain access over the other VM. This can be achieved if both the VMs are running on the same host. Because there are several VMs running on the same machine, there would be several victims of the VM hopping attack. An attacker can falsify the SaaS user's data once he gains access to a target VM by VM hopping, endangering the confidentiality and integrity of SaaS. 3) VM mobility: This enables the moving or copying of VMs from one host to another over the network or by using portable storage devices without physically stealing or snatching a hard drive. Although this makes the process of deployment easier, it could lead to security problems such as spread of vulnerable configurations. The severity of the attack ranges from leaking sensitive information to completely compromising the OS. 4) VM escape: This means gaining access over the hypervisor and attacking the rest of the VMs. If an attacker gains access to the host running multiple VMs, the attacker can access to the resources shared by the other VMs. The host can monitor the memory being allocated and the CPU utilization. If necessary, an attacker can bring down these resources and turn off the hypervisor. If the hypervisor fails, all the other VMs turn off eventually.

Some of the issues related to the cloud platform as discussed in [4] consist of the following: 1) Are the cloud data centers physically secured against security breaches? 2) How are the applications secured in a shared virtualized infrastructure against malicious attacks? Can the APIs and interfaces provided by cloud services be trusted?

3 NIST Guidelines on Security and Privacy in public cloud computing

In this section, we discuss in detail the guidelines described by NIST in [2] to achieve security and privacy in cloud computing.

1) Governance: It involves controlling and monitoring deployed applications over standards, procedures, and policies. It also involves the implementation, testing, design, and monitoring of deployed cloud services. Cloud computing services are widely used among employees and lack of control over the employees' access to the cloud services by the organization can cause problems.

Roles and responsibilities involved in accessing the cloud services need attention to ensure systems are secure and risks are managed. To determine how data is stored, protected, and used, to verify policy enforcement, and to validate services, audit mechanism and tools should be in place. Risks in cloud computing are continuously evolving and to deal with them a risk management program should be in place.

2) Compliance: Conformance with an established standard, specification, law, or regulation is involved. Compliance becomes a complicated issue due to the existence of different types of security laws at the national, state, and local levels within different countries. Any data that is processed or stored outside the bounded spaces of an organization inherently brings a level of risk and it is important to carefully address this issue. Data location is one of the most common compliance issues faced by any organization.

Any organization will structure its computing environment according to their needs and will know in detail where the data is stored, what measures they have taken to protect unauthorized access to the data, and if they use an in-house computing/storage center. But, in case of the usage of cloud computing technology this detailed information about the exact location of an organization's data is not known, then this lack of detailed information leads to a situation and makes it difficult to ascertain whether the specified compliance requirements are met. Usage of external audits and security certification could to some extent help in handling this issue.

3) Trust: In cloud computing an organization places an unprecedented level of trust in the cloud provider by giving away the direct control of many security aspects involved in the cloud. To enable a basis of trust the ownership rights of the organization over the data must be firmly established in the service contract.

It is challenging to assess and manage risk in systems that use cloud services. It is important for organizations to ensure that security controls are implemented and operated correctly as intended to manage risks. Based on the degree of control an organization is able to achieve on the provider, to provision the security controls which are necessary to secure the organization's data and gain assurance that those controls have been placed, it is possible to establish a level of trust in a cloud service. The organization must reject the service or be ready to take a greater degree of risk, if the level of trust provided by the service is below the specified and negotiated expectations and is unable to employ other suitable controls.

4) Architecture: The hardware and software residing in the cloud comprises the architecture used to deliver cloud services. The implementation, scalability logic of the framework, and the physical location of the infrastructure is determined by the cloud provider. Virtual machines are loosely coupled with cloud storage and is the basic unit of deployment in cloud computing. Cloud components communicating with each other using application programming interfaces are typically used to build applications. Underneath the complexity that affects security, many of the simplified interfaces and service abstractions are involved.

5) Identity and Access Management: Unauthorized access to data in the cloud is a major concern and the issues related to data security and privacy are widely discussed for the wide usage of cloud. The existing identification and authentication framework used by organizations may not naturally extend into the cloud and it will be difficult to modify the existing framework to support cloud services.

One possible solution could be to employ authentication systems, one for the internal organizational systems and another for external cloud-based systems.

To administer and authenticate the users so that they can access applications and data, cloud providers support the standard named Security Assertion Markup Language (SAML) which is used to provide cloud based identity and access management services. This alone is not sufficient to maintain identity services, but the capability to adapt cloud to the subscriber privileges and maintain control over access to resources is also needed.

6) Software Isolation: High degrees of multi-tenancy over large numbers of platforms are needed for cloud computing to achieve the envisioned flexibility of on-demand provisioning of reliable services and the cost benefits and efficiencies due to economies of scale. To reach the high scales of consumption desired, cloud providers have to ensure dynamic flexible delivery of service and isolation of subscriber resources.

7) Data Protection: Since the cloud environment is shared, the data stored in cloud co-exists with other customers' data. Before moving the data to the cloud it is very important that organizations reassure the means and control measures that have been established to keep the data secure and to establish the controlled access to the data.

8) Availability: The extent to which an organization's computational resources are accessible and usable is termed as availability. Different threats to availability consist of denial of service attacks, natural disasters, etc. Availability can be affected either temporarily or permanently, and a loss can be partial or complete and can impact the mission of the organization.

9) Incident Response: The security of a computer system is compromised by attacks and incident response, which is an organized method and is essential to deal with attack consequences. Incident verification, attack analysis, problem remediation, service restoration, etc., are some of the incident response activities cloud providers need to perform.

4 Overview of Microsoft Windows Azure Architecture

As defined in [6], Windows Azure is a cloud services operating system that serves as the development, service hosting and service management for the Windows Azure platform. This platform helps developers to host and manage web application through Microsoft datacenters with on-demand compute and storage options.

This section discusses the Microsoft Windows Azure architecture and each of its components as described in [7]. This Windows Azure architecture mainly consists of four components: 1) Windows Azure 2) SQL Azure 3) Windows Azure AppFabric and 4) Windows Azure Marketplace.

1) Windows Azure: This is a Windows environment for running applications and storing data on computers in Microsoft data centers. It consists of five components namely: a) Compute – Applications that are built using C#, Visual Basic, C++, Java can be executed using the Compute service on a Windows Server Foundation. b) Storage – Binary large objects (blobs) can be stored using this service and also provides tables with a query language. c) Fabric Controller – It is responsible for creating VMs and starting the applications that run on them. d) Content Delivery Network – It stores the copies of the data that are frequently accessed by the users closer to them which helps in speeding up access to the data. e) Connect – This service helps the Windows Azure applications to access database that is on the premise of the organization.

2) SQL Azure: This can be used for storing data in the cloud and is built on Microsoft SQL Server. It includes the following three components: a) SQL Azure Database - It is a cloud-based database management system (DBMS) and it allows both the on-premise and cloud applications to store data on Microsoft servers. b) SQL Azure Reporting - is used with SQL Azure database and it is responsible for creating SQL Server Reporting Services (SSRS) reports on the cloud data. c) SQL Azure Data Sync - is used to synchronize data between SQL Azure Database and on-premise SQL Server databases. Different SQL Azure databases present in different Microsoft data centers can be synchronized using Azure Data Sync.

3) Windows Azure AppFabric: This provides infrastructure for applications. It consists of the following three components: a) Service Bus - it exposes applications endpoints in the cloud so that other applications in the cloud or on-premise can access them. b) Access Control - used to define rules that help to control what services each user will be able to access. c) Caching - it is used to cache frequently accessed data by users so that performance is increased and reduces the need to query the database by the application every time to retrieve the data.

4) Windows Azure Marketplace: It lets the customers find as well as buy cloud applications and cloud-accessible data. It consists of the following two components: a) DataMarket – datasets are made available to content providers with the help of this component. b) AppMarket – cloud applications developed are exposed using this component so that other customers can buy them.

5 Security Features in Microsoft Windows Azure

Data and programs belonging to customers are hosted in the cloud by Microsoft using the Windows Azure. So it is essential to maintain the security and privacy of the data and applications residing in the cloud. In this section, we discuss in detail about the different features implemented by Microsoft in the Windows Azure cloud platform to accomplish the security of user's data as described in [6].

1) Identity and Access Management: This feature ensures that only authorized and authenticated users are allowed to access the required cloud services. Following are the different mechanisms used to accomplish the Identity and Access Management security feature of the cloud: a) SMAPI Authentication – The Service Management API provides web services via the Representational State Transfer (REST) protocol. High degree of assurance is accomplished with this mechanism and that only the authorized representatives of the customer can access the service. b) Least Privilege Customer Software – This is a security best practice that is widely used in which applications are executed with least privileges. Also, customers are not granted administrative access to their VMs. This helps in reducing the potential impact and protects from attacks as an elevation in privileges is required to perform attacks. c) SSL Mutual Authentication for Internal Control Traffic – SSL is used to communicate between the internal components of Windows Azure.

2) Isolation: This involves keeping different data segregated from one another. Isolation can be accomplished at different levels in the Windows Azure using the following: a) Isolation of Hypervisor, Root OS and Guest VMs – The root OS and the hypervisor manages the root VM and the guest VMs and so isolation of the root VM from the guest VMs helps to accomplish security to a certain extent. b) VLAN Isolation – Fabric Controllers and other devices are isolated using VLANs. A network is partitioned using VLANs and without passing through a router no communication is possible. This prevents a compromised node from faking traffic outside its VLAN, and also it cannot eavesdrop on traffic that is not to or from its VLANs. c) Isolation of Customer Access – Customer access environments are separated from customer applications and storage.

3) Encryption: Data in storage and in transit is encrypted to accomplish data protection of user's data. .NET libraries in Windows Azure SDK are extended with .NET Cryptographic Service Providers (CSPs) so that developers can implement encryption, hashing and key management functionalities for their data either in storage or in transit. Encryption algorithms like AES, cryptographic hash functionality like MD5 and SHA-2, etc. can be easily accessed by Windows Azure developers.

4) Availability: Data is replicated to three separate nodes within the Fabric in Windows Azure to minimize the impact of hardware failures. Different levels of redundancy are provided to accomplish greater availability of customer's data.

6 Mapping of Microsoft Windows Azure Security Features to NIST Security & Privacy Guidelines

In this section, we map the different areas related to security and privacy as discussed by NIST in [2] to the security features implemented in Microsoft Windows Azure Platform as described in [6].

NIST Areas	Microsoft Windows Azure Security Features
Governance	* Multiple levels of monitoring, logging, and reporting are implemented. * The monitoring and diagnostic log information are gathered by the Monitoring Agent (MA) from many places including the FC (Fabric Controller) and the root OS and are written into the log files. * Various monitoring and diagnostic log data are read and summarized by the Monitoring Data analysis Service.
Compliance	* It is certified by one of the premier international information security management standards i.e. ISO27001.
Trust	* Customer's data are made unavailable once the delete operations are called by the Windows Azure's Storage subsystem. * Execution of delete operation removes all references to the associated data item and it cannot be accessed via the storage APIs. All copies of the deleted data item are then garbage collected. * When the associated storage block is reused for storing other data the physical bits are overwritten.
Architecture	* Windows Azure fully integrates Microsoft's Security Development Lifecycle (SDL) guidelines to provide security assurance within Windows Azure's development processes. * Microsoft scrutinizes places where data from a less-trusted component is parsed by a more trusted component like when Windows Azure portal and SMAPI processes requests coming over the network from sources controlled by customers.

Identity and Access Management	* Customers access the Windows Azure Portal through a web browser or access SMAPI through standalone command line tools, either programmatically or using Visual Studio. * Customers upload developed applications and manage their Hosted Services and Storage Accounts through the Windows Azure Portal web site or programmatically through the Service Management API (SMAPI). * Customers can monitor and manage their applications via the portal or programmatically through SMAPI using the same authentication mechanism. * SMAPI authentication is based on a user-generated public/private key pair and self-signed certificate registered through the Windows Azure Portal. The certificate is then used to authenticate subsequent access to SMAPI. * Access to Windows Azure storage is governed by a storage account key (SAK) that is associated with each Storage Account. Storage account keys can be reset via the Windows Azure Portal or SMAPI.
Software Isolation	* Microsoft's Hyper-V is used to provide strong isolation of guest VMs. * The hypervisor and the root OS provide network packet filters that assure that the untrusted VMs cannot generate spoofed traffic, cannot receive traffic not addressed to them, cannot direct traffic to protected infrastructure endpoints, and cannot send or receive inappropriate broadcast traffic. * VLANs are used to isolate the FCs and other devices.
Data Protection	* Critical internal communications are protected using SSL encryption. * Windows Azure SDK extends the core .NET libraries to allow developers to integrate the .NET Cryptographic Service Providers (CSPs) within Windows Azure. * Developers familiar with .NET CSPs can easily implement encryption, hashing, and key management functionality for stored or transmitted data.
Availability	* Customers can create a second Storage Account to provide hot-failover capability. * Customers can create custom roles to replicate and synchronize data between Microsoft facilities. * Customers can also write customized roles to extract data from storage for offsite private backups. * Data is replicated within Windows Azure to three separate nodes within the Fabric to minimize the impact of hardware failures. * Each datacenter facility has a minimum of two sources of electrical power, including a power generation capability for extended off-grid operation.
Incident Response	* Microsoft security vulnerabilities can be reported to the Microsoft Security Response Center or via email to secure@microsoft.com. * Microsoft follows a consistent process to assess and respond to vulnerabilities and incidents reported via the standard facilities.

7 Conclusion

Cloud computing technology is in constant development and has recently emerged as a paradigm for delivering and managing services over the Internet. With the wider adoption of this technology, cloud security issues have also emerged. In this paper, we first analyze the guidelines provided by NIST to address security and privacy issues in public cloud computing. Then we provide analysis of the Microsoft Windows Azure cloud platform describing how the NIST guidelines have been implemented in this platform.

The data and programs belonging to customers are hosted by Microsoft using Windows Azure. It provides different security features, controls and mechanisms for customers to choose so that they can achieve their required level of security. The analysis performed in this paper will provide customers a good understanding of how the privacy and security-related issues that are considered to have long-term significance on the cloud computing technology have been addressed by Microsoft Windows Azure, making it one of the most popular cloud computing platforms to provide a better level of data security.

8 References

[1] P. Mell and T. Grance, The NIST Definition of Cloud Computing, National Institute of Standards and Technology, Spetember 2011.

[2] W. Jansen and T. Grance, NIST Guidelines on Security and Privacy in Public Cloud Computing, January 2011.

[3] S. Sengupta, V. Kaulgud, and V. S. Sharma, Cloud Computing Security – Trends and Research Directions, IEEE World Congress on Services, 2011.

[4] B. Grobauer, T. Walloschek, and E. Stocker, Understanding Cloud Computing Vulnerabilities, IEEE Security & Privacy, April 2011.

[5] Cloud Enterprise Architecture, Pethuru Raj, CRC Taylor and Francis, 2012.

[6] C. Kaufman and R. Venkatapathy, Windows Azure Security Overivew, Microsoft, August 2010.

[7] D. Chappell, Introducing the Windows Azure Platform, David Chappel and Associates, Sponsored by Microsoft Corporation, Oct 2010.

[8] Q. Zhang, L. Cheng and R. Boutaba, Cloud computing: state-of-the-art and research challenges, Journal of Internet Services and Applications, May 2010, Volume 1, Issue 1, pp 7-18.

[9] G. Tajadod, L. Batten and K. Govinda, Microsoft and Amazon A comparison of approaches to cloud security, Fourth International Conference on Cloud Computing Technology and Science, 2012.

[10] X. Jing and Z. Jian-jun, A Brief Survey on the Security Model of Cloud Computing, Ninth International Symposium on Distributed Computing and Applications to Business, Engineering and Science, 2010.

[11] Z. Wang, Security and privacy issues within the Cloud Computing, International Conference on Computational and Information Science, 2011.

[12] T. Yu and Y. Zhu, Research On Cloud Computing And Security, Eleventh International Symposium on Distributed Computing and Applications to Business, Engineering & Sciences, 2012.

[13] X. Ma, Security Concerns in Cloud Computing, Fourth International Conference on Computational and Information Science, 2012.

An Approach for QoS-aware Cloud Service Selection Based on Genetic Algorithm and Simplex Method

Chengwen Zhang[1], **Jian Kuang**[2], **Zhitao Dai**[3], **Bo Cheng**[4], **and Lei Zhang**[5]

[1]Beijing Key Laboratory of Intelligent Telecommunications Software and Multimedia, Beijing University of Posts & Telecommunications, Beijing, China

[2]Beijing Key Laboratory of Intelligent Telecommunications Software and Multimedia, Beijing University of Posts & Telecommunications, Beijing, China

[3]Beijing Key Laboratory of Intelligent Telecommunications Software and Multimedia, Beijing University of Posts & Telecommunications, Beijing, China

[4]State Key Lab of Networking and Switching Technology, Beijing University of Posts & Telecommunications, Beijing, China

[5]Key Laboratory of Trustworthy Distributed Computing and Service (BUPT), Ministry of Education, Beijing, China

Abstract - *For the problem of cloud service selection, this paper gives a hybrid algorithm. The hybrid algorithm is composed mainly by Simplex Method and Genetic Algorithm. In this algorithm, a tree traversal sequence encoding scheme and some Simplex Method operations are proposed. The design of the tree traversal sequence encoding can support various types of service combinations. In addition, the hybrid algorithm uses Simplex Method operations to further improve local convergence of Genetic Algorithm. The global convergence ability and local convergence capacity of Genetic Algorithm can be gotten better at the same time. Passed tests and analyses show that the algorithm proposed in this paper can be a good choice to solve QoS-based cloud service selection problems.*

Keywords: Genetic algorithm, QoS-aware, Simplex method, Cloud service selection

1 Introduction

In cloud computing [1-4] environment, there are inevitably many service providers to provide services with same functionalities and different QoS. These services can combine tens of thousands composite services with same functions and different QoS. That is, there are many different combination plans. Therefore, in a service composition process, we need to choose service components from massive services with same functions and different QoS based on user's QoS requirements. How to select the most suitable composite service among many available candidate services for consumers is an interesting practical issue [24, 25]. The service selection with global QoS constraints possesses a considerably big proportion in the problem of QoS-based cloud service selection. QoS-based cloud service selection plays an important role in the combination of cloud services. Researches in this area have aroused widespread concern in academic circles [5-11, 14-21, 23-27].

QoS-based cloud service selection problem is one of the hot research areas. The calculation algorithms based on QoS properties is a kind of QoS-based service selection algorithm. Exhaustive methods and approximate algorithms are two kinds of QoS properties calculation methods. To meet the global constraints and to find the optimal combination are under the scope of combinatorial optimization, and QoS-based service selection is NP-hard problem [11], therefore, approximate algorithm is more suitable to solve optimization combinatorial problems. Genetic Algorithm is a kind of approximate algorithm. It is a good method to solve optimization combinatorial problems [12-13]. But, Genetic Algorithm is not advantageous for the local convergence. To compensate for local search capability of Genetic Algorithm itself, the combination of Genetic Algorithm and some kind of local search algorithms is needed to enhance the local search capabilities of Genetic Algorithm.

Based on the above analyses, this paper presents an improved Genetic Algorithm. Firstly, a tree traversal sequence encoding of Genetic Algorithms is described. Secondly, to compensate for the local search capabilities of Genetic Algorithm itself, a hybrid algorithm of Genetic Algorithm and Simplex Method is introduced.

The remaining sections of this paper are as follows. Section two described researches of QoS-based cloud service selection computing. The proposed hybrid GA was discussed in detail in section three. Section four presented some simulation works and discussed the simulation results. Section five came to conclusions and noted that the next step in research content.

2 Quality-based cloud service selection

Based on all global QoS constraints, to select the best plan from a large number of service composition plans is the area of combinatorial optimization. To solve such problems, the calculation methods based on QoS attributes are divided into two categories. One category is exhaustive algorithm. In this kind of algorithm, all of candidate plans are calculated according to certain rules in order to choose the best plan. It needs to figure out all possible solutions in order to obtain the optimal solution. So the exhaustive combinatorial optimization method is poor scalability and has large calculation. The other is approximate algorithm. In this type of algorithm, an ideal composition plan is infinitely close to the best one. At last, a plan that meets all QoS requirements but is not the best one will be gained. The methods in [10-11, 16-21] fall into this category.

In the field of combinatorial optimization, there is a random search algorithm based on probability. Genetic Algorithm is suitable for solving such problems [12], and it can effectively prevent exhaustive algorithm limitations. The solution based on Genetic Algorithm is a global optimization one. [10-11, 17-21] used Genetic Algorithm for the optimization of service composition.

Genetic Algorithm and some kind of local search algorithms need to be combined to enhance its local search capabilities and to achieve fairly good results in order to compensate for the local search capability of Genetic Algorithm itself.

3 Genetic algorithm with simplex method

In this section, we present a hybrid algorithm with Simplex Method and GA in order to solve quality-driven selection, mainly including the design of a tree traversal sequence encoding scheme and some Simplex Method operations.

3.1 Tree traversal sequence encoding scheme

A chromosome encoding approach is the basis of the running of Genetic Algorithm. All of subsequent genetic operations should be based on coding design. Different issues should use different coding techniques. The encoding method for solving QoS-based service selection problem should not only reflect every service in services combination but also reflect the structure information of services combination itself. Therefore, the chromosome coding scheme needs to be improved.

This paper designed a tree traversal sequence encoding scheme. The encoding is based on a tree combination template of services combination. The following will in turn introduce the establishment of the tree combination template and how to create chromosomes of GA.

3.1.1 Building tree combination template

A service combination process can be recursively decomposed into four kind of basic models (that is, series model, parallel model, choice model and loop model). Here are four abbreviations SM, PM, CM and LM that express respectively series model, parallel model, choice model and loop model. To describe complicated service combination process, the service combination process can be expressed as an equivalent tree structure that is called tree combination template. In this tree combination template, root node, non-leaf nodes and leaf nodes represent respectively composition model of entire service combination process, logical relationships among tasks and tasks themselves.

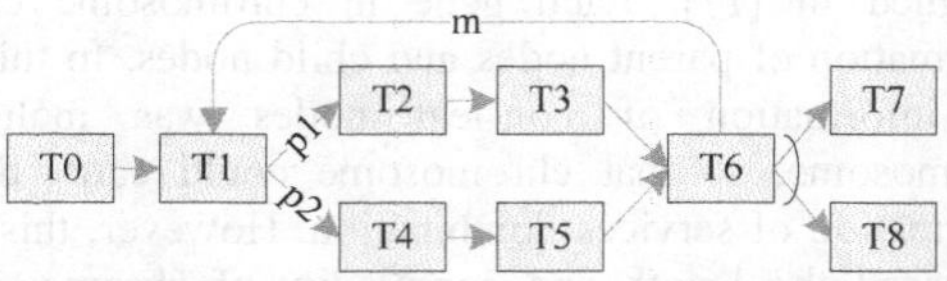

Fig. 1. An example about a service combination process

Figure 1 is an example of a service combination process. In this example, all of four models are included. In figure 1, T0 and T1, T2 and T3, T4 and T5 are all sequence type. The relationship among tasks T1, T2, T3, T4, T5 and T6 is cycle and its circulation number is *m*. The two branches of T2 and T4 are selection relationship and their choice probabilities are *p1* and *p2* respectively. The sum of *p1* and *p2* is 1. T7 and T8 are parallel type. Figure 2 is the tree combination template that expresses the service combination process in figure 1.

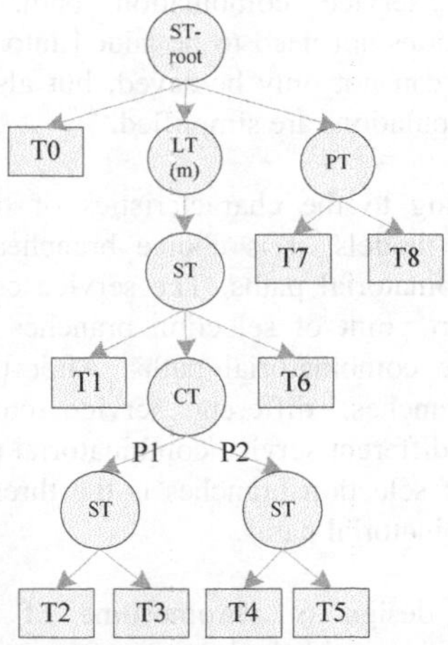

Fig. 2. A tree combination template corresponding to the service combination process in Figure 1

In Figure 2, all leaf nodes express all of tasks T0 ~ T8 in the service combination process. Each task can have a number of candidate services. The non-leaf nodes ST, PT, CT and LT express respectively series type, parallel type, choice type and loop type. They are four kinds of expression of their sub-tree relationships. The non-leaf node CT contains the implementation probability of its sub-trees. The non-leaf node LT involves the number of loop of its sub-trees. During calculating an individual's fitness value, non-leaf nodes will save values of all QoS attributes of its sub-trees.

Before the running of service selection algorithm, it is necessary to express the process of service combination with a unified description. In this paper, a tree-form combination template is used to unify the different formats of services combination processes. After the running of service selection algorithm, the original expression of the services combination processes will be restored.

3.1.2 Creating chromosomes of GA

It is very important to design adequate chromosome to solve the problem of service selection. A tree-encoding is designed in [17]. Each gene in chromosome carries the information of parent nodes and child nodes. In this method, the information of non-leaf nodes was included into chromosome, so that chromosome could carry the logical information of services combination. However, this approach increased the length and complexity of chromosome. Each chromosome must carry same logical information of services combination. This method is a waste of space. And, non-leaf nodes will not participate in follow-up genetic manipulations.

The combinational logic information needs to be kept in tree template and does not need to be included in every chromosome. Chromosome only need include leaf nodes of tree template. The genes of a chromosome arrange in accordance with the result of preorder traversal of tree template. The length of chromosome is equal to the number of tasks in a service combination path. Any additional information does not need to be added into the chromosome. Thus, space can not only be saved, but also the subsequent genetic manipulations are simplified.

According to the characteristics of the four kinds of combination models, it is choice branches to create many service combinatorial paths. The service composition logics until the start point of selection branches are same among some service combinatorial paths. After the start point of selection branches, different service composition logics distribute in different service combinatorial paths. That is, the start point of selection branches is the threshold of different service combinatorial paths.

In the design of chromosome of the hybrid GA, chromosome is established in the form of unidimensional code. All of gene positions in chromosome correspond to tasks in service composition logic. Each task executes in turn successively based on gene position order from left to right. In the relationship between chromosomes and combinatory logic, different combinatorial path corresponds to different chromosome. That is, the number of chromosomes and the number of combinatorial paths are same.

The creation process of chromosome is as follows.

Firstly, according to the definition of tree combination template, a tree combination template is built based on service composition logic.

Secondly, an unidimensional chromosome is initialized. The leftmost gene locus in the chromosome is the starting point to be treated. A pointer is initialized and points to the leftmost gene locus in the chromosome.

Thirdly, from the root node of the tree combination template, all of nodes are traversed from left to right according to a preorder traversal way.

The tree combination template in Figure 2 can be encoded into chromosomes shown below. In this example, there are two chromosomes that express two composition paths.

T0, T1, T2, T3, T6, T7, T8

T0, T1, T4, T5, T6, T7, T8

After the chromosome has been coded, it could then generate a specific individual (ie, service combination instance). The following is the specific method to build an individual. Every gene in the chromosome expresses a task of service composition. There are a lot of candidate services for a task. A specific atomic service needs to be selected from every set of candidate services. All of atomic services will form a composite service instance that is an individual in population. A certain number of generated individuals can compose an initial population. Through main genetic manipulations, new generations of population constantly are gotten until a satisfactory solution is obtained.

3.2 SM operations

GA can not be restricted by restrictive assumptions constraints in search space. It does not require continuity, derivative existence and single peak assumptions. In addition, Genetic Algorithm with global optimization capability uses populations to organize optimization operations. It searches multiple regions in the solution space at same time, so it has the inherent parallelism. However, local convergence of Genetic Algorithms is not an advantage. Therefore, in order to compensate for Genetic Algorithm itself in lack of local search capability, Genetic Algorithm needs to be integrated with some kind of local search algorithms to enhance its local search capabilities.

Simplex Method (SM) is a common approach to solve mathematical programming problem. Genetic Algorithm and Simplex Method also have their own advantages. Genetic Algorithm has global optimization capability, and it can search simultaneously multiple regions of solution space. Simplex Method has local space search ability, fast convergence speed. It can change search direction according to the trend of fitness values and the use of local information.

Existing researches primarily solve the problem of combination service selection through local optimization or global optimization algorithms. The running time of the local optimization algorithm is less than the global optimization algorithm, but it can not take into account the global QoS constraints, and often can not meet non-functional requirements that customers bring forward. The global optimization algorithms can consider the global QoS constraints, but the amount of calculation is larger than the local optimization algorithm. Thus, these two algorithms both have some limitations.

As described above, a combination of Genetic Algorithm and Simplex Method can form a hybrid algorithm [22] that includes the global optimization algorithm and the local optimization algorithm. Genetic Algorithm ensures that the hybrid algorithm has the global search capability and can find the global optimal point. Simplex Method can add a number of parallel searches in many local areas and it can use local search methods to direct the search. It can not only speed up the process of global optimization, but also solve the "premature" problem of Genetic Algorithm to a certain extent. Better convergence speed and search capability can be gotten at the same time.

Based on the research about the combination of simplex method and Genetic Algorithm, this paper presents a hybrid algorithm that is the Combination of Genetic Algorithm and Simplex Method. This hybrid algorithm will be used to solve the service choice problem.

The following is the main idea of the hybrid algorithm. After Genetic Algorithm produces a new generation of population, some local initial simplexes are composed by some randomly selected individuals in a certain probability. Individuals with higher fitness values are introduced through continuous reflection operations and they will replace the individuals whose fitness values are lower. So, a number of new better individuals will be included into the next generation of population and will participate in genetic manipulations in the next generation of population. In addition, during the reflection operation, the decision variable matrix will be used.

Some Simplex Method operations are joined between two generations of population. After a series of reproduction, crossover and mutation operators, a number of individuals are randomly selected to form a certain number of initial simplexes. Some local Simplex operations are run in parallel. After all initial simplexes have completed their simplex operations, more excellent individuals are obtained. We can proceed with the next generation of genetic manipulations.

$$N_{is} = ceil(\frac{Sp}{N_{task}+1}) \tag{1}$$

In the above equation, The number of generated initial simplexes is N_{is}. Sp is the population size of Genetic Algorithm. N_{task} is the number of tasks.

The main steps of simplex operations of each initial simplex are the following ones:

1), Establishing an initial simplex

An initial simplex is formed in a n-dimensional space by n+1 individuals that are selected randomly From the current population.

2), Selecting the worst individual

The vertex with the smallest function value among *n+1* vertices is found and its corresponding individual is denoted by I_{n+1}. The individuals corresponding to the remaining *n* vertices are indicated respectively by $I_1, I_2, \cdots, I_n$.

3), Constructing decision variable matrix of every vertex

The decision variable matrixes $D_1, D_2, \cdots, D_n, D_{n+1}$ are built respectively for individuals $I_1, I_2, \cdots, I_n, I_{n+1}$. In the decision variable matrix, each row represents the decision variable vector of all candidate services of a task. As shown below is the specific method to construct. Only when the *j*th candidate service of the *i*th task is selected, the component d_{ij} is 1 in the decision variable matrix D_k, otherwise the value of d_{ij} is 0.

4), Calculating decision variable matrix of reflection center

The reflection center is I_c that is about *n* individuals except the worst individual I_{n+1}. The decision variable matrix D_c about I_c can be built according to the following equation.

$$D_c = (\sum_{i=1}^{n} D_i) / n \tag{2}$$

5), Computing decision variable matrix about the reflection point

I_0 is the reflection point of the worst individual I_{n+1} on I_c. Its decision variable matrix is D_0.

$$D_0 = 2D_c - D_{n+1} \quad (3)$$

6), Boolean the decision variable matrix of the reflection point

Boolean-oriented approach is to reassign 0 or 1 to each component d_{ij} in the decision variable matrix D_0. The value 1 will be set to the largest component in each row vector D_k of D_0 and the remaining components are assigned the value of 0. Thereby, a boolean decision variables matrix D_0' will be generated. In the Boolean process, if there are multiple components with the same and maximum value in a row vector, the value 1 will be set to random component among them. The remaining components in the row vector are 0.

7), Generating a new individual corresponding to the reflection point

A new individual I_0 is generated on the basis of the decision variable matrix I_0'. For each row vector in D_0', the only component with the value of 1 is used to select its atom service instance. The atom service instance will is assigned to corresponding gene locus on a chromosome. After all of gene loci are set atom service instances, the formation of a new individual I_0 will be done.

8), Determining whether new individuals meet user's global constraints

Based on the search thinking of that the best point should be almost the opposite of the worst one, the fitness value of a new individual I_0 always is greater than the worst individual I_{n+1} in the initial simplex. Therefore, if the new individual's fitness is greater than the worst individual and the new individual meets the user's global QoS constraints, the new individual will replace the worst one in population and joins the next generation population evolution. Otherwise, if the new individual's fitness is less than the worst individual or the new individual does not meet the user's global QoS constraints, the new individual will also replace the worst one in population and form a new simplex to continue with the next iteration of the simplex algorithm. We can end the operation of the simplex until a new individual's fitness is greater than the worst individual and the new individual meets the user's global QoS constraints.

Simplex operations are done in N_{is} initial simplexes in turn. After every simplex has gained a new individual whose fitness value is better than the worst individual in the simplex and that is able to meet the global user constraints, these new individuals will be generated and added into the population to participate in the next generation of population genetic manipulations.

Because individuals are randomly selected to build an initial simplex, the randomness of Genetic Algorithm can be ensured. And the opportunities to generate new individuals are increased. On the other hand, Simplex Method can control the evolution direction of Genetic Algorithm to make better solutions. It is parallel searches in a number of local solution spaces not only that enhances the local search ability bus also that accelerates the global convergence and solves the "premature" problem of GA to a certain extent.

4 Tests and analyses of hybrid GA

The proposed service selecting algorithm in this paper improves simple Genetic Algorithm in two ways. One is the improvements of simple Genetic Algorithm including tree traversal sequence encoding. The other hand is to build a more powerful and efficient hybrid search algorithm that is composed by Genetic Algorithm and Simplex Method. Through the above two improvements, the hybrid GA has better search ability. Here are the tests and test analyses through which the capacity of the presented hybrid GA will be validated.

4.1 Test data preparation

In order to verify the effect of services choice done by the hybrid GA, some comparison tests between simple Genetic Algorithm and the hybrid GA algorithm were made.

In order to fairly test the two algorithms, they would run in the same hardware and software operating environment, including CPU, memory, OS, development language and IDE, etc.

The simple Genetic Algorithm and the hybrid GA used initialization parameters as follows. The population size is 500. The crossover probability is 0.7 and the mutation probability is 0.1.

Based on the above preparation of test data, simple Genetic Algorithm and the hybrid GA were run respectively. The test results were analyzed from search capability

4.2 Tests and analyses of search capability

Search capability is that the algorithm can find the optimal solution in a solution space. It can be measured by the quality of the solution that the algorithm searches. In Genetic Algorithm, the algorithm search capability can be measured through the fitness value of the final selected individual.

The hybrid GA took a tree traversal coding as well as the combination of Simplex Method to improve global search ability and local search capability from different aspects of Genetic Algorithm. In order to verify these strategies, simple Genetic Algorithm and the hybrid GA were run for 50 times at different scale of problems (that is, the number of different tasks and different number of candidate services) respectively. The average values of the final fitness values at all running time were taken. A few set of test data are listed in Table I.

TABLE 1 Average value of maximum fitness

task number	average number of candidate services for each task	average fitness value of simple GA	average fitness value of hybrid GA
5	6	0.227	0.239
12	10	0.106	0.197
25	35	0.027	0.09

As shown in Table 1, when in the face of the selection problem with the same size of combination services, the hybrid GA can get higher average final fitness value than the simple Genetic Algorithm. When the scale of the composition problem is small, the advantage of the hybrid GA is not clear. But, when there are a larger number of tasks in a combined service flow, the hybrid GA can get much better solutions than the simple Genetic Algorithm. In the test conditions of this article, when the number of tasks is more than 12, the hybrid GA clearly has stronger search capabilities. This shows that the hybrid GA has better search capabilities, especially in the larger scale of service selection, that the search capabilities are more prominent.

The crossover operation of chromosomes and the mutation operation of chromosomes can search optimal results not only in same path but also in different composition paths. The search areas of the crossover operation and the mutation operation are broadened. This is one reason why the hybrid GA can get more fitness than the simple GA. Another reason is the use of Simplex Method operations. These Simplex Method operations enhance the local search capabilities of Genetic Algorithm.

5 Conclusions

As a kind of distributed computing model, academia and industry have been greatly concerned about cloud services in recent years. With the cloud services technologies have become more sophisticated, more and more easily used cloud services with the stability characteristics are shared on network. But a single atomic cloud services can provide limited functionalities. In order to more fully utilize the shared cloud services, it is necessary to combine shared cloud services to form a new combination of cloud services to provide more powerful service functions.

With the progressive development of cloud services technology and application, it is inevitable for a task to appear a large number of candidate services with the same function properties and different non-functional attributes (mainly referring to QoS attributes). It has become an urgent problem that how to fast and flexibly select a high-availability, high reliability, high performance and the best services to meet user' needs from massive candidate services. Namely, it is QoS-based service selection problem.

This paper presents a combination services selection algorithm based on the hybrid GA. Based on the analyses of the 0-1 integer programming model of composite service selection problem, the simple Genetic Algorithm is improved itself and combines a local optimization algorithm – Simplex Method. The improvements of the simple Genetic Algorithm itself includes that the design of a tree traversal sequence encoding to support a variety of combination types. In addition, in order to compensate the lack of the ability of local search of Genetic Algorithm itself, Genetic Algorithm and Simplex Method are applied to the formation of a new hybrid algorithm. In the result, the search ability can be improved at the same time.

Through the realization of the above-mentioned algorithm, testing and analyses of test results, some strong validations of the proposed algorithm in capacity effect were done. The hybrid GA can be a good solution to QoS-driven cloud services selection.

In the above experiments, the number of individuals in populations is same in the face of different combination sizes. If the populations with different sizes can be adopted for different composition scales, the efficiency of algorithm will be greatly improved. Therefore, the next study will examine the dynamic adaptive mechanism of population size. The other next step is to apply the proposed hybrid algorithm into a number of practical large-scale services computing environments, in order to improve the efficient and reliable operations of the hybrid GA further.

Acknowledgments: This work was supported by NSFC under Grant Nos. 60872042, the Fundamental Research Funds for the Central Universities (2011RC0203) and the Co-construction Special Funds of Beijing.

6 References

[1] B. Rochwerger, D. Breitgand and E. Levy, et al. "The reservoir model and architecture for open federated cloud computing"; IBM Journal of Research and Development, 53, 4, 1—17, 2009.

[2] B. Hayes. "Cloud computing"; Comm. ACM, 51, 7, 9—11, 2008.

[3] A. A. Ahson and M. Ilyas. "Cloud computing and software services". CRC Press, 2010.

[4] M. Armburst, et al. "Above the clouds: a Berkeley view of cloud computing". Tech. report UCB/EECS-2009-28, Electrical Eng. and Computer Science Dept., Univ. of California, Berkeley, 2009.

[5] Laiping Zhao, Yizhi Ren, Mingchu Li. "Flexible service selection with user-specific QoS support in service-oriented architecture"; Journal of Network and Computer Applications, 35, 3, 962—973, 2012.

[6] Z. ur Rehman, F. K. Hussain, O. K. Hussain. "Towards multi-criteria cloud service selection". 2011 Fifth International Conference on Innovative Mobile and Internet Services in Ubiquitous Computing (IMIS), 44—48, 2011.

[7] Y. Liu, A. H. Ngu and L. Zeng. "QoS computation and policing in dynamic web service selection". In Proceedings of the 13th International Conference on World Wide Web (WWW), ACM Press, New York, USA, 66—73, 2004.

[8] L. Zeng, B. Benatallah, M. Dumas and Q. Z. Sheng. "Quality driven web services composition". Proc. 12th Int'l Conf. World Wide Web (WWW), ACM Press, Budapest, Hungary, 411—421, 2003.

[9] Liang Zhao Zeng, Boualem Benatallah, etc. "QoS-aware middleware for web services composition"; IEEE Transactions on Software Engineering, 30, 5, 311—327, 2004.

[10] Liang Jie Zhang, Bing Li and Tian Chao, etc. "On demand web services-based business process composition". IEEE International Conference on System, Man, and Cybernetics (SMC'03), Washington, USA, 4057—4064, 2003.

[11] G. Canfora, M. Di Penta and R. Esposito, etc. "A lightweight approach for QoS–aware service composition". In Proc. 2nd International Conference on Service Oriented Computing (ICSOC'04), New York, USA, 36—47, 2004.

[12] M. Srinivas and L. M. Patnaik. "Genetic algorithm: a survey"; IEEE Computer, 27, 6, 17—26, 1994.

[13] R. Ignacio, G. Jesús and P. Héctor, etc. "Statistical analysis of the main parameters involved in the design of a genetic algorithm"; IEEE Transactions on Systems, Man, and Cybernetics—Part C: Applications and Reviews, 32, 1, 31—37, 2002.

[14] Jun Huang, Yanbing Liu, Ruozhou Yu. "Modeling and algorithms for QoS-aware service composition in virtualization-based cloud computing"; IEICE Transactions on Communications, E96B, 1, 10—19, 2013.

[15] A. Danilo and P. Barbara. "Adaptive service composition in flexible processes"; IEEE Transactions on Software Engineering, 33, 6, 369—384, 2007.

[16] T. Yu, Y. Zhang and K. J. Lin. "Efficient algorithms for web services selection with end-to-end QoS constraints"; ACM Transactions on the Web, 1, 1, 1—26, 2007.

[17] C. M. Gao, M. L. Cai and Chen Huowang. "QoS-aware service composition based on tree-coded Genetic Algorithm". 31st Annual International Computer Software and Applications Conference (COMPSAC 2007), 1, 361—367, 2007.

[18] C. W. Zhang, S. Su and J. L. Chen. "DiGA: population diversity handling Genetic Algorithm for QoS-aware web services selection"; Computer Communications, Elsevier, 30, 5, 1082—1090, 2007.

[19] Y. H. Yan and Y. Liang. "Using genetic algorithms to navigate partial enumerable problem space for web services composition". 3rd International Conference on Natural Computation (ICNC 2007), China, 475—479, 2007.

[20] Y. Ma, C. W. Zhang. "Quick convergence of genetic algorithm for QoS-driven web service selection"; Computer Networks, 5, 1093—1104, 2008.

[21] G. Canfora, M. Dipenta and R. Esposito. "An approach for QoS-aware service composition based on genetic algorithms". Proceedings of the 2005 Conference on Genetic and Evolutionary Computation, Washington, 1069—1075, 2005.

[22] J. Yen, C. Liao, B. Lee, et al. "A hybrid approach to modeling metabolic systems using a genetic algorithms and simplex method"; IEEE Trans. on Systems, Man, and Cybernetics-part B: Cybernetics, 28, 2, 173—191, 1998.

[23] Cang Hong Jin, Ming-hui Wu and Tao Jiang, etc. "Combine automatic and manual process on web service selection and composition to support QoS". 12th International Conference on Computer Supported Cooperative Work in Design (CSCWD 2008), Xi'an, China, 459—464, 2008.

[24] Q. Liang, X. Wu, and H. C. Lau. "Optimizing service systems based on application-level QoS"; IEEE Transactions on Services Computing, 2, 108—121, 2009.

[25] Q. Z. Sheng, B. Benatallah, Z. Maamar, and A. H. H. Ngu. "Configurable composition and adaptive provisioning of web services"; IEEE Transactions on Services Computing, 2, 34—49, 2009.

[26] S. N. Huang and ATS. Chan. "Dynamic QoS adaptation for mobile middleware"; IEEE Transactions on Software Engineering, 34, 738—752, 2008.

[27] M. Alrifai and T. Risse. "Combining global optimization with local selection for efficient QoS-aware service composition". 18th international conference on World Wide Web (WWW 2009), 2009.

Maximizing SLA and QoE in Heterogeneous Cloud Computing Environment

Md Sabbir Hasan[1], **Eui-Nam Huh**[2]
[1]Department of Computer Engineering, Kyung Hee University, Suwon, South Korea
[2]Department of Computer Engineering, Kyung Hee University, Suwon, South Korea

Abstract - *Cloud Computing delivers users a proficient way to dynamically allocate computing resources to meet demands. The use of Server virtualization techniques for Cloud Computing platforms provide great elasticity with the capability to consolidate several virtual machines on the same physical server, to resize a virtual machine capacity and to migrate virtual machine across physical servers. A key challenge for Cloud Service providers is proper resource management while taking into account of Service Level Agreement and Quality of Experience of users. Reserving resources would be beneficial to improve the quality of service, if the actual demand of the user is known in advance. However, in reality, the actual computing demand can be pragmatic only at the point of actual usage. In this paper, we propose a demand prediction method constructed on present usage of resources, aiming better provisioning of resource demand. Our proposed VM allocation is mapped into the multidimensional bin-packing problem, which is NP-complete. To solve this problem, we have designed heuristics for quantitatively optimizing the VM allocation. The simulation results show that our scheme performs better comparing to the existing VM allocation schemes in cloud computing environment, in terms of maintaining SLA and better QoE.*

Keywords: Quality of Experience, Service Level Agreement, Cloud Computing, VM Resource Allocation.

1 Introduction

Cloud Computing has received significant attention recent times as the hype is created and responded largely by the companies like Amazon, IBM, Google, Yahoo!, Microsoft, Sun, NASA and RackSpace by making their own cloud platforms for consumers and enterprises to access the cloud resources through services. With the rapid development of Virtualization technology including the advantage of isolation, consolidation and multiplexing of resources, became key role to deploy in modern data centers [1]. Due to virtualization, numerous tasks are seen as a single entity in a virtual machine. Since Infrastructure-as-a-Service (IaaS) is a computational service model applied in the cloud computing paradigm, Virtualization technologies are used these days to support computing resource access by the users in this model. Users can specify required software stack such as operating systems, software libraries, and applications; then package them all together into virtual machines (VMs). Finally, VMs will be hosted in a computing environment operated by cloud providers. [2].

QoS requirement can be formalized in Service Level Agreement that serves as the foundation for the expected level of service between the Cloud consumer and the Service or Cloud provider. However, Infrastructure providers often end up over provisioning of resources to maximize the Service Level Agreement that results poor Resource Management and Large Operational cost. Contrary to that, under provisioning of resources will increase SLA violation and affect QoE of Users. Quality of experience (QoE), sometimes also known as Quality of Service, is a subjective measure of a user's experiences with a service in Cloud Computing Environment. The poor QoE will dissatisfy the User. A typical user-related measure is the mean opinion score (MOS), which can be determined from subjective analysis, usually used to measure the Quality of Experience of the User's. Nevertheless, Subjective analysis is not enough while predicting the resource demand of User that might require during execution time. So we build an exponential relationship between SLA violation and QoE, based on Subjective and Quantitative analysis to maintain better Service Level Agreement.

However, the research in SLA and QoE in Cloud Computing Environment is still in its infancy, and several technical issues remain open. One important issue is to meet the QoS requirements of Cloud services that require a different quantity of VM resources at run-time [3]. Inappropriate VM resource allocation in this environment may result in resource waste and Service quality degradation.

Nevertheless, the VM resource allocation is challenging due to the dynamic nature of the workload and cloud platform. Specifically, this is demanding in terms of the VM resource requirement, multimedia service heterogeneity and the heterogeneous network conditions [3], [4], [5]. It is cumbersome for a cloud provider to perform over commitment of VM resources for processing media service tasks, which may have different QoS requirements and unpredictable resource consumption. Moreover, the irregular spikes and bursts of user activities in interactive cloud-based applications complicates the over commitment estimation of VM resources.

In this paper, we tackle the aforementioned challenges of VM resource allocation in heterogeneous cloud environment. We propose a VM resource allocation model that optimally allocates VM resources to a set of physical machines/servers by considering the dynamic VM resource requirements of cloud multimedia services. It ensures the minimum SLA Violation, while maintaining high system utilization by avoiding over provisioning the VM resources to the services. The proposed VM resource allocation model is designed to:

- Minimize the number of physical servers/machines for energy savings;
- Reduce SLA violation to improve QoE;
- Achieve load balancing or overall utilization of physical resources.

Several experiments are carried out to validate the efficiency of our proposed VM resource allocation model in heterogeneous cloud platform. These experiments are conducted for different patterns of workload for various environments. We also have compared our proposed algorithm with three other existing algorithms in cloud platform, which comprised of LR-MMT [6], BFD, FFD [7]. The results include the performance of SLA Violation reduction and better QoE of Users.

The rest of the paper is organized as follows: Section 2 presents the related work. Section 3 describes our VM resource allocation model and heuristics for the current multidimensional bin packing problem. Section 4 presents experimental results and performance comparisons. Finally, Section 5 concludes the paper.

2 Related Works

Our work is based on Dynamic Consolidation of Virtual Machine's retaining strict Service Level Agreement. There are several research groups in both academia and industry, working on Energy aware resource allocation and management by performing static and dynamic consolidation of VM's and servers.

Cardosa et al. [8] proposed a solution for VM placement and power-efficient consolidation of VMs in modern data centers where it runs heterogeneous applications. They have adopted min, max, share parameters of XEN and VMware that represents the Utilization limit of upper and lower of CPU allocation and sharing same resources by different VMs. They also considered a priority based approach for peak load of enterprise environment. As a result it does not support strict SLA and VM allocation is static. Verma et al [9] described a power aware application placement framework in which at each time frame the placement of VMs is optimized to minimize the power consumption and maximize the performance at certain level. The main difference with his work is that, our proposed algorithm doesn't violate Strict SLA requirement when workload is varied and unpredictable.

Stilwell et al [10] proposed a formulation of the resource allocation problem in shared hosting platform for static workloads with servers that provide multiple types of resources. Their algorithm runs faster in large systems and fulfill QoS requirement but it lack dynamicity when workload in unpredictable and dynamic. Like him other researchers [11], [12] also studied VM resource management techniques to maintain QoS requirement when workload is static in Cloud Computing. Wood et al [13] developed the Sandpiper System that monitors and detects hotspots and reconfigure VMs when is necessary. In order to choose which VMs to migrate , their system sorts them using volume-size-ratio, which is a metric based on CPU, network and memory loads where as we considered both size of VM and the migration time required to maintain strict SLA.

In contrast to above approaches, Our algorithms that includes Host Utilization, power consumption increment of Hosts and migration time of VMs and further modification from their approach shows better result in terms of SLA Violation and QoE of Users. Our Estimator for Host overload detection provides better consolidation of VMs as it reduces the number of unnecessary VM Migration.

3 Problem Statement

As depicted in figure (1) the system model of Cloud Computing environment consists of three components, i.e., user, Cloud Broker and Cloud Provider. Each Cloud Provider supplies a pool of resources to the User. Cloud Broker works as a Centralized Unit or 3rd party which interacts with both Users and Cloud Providers having some core functionalities. Our approach in this paper is to predict the resource demand based on the current usage of resources by Cloud Providers and their workload of the servers, later allocate VM based on the actual demand to improve SLA and QoE of Users. So, we ignore to describe other functionalities of Cloud Broker. We propose the VM resource Allocation model as Multidimensional Bin Packing Problem [14], which is NP complete. The target is to find the minimum number of Physical Host to place the VM's, with respect to Physical Host's capacity. To solve this problem, we have designed a linear Programming (LP) model, as well as heuristics to quantitatively optimize the VM allocation. The VM resource allocation process can be static or dynamic. In static VM allocation, VM capacities are configured using peak load demands of each workload. The utilization of the peak load demand ensures that the VM does not overload and stay in the same physical servers during their entire lifetime. However, it leads to idleness due to the variable VM resource demand. In dynamic VM allocation, VM capacities are configured dynamically according to the current media workload demands. However, it may require migrating VMs between physical servers in order to: (i) pull out physical servers from an overloaded state when the sum of VMs capacities mapped to a physical server becomes higher than its capacity; (ii) turn off a physical server when the VMs mapped to it can be moved to other physical servers. In our scenario, we allow the virtual machine capacities to be varied on demand. We also introduce a VM migration policy to overcome from overloading the host, resulting better Quality of Service to User's.

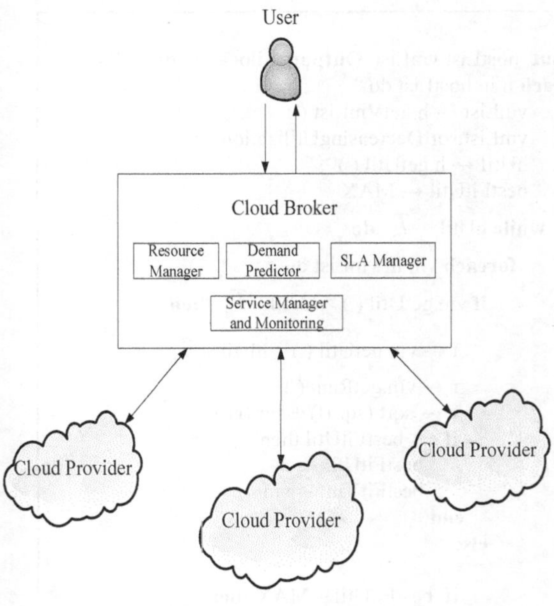

Figure (1): Cloud Computing Environment

3.1 Resource Demand Prediction

Predicting the actual VM demand greatly minimizes the VM allocation problem that results less energy consumption and service downtime. However, the demand cannot be known in advance. Therefore, present usage pattern of all the cloud providers is used to determine the future VM demand and provide on demand resource addition if needed in our approach. The Broker is responsible for accumulating the information as a centralized entity. The usage history might unravel some patterns that might help to predict the actual usage amount. For our experiments, we use different pattern of workload to create uncertainty predicting the actual demand, but the functions we considered to measure the resource demand, improves resource utilization and performance. So we formulate, resource required to satisfy present demand, $R_q \geq \{Q(n), W_{avg}, SLA_t\}$. We carefully choose the functions to get better likelihood depending on the present usage of resources.

Definition 1(Service Queue Length): $Q_m(i)$ denotes the number of class-m requests arrive at the time instant t, $t \in \{1,2,3...T\}$ and $m \in \{1,2,3...k\}$. Every class-m request has deadline d_m. So if a class- m request arrives at t time that must be served no later than $\{t+d_m\}$. We consider the arrival rate is Poisson process. So the arrival rate of incoming request is λ and mean duration of served request is $1/\lambda$. So for class-m request, arrival service request will be λ_m and that should be $\lambda_m < \lambda$. Using little's law, average number of request in the queue $Q_m(t)$ = Arrival rate$\times$time to serve request. For Multimedia application (Instant Channel Change in IPTV), where deadline $d = 0$, each request must be served at the instant time. So number of servers needed at time l will be Q_t. If we have number of servers at the Cloud provider side as $(S_1, S_2, S_3 .... S_T)$, then to satisfy the entire request at time instant t, we have to have $S_t \geq Q_t$.

So for a time frame from t_0 to $t_0 + t_n$:

$$\sum_{n=t_0}^{t_0+t_n} S_n \geq \sum_{n=t_0}^{t_0+t_n} Q(n) \ ; \ \forall t_0, t_n \in t \quad (1)$$

For a strict condition:

$$\sum_{n=t_0}^{t_0+t_n} S_n = \sum_{n=t_0}^{t_0+t_n-d} Q(n) \ ; \ \forall t_0, t_n \in t \quad (2)$$

But that would miss some of the deadlines that have been requested.

Definition 2 (Server Workload): In heterogeneous cloud environment, servers workload fluctuates depending on the behavior of different applications resource requirements. We consider, the average arrival rate of lock to a data item is λ_l and locks the data item for t_h. Then the contention to that data item appears $C = \lambda_l \times t_h$. The probability of application contention in the server can be formulated $P_{cont} = 1/_d \lambda_l t_h$, where $0 \leq d \leq 1$. So average workload for Application on the server:

$$W_{avg} = \frac{1}{t_n - t_0}(1/_d \lambda_l t_h); \quad 0 \leq d \leq 1 \quad (3)$$

For all the servers from different Cloud provider's workload can be statistically measured by using the formula for t_0 to t_n timeframe.

Definition 3 (SLA Violation rate): Maintaining Strong Service Level Agreement (SLA) and meeting QoS requirement is enormously important for Cloud Computing Environment. Overprovisioning of resources to meet target SLA can increase the power consumption whereas Energy-aware resource management is highly important these days. Basically QoS requirements can be governed by service response time or throughput, and that can be varied for different application. However for Cloud providers, workload independent metrics should be considered to calculate SLA percentage or violation. For measuring SLA violation in IaaS environment, we considered two metrics: (1) the percentage of time an active Host have experienced 100% CPU Utilization. (2) Performance degradation due to VM migration from one Host to another. Same metrics has been considered by past researchers [6], but our result shows better improvement in maintaining SLA considering these two metrics. We considered SLAs are delivered when 100% requirement of an application has been served by a VM. However, when a Host experience CPU Utilization of 100%, the performance of Application degrade due to leaping the capacity.

$$\text{SLA time per active Host} = \frac{1}{x}\sum_{P=1}^{x}\frac{H_{sP}}{H_{aP}} \tag{4}$$

$$\text{Performance degradation due to migration} = \frac{1}{y}\sum_{M=1}^{y}\frac{V_{dM}}{V_{aM}} \tag{5}$$

Where and are the number of Hosts and VMs respectively; is the total time when host has experienced 100% CPU utilization caused SLA violation; is the total time host was active; is the approximation of performance degradation due to migration of VM and we consider it 10% ; is the total CPU capacity requested by the VM during its epoch.

3.2 Heuristic for dynamic resource allocation

The multidimensional bin packing problem can also be solved using heuristics. So, the problem of VM allocation can be divided in two ways. Those can be mentioned as- admission of new requirements for VM provisioning and enlisting the VMs in the host, and optimization of current VM allocation. The first part can be seen as a bin packing problem with variable bin size and prices, whereas bins represent the physical hosts, bin sizes are the available CPU capacity and bin process are the energy consumption. Although Heuristic solution will not guarantee an optimal solution, the required time to obtain a feasible solution is much shorter than LP. We solved the first problem by using Best Fit Decreasing Algorithm that is shown to use no more than $11/9 . OPT + 1$ bins [14]. However, for solving the second problem, we consider power consumption of Hosts and CPU utilization of Hosts. The pseudo-code of VM selection and VM placement is presented in the Algorithm. We calculate the other available host's current CPU Utilization and increase of Power consumption if the selected VM had have migrated. By using $\sqrt{x^2+y^2}$, we get a point where it indicates the tradeoff point between CPU Utilization and incremental of Power Consumption of Hosts and find the suitable Host for VM. Otherwise it will find a Host which Utilization is higher calculating that the Host doesn't get overloaded if the VM migrated to that Host.

Algorithm 1: VM Allocation Algorithm

```
Input: hostList vmList  Output: Allocation of VM's
foreach h in hostList do
    vmList ← h.getVmList ( )
    vmList.sortDecreasingUtilization ( )
    hUtil ← h.getUtil ( )
    bestFitUtil ← MAX
  while hUtil > T_u do
    foreach vm in vmList do
      if vm.getUtil ( ) > hUtil – T_u then
        t ← vm.getUtil ( ) – hUtil + T_u
        r ← vm.getRam ( )
        c ← sqrt (sqr (t) + sqr (r) )
        if c < bestFitUtil then
          bestFitUtil ← c
          bestFitVm ← vm
        end
      else
        if bestFitUtil = MAX then
          bestFitVm ← vm
        break
      end
    end
  end
  hUtill ← hUtil-bestFitVm.getUtil ( )
  migrationList.add(bestFitVm)
  vmList.remove(bestFitVm)
foreach bestFitVm in vmList do
  minPower ← Max
  allocatedHost ← Null
  maxHost ← MIN
  mindiagonal ← MAX
  foreach host in hostList do
   if bestVmUtil() < THRESH_UP – hUtil()
then
powerdiff ← powerAfterAllocation – getPower (host)
hUtil ← getUtilizationOfCpu (host)
   A← sqrt (sqr (powerdiff) + sqr (hUtil))
   if  A < mindiagonal then
      allocatedHost ← A
   end
  else
   if hUtil > maxHost
     allocatedHost ← host
   end
```

```
        end
    end

    if allocatedHost ≠ NULL then
        allocate vm to allocatedHost
    end
end
return allocation
```

3.3 QoE and SLA Violation

Addressing quality from the view points of the end user's communication experience and their perceived QoE is relatively new approach to the Cloud Computing environment while so many efforts have been made to improve QoS of Networks to fulfill the targeted SLA. Although QoE is very subjective in nature, it is very important that a strategy is devised to measure it as realistically as possible (1). Based on the method we discussed earlier we make a subjective and quantitative formulation to get QoE, which is related to SLA violation. We build a relationship between QoE and SLA violation as our proposed approach that deals with dynamic VM allocation technique for proper resource management rather network parameter analysis. A typical user-related measure is the mean opinion score (MOS), which can be determined from subjective ratings by real users or predicted from objective measurements of properties of the delivered service [17], which is used as a part of our subjective analysis. So, the numerical formula to get QoE is as follows:

$$QoE = e^{-(SLA_v)^{\frac{SLA_{C_i} \times C_i}{\Delta t}}} \times \left(\sum_{i=1}^{n} W_i X_i^* - \alpha^+ + \alpha^-\right) \quad (6)$$

where, $C_{i,j,k} \in C$; $C_i \neq C_j \neq C_k$ and $W_i = 0 \sim 1$

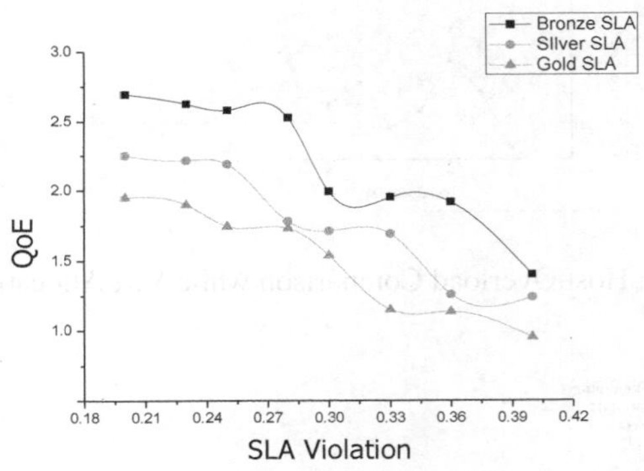

Figure (2): Relationship between QoE and SLA Violation

In equation (6), SLA_v denotes the SLA violation rate during the workload execution; C_i represents the subscribed SLA class priority, if the subscribed service class is high, the constant will have high priority value. It means the QoE level of premium service subscriber's will be lower comparing to other subscriber's at same SLA violation rate; SLA_{C_i} symbolizes the subscribed SLA Class (Gold, Silver, Bronze), Different class will have different priority e.g. C_i, C_j, C_k; we define Mean Opinion Score (MOS) by $(\sum_{i=1}^{n} W_i X_i^* - \alpha^+ + \alpha^-)$, where W_i and X_i epitomizes i^{th} criterion and positive weight of ith criterion respectively; α^+ and α^- are determined as overestimation and underestimation error.

Figure (2) depicts that, for the same SLA violation how QoE differs to different subscribed class. We set priority $C_{i,j,k} = 1,2,3$ for gold, silver and bronze class SLA having different subscriber value. QoE was measured at the scale of 3 having SLA Violation ranging from 20%-40%.

4. Performance Evaluation

4.1 Test bed Setup:

We evaluate our proposed algorithm in CloudSim toolkit. CloudSim is an extensible simulation toolkit that enables modeling and simulation of Cloud Computing systems and application provisioning system created by CLOUDS Lab, University of Melbourne [17]. We choose to do that as it is enormously difficult to conduct large-scale experiments in real infrastructure. 800 heterogeneous physical nodes is used to do the experiment. Three types of VM was used as High-CPU medium instance (2500 MIPS, 0.85 GB), Extra Large instance (2000 MIPS, 3.75 GB) Small instance (2000, 3.75 GB) and Micro Instance (1000 MIPS, 1.7). We have conducted experiment with real life data provided by the CoMon project, a monitoring infrastructure for PlanetLab. We have used CPU Utilization data of more than thousand VMs from different geographic Places. We have traced random 10 days' workload data from March and April, 2011 and the average CPU load was below 70% and workload was assigned to VMs randomly. We compared with LR-MMT (Local Regression- Minimizing Migration Time) [6], BFD (Best Fit Decreasing), FFD (First Fit Decreasing) [7] to show the improvement of our result. LR-MMT method was so far the best approach in this area (1).

Table 1

Summary of Test Bed characteristics

Simulator	CloudSim
Number of Host	800
Host features	Intel Xeon 3040, 2 cores × 1860 MHz, 4 GB, Intel Xeon 3075, 2 cores × 2660 MHz, 4 GB

Number of VMs	1052,898,1061,1516,1078, 1463,1358,1233,1054,1033
VMs Feature	Amazon EC2 instance type
Workload Data	CPU Utilization From PlanetLab for 10 days
Control Time	5 minutes

4.2 Analysis

In order to compare the efficiency, we have evaluated SLA Violations with other researcher's proposed algorithms. Our proposed approach outperforms the algorithm provided by Anton et al. [6] and solution proposed by [7]. From the experiment we calculated the amount of time an Active Host experienced 100% CPU Load that caused performance degradation for the application in its epoch and number of VM migration occurs due to VM consolidation. We haven't done aggressive consolidation otherwise it has been resulted in other way, increasing the SLA violation. Due to dynamically selecting the Upper threshold and efficiently placing of VMs in the Hosts, lesser number of migrations and higher rate of maintaining SLA occur. Fig: (4.a) shows 8.5%, 52.63%, and 59% less SLA Violation comparing to LR-MMT algorithm, BFD and FFD algorithm while experimenting with 10 days' workload with CloudSim. During the workload execution, LR-MMT, BFD and FFD algorithm suffers from 100% Host overloading by 2.3%, 5.6% and 4.3% than our proposed approach resulting more SLA Violation. Moreover, SLA Violation reflects on measuring QoE and our approach shows significant improvement. Fig: (4.c) indicates QoE enhancement of 9.3%, 23% and 25.9% comparing with LR-MMT, BFD and FFD respectively.

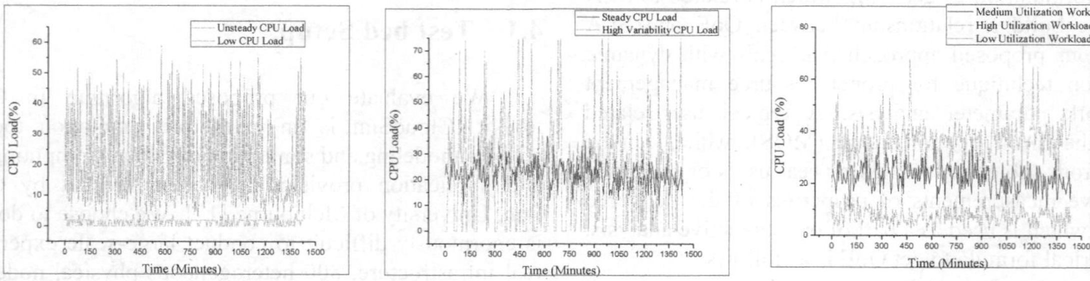

Figure (3): Workload Variation

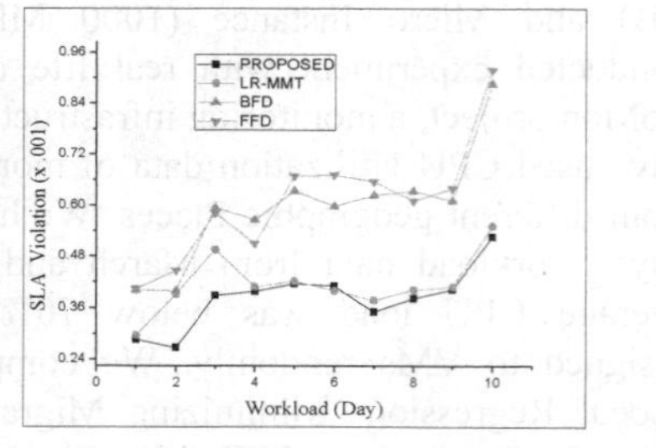

Figure (4.a): SLA Violation Comparison

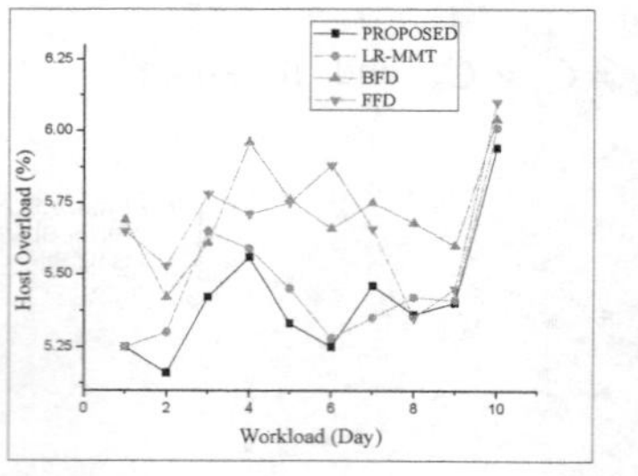

Figure (4.b): Host Overload Comparison while VM Allocation

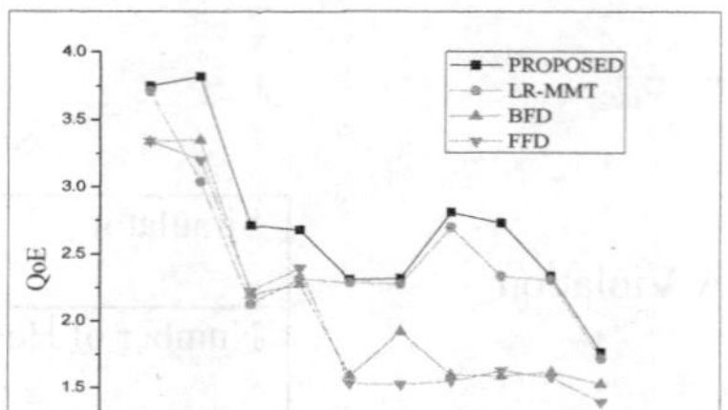

Figure (4.c): QoE Comparison with 10 days SLA Violation

5 Conclusions

In this paper we propose a demand prediction method based on the current usage of resource. In addition to that we also solved resource allocation problem heuristic solution. Performance comparison shows that our resource management/allocation approach performs very competitively providing better QoE. This work does not include the cost analysis model for different cloud providers, broker intelligence and how resource can be distributed by different types of Cloud Providers from different geographic sites. As for the future works, we would incorporate some of the above as a part of the future work.

6 Conclusions

This work was supported by a grant from the NIPA (National IT Industry Promotion Agency) in 2012. (Global IT Talents Program) . Professor Eui-Num Huh is corresponding Author.

7 References

[1] B. Sotomayor, R. Montero, I. Llorente, and I. Foster, "Virtual infrastructure management in private and hybrid clouds", IEEE Internet Computing, pp. 14–22, 2009.

[2] S. Chaisiri, B.-S. Lee, and D. Niyato, "Optimal virtual machine placement across multiple cloud providers," in Services Services Computing Conference (APSCC), pp. 103-110, 2009.

[3] W. Zhu, C. Luo, J. Wang, and S. Li, "Multimedia cloud computing," Signal Processing Magazine, IEEE, vol. 28, no. 3, pp. 59 –69, may, 2011.

[4] N. Tolia, D. Andersen, and M. Satyanarayanan, "Quantifying interactive user experience on thin clients," Computer, vol. 39, no. 3, pp. 46 – 52, march, 2006.

[5] M. Satyanarayanan, P. Bahl, R. Caceres, and N. Davies, "The case for vm-based cloudlets in mobile computing," Pervasive Computing, IEEE,vol. 8, no. 4, pp. 14 –23, oct.-dec. 2009.

[6] A. Beloglazov, R. Buyya, "Optimal Online Deterministic Algorithms and adaptive heuristics for energy and performance efficient dynamic consolidation of virtual machines in cloud data center s". Concurrency and Computation: Practice and Experience (CCPE), 2012.

[7] Tiago C. Ferreto, Maco A.S. Netto, Rodrigo N. Calheiros, Cesar A.F De Rose, "Server Consolidation with migration control for virtualized data centers", Future Generation Computer System, pp. 1027-1034, 2011.

[8] M. Cardosa, M. Korupolu, and A. Singh, "Share and utilities based power consolidation in virtualized server environments," in Proc of IFIP/IEEE International Symposium on Integrated Network Management IM'09, 2009.

[9] A. Verma, P. Ahuja, A. Neogi, pMapper: Power and migration cost aware application placement in virtualized systems, in Proc of the 9th ACM/IFIP/USENIX International Conference on Middleware, Springer, pp. 243-264, 2008.

[10] M. Stilwell, D. Schanzenbach, F. Vivien, H. Casanova, "Resource allocation algorithms for virtualized service hosting's platform," Journal of Parallel and distributed Computing, vol.70, no. 9 pp. 962-974, 2010.

[11] Jeffrey M. Galloway, Karl L. Smith, Susan S. Vrbsky, "Power aware load balancing for Cloud Computing," in Proc of the World Congress on Engineering and Computer Science 2011 Vol I October 19-21, WCECS 2011.

[12] Kuo-Qin Yan ; Wen-Pin Liao ; Shun-Sheng Wang , "Towards a Load Balancing in a three-level cloud computing network ", in Proc of 3rd IEEE International Conference on Computer Science and Information Technology (ICCSIT), 2010, Vol-1, pp.-108-113, 2010.

[13] T. Wood, P. Shenoy, A. Venkataramani, M. Yousif: "Sandpiper: Black-box and gray-box resource management for virtual machines." Computer Networks 53(17), 2923-2938, 2009.

[14] Yue M. "A simple proof of the inequality FFD (L) < 11/9 OPT (L) + 1, for all 1 for the FFD bin packing algorithm." Acta Mathematicae Applicatae Sinica (English Series) ;7(4): 321-331, 1991.

[15] A. Beloglazov, J. Abwajy, R. Buyya, "Energy-aware resource allocation heuristics for efficient management of data centers for cloud computing" Future Generation Computer Systems 755–768, 2012.

[16] M. Fiedler, T. Hoßfeld, and P. Tran-Gia, "A Generic Quantitative Relationship between Quality of Experience and Quality of Service," IEEE Network Special Issue on Improving QoE for Network Services, vol. 24, June. 2010.

[17] RN Calheiros, R. Ranjan, A. Beloglazov, CAFD Rose, R. Buyya. "CloudSim: a toolkit for modeling and simulation of cloud computing environments and evaluation of resource provisioning algorithms." Software: Practice and Experience; 41(1): 23-50. 2011.

Social Network Storage Allocation

Faruk Bagci
Department of Computer Engineering
Kuwait University
Kuwait City, Kuwait
dr.faruk.bagci@gmail.com

Mohamed Esam
Department of Information Engineering & Technology
German University in Cairo
Cairo, Egypt
mohamed.esameldin@guc.edu.eg

Aya Kamel, Iman Mansour, Rimon Hanna, Seif El-Din Allam, Taher Galal
Department of Media Engineering and Technology
German University in Cairo
Cairo, Egypt
{aya.kamel, iman.mansour, rimon.hanna, seif.allam, taher.galal}@student.guc.edu.eg

Abstract

Today, social networks present massive amounts of data by the hour that need storage, therefore, along with the aid of cloud computing, social networks users can have their data stored in data centers anywhere around the globe belonging to the cloud. This paper will be focusing on how to allocate user data to the appropriate global data centers from a social networking point of view. The method is carried out using the proposed algorithm where a number of factors are involved such as; read-rate, write-rate, and the number/location of friend connections are used to calculate which data center would yield shorter latency and therefore better results if the user data was to be stored at that location. After validating which was done via simulation, the algorithm proved to yield sufficiently improved data-access latency scores in all test cases.

Keywords: social networks, storage allocation, cloud computing

1. Introduction

In the present day, the use of social networks as means of communication have almost become a part of people's everyday routine for generations both young and old. The online social network industry has boomed over the last decade due to the high demand of the willing public. The modern internet-using public currently depends on social networks to maintain relations with friends, family, work related contacts, and even business marketing while also keeping track of events, meetings, etc. Social networks could be divided into either purely social (e.g. Facebook) or business driven (e.g. LinkedIn) each serving different purposes. Social networks are made to support massive amounts of data traffic, in which users post, upload photos or videos, and connect with friends. Furthermore, many businesses nowadays are turning to social networks, such as Facebook or Twitter, as major marketing tools, where they can create 'fan' pages and monitor various aspects regarding the business such as; keeping track of positive or negative comments regarding the company or its products, and spotting new product/service opportunities [1] [2]. Considering all the services available in social networks from uploading pictures on Flickr, videos on Youtube, joining a project via LinkedIn or simply posting to your friends on Facebook, all this data needs to be stored 'somewhere'. That 'somewhere' is the cloud [3].

Cloud computing as a system is a complex combination of hardware, software, storage and processing distributed around the globe which work together to form one major entity, i.e. the cloud. The system allows a user connected to the cloud to immediately access latter resources wherever their location is [3]. Therefore, instead of using stand-alone servers, each with its own individual resources and storage, the cloud offers multiple units which hold thousands of computers, storage devices, and networks performing. These units are known as data centers. The process of making these data centers, and the vast numbers of machines of which they are comprised of, able to be viewed as one single entity (cloud) to the user is done by virtualization. With virtualization as a tool, the cloud can provide users with virtual storage to store user information, create virtual networks to connect clients, as well as virtual servers to process the vast amounts of data traffic being transmitted through the cloud. As a result, the cloud offers storage, processing and many other features to various users without burdening the user on where and how her data is to be handled and stored.

Finally, putting in mind that clouds are currently the main storage system for most social networks, where all users are instantly able to share the pool of resources which the cloud offers. This combination gave rise to the question of which data (belonging to which user) should be stored in which location (data center).

The aim of this paper is to improve data retrieval latency i.e. the time taken to retrieve the data required from the data center to the demanding user and vice versa and therefore improve overall performance of the storage system in the social networking context.

2. Related Work

As the social networking systems are growing more and more popular, it becomes more and more important to start looking at how the data is being stored [4]. Moreover as social networking started to give extra features such as games, video sharing and storing all of the users' statuses, the need increases to have better means of storing such enormous amounts of data.

New methods of data storage needed to be implemented. Here arises the use of cloud computing [5], allowing the ability to have more data centers located over different parts of the world, while having all these data centers connected together, and giving rise to easier means of communication between the data centers. This is mainly because different people's data will be stored over different data centers, but it could be for some reason that someone needs access to data of her friend which lives in a different country and has her data stored on a different data center [6].

Here the cloud computing technology comes in handy. As we can have all data centers connected together in one large cloud therefore wherever the data of the user lies it can be accessed by herself or any of her friends. Also the use of social networking increases the efficiency of data flow. Therefore the use of new services should arise so that could add extra features to the user.

Some research was first performed on the topic of social networking and cloud computing. In [7] the main research concentrates on how security issues can arise and how to solve them when information is placed over the cloud. Methods of how to overcome these issues are taken into consideration and tested.

Also, in [8] authors regard the same aspects as before but from a different perspective where practices were analyzed that can be used to maintain a secure system while using social network platforms. Moreover, [9] elaborates how the use of cloud computing would address the utilization of memory and data flow from the perspective of the network communication.

Other research projects elaborate how to increase the usability of social networks and how the use of these social networks would use cloud computing technologies to better share resources between the social network users [10] [11].

In [12] authors specify which place a developer should host her application regarding the geographical position of the application users, and how the cloud technology should handle peeks in the usage of this application.

3. Problem Formulation

The problem this paper aims to solve is basically that the optimum location i.e. data center, to store the user's data is not necessarily the actual location of the user. However, this depends on the location of the user's friends with respect to the user's current location i.e. the users who send or receive data to/from the targeted user.

Figure 1: A case where the optimum location to store user's data is not her actual location

	User 1	User 2	User 3	User 4	User 5
User 1	0	1	0	1	0
User 2	1	0	1	1	0
User 3	0	0	0	1	1
User 4	1	1	1	0	1
User 5	0	0	1	1	0

Table I: Friendship Matrix showing friendship relations between 5 users

Figure 1 shows an example of the latter case where the optimum location to store the user's data is not the actual user location. This example shows a user whose data is stored in her actual location while on the other hand most of this user's friends are logged in from a different location. In this case, every time this user communicates with one of her friends, the data has to propagate all the way from the user's actual location to the friend's location which implies a very high delay and cost. However, if the user's data is stored in the same location of the friend, the data will only propagate within the same data center which is definitely lower in cost.

Table I shown above represents the friendship relationship *f* between users of the social network where *f(a, b)* = 1 when users *a* and *b* are friends and *n* represents the number of users in the system. Therefore, for a user u_i, the number of friends can be calculated as

$$k = \sum_{j=1}^{n} f(i,j)$$

The measure from which the optimum position will be calculated is the time taken for data transmission between users, called *cost*. Calculating cost depends on various attributes including user's post rate, read rate, and location of both the user and her corresponding friends.

Assuming that *T(a, b)* is the cost of data transfer between data centers *a* and *b*, *l* is the location of u_i, d_i is the data center where user *i*'s data is stored, *post(x)* is the post rate of user *x* and *read(x)* is the read rate of user *x*, then the cost of user u_i in the system can be represented as

$$Cost(u_i) = T(l, d_i) \times post(u_i) + \sum_{j=1}^{k} T(l, d_j) \times read(u_i)$$

The aim of the research presented in this paper is to mitigate the total cost of the system which can be represented by

$$Cost_{total} = \sum_{j=1}^{n} Cost(u_i)$$

constrained by the facts that per data center:

$$\sum_{i=1}^{num} Capacity(u_i) \leq Capacity(datacenter)$$

$$\&\&$$

$$\sum_{i=1}^{num} CPU(u_i) \leq CPU(datacenter)$$

$$\&\&$$

$$\sum_{i=1}^{num} RAM(u_i) \leq RAM(datacenter)$$

where *num* is the number of users whose data is stored in the data center, *Capacity(x)* is amount of storage needed for user x or available in data center *x* (in TB). *CPU(x)* is the processing capabilities/requirements of data center/user *x* and *RAM(x)* is the memory capabilities/requirements of data center/user *x*. The algorithm explained in the following section presents a solution for the latter problem.

4. Algorithm

We are living in the world of Web 2.0, where hundreds of millions of people are connected to the Internet and millions of those people are connected on social networking sites. Facebook for example has a widespread all over the world as shown in Figure 2 which shows the distribution of Facebook users all over the world in white color. Other means of social networks like LinkedIn, MySpace, and Twitter are also massively used as well as blogs, YouTube and Flickr. The vast amount of ways in which people can be connected online has sparked the interest of cloud computing services. Cloud computing services have been developing ways to tap into the Web 2.0 world and establish means of turning the flow of information and communication into business potential.

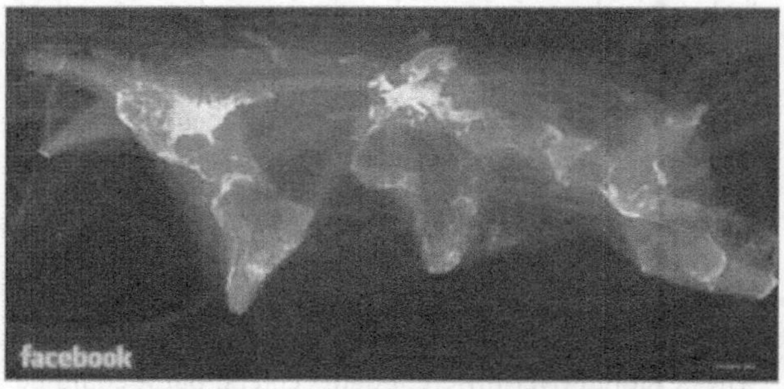

Figure 2: Distribution of Facebook Users around the World [13]

In order to optimize locating the users' data so as to reduce the cost of retrieving it, the proposed algorithm chooses the optimal data center to store the users' data according to some parameters. According to these parameters, the cost of storing the users' data in each possible data center is calculated and the optimal location is chosen accordingly i.e. the data center with minimum cost.

There are multiple factors affecting this decision. The first factor being the percentages of the user's friends in each country, these percentages is then multiplied by the weight of their distance from the user. The second of these factors is how often the user interacts with her friends and what is the form of these interactions, does she read posts by her friends more or does she create her own posts?

Each of these interactions is assigned a different weight; posting is assigned a bigger weight than reading since the write penalty to a storage device is greater making it essential to reduce this penalty by storing the user's data closer to her location. Last but not least we had to put in consideration the performance differences between the servers and data centers in each country in terms of CPU, RAM, storage capacity, and storage performance; assigning better weights to servers with higher performance.

Finally all of these factors were combined together to form a performance evaluation algorithm of each of the cases of the user's data being stored in one of the data centers and the data is then moved to the data center with the best performance value. Figure 3 shows the sequence of steps carried out in the algorithm in order to reach the decision which location is the optimum location for storing user's data.

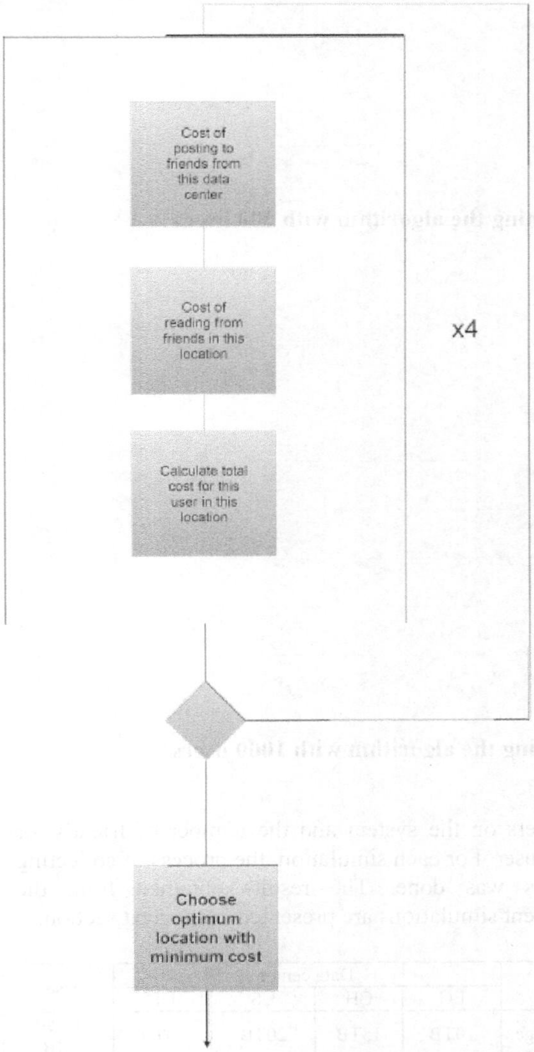

Figure 3: A flow chart showing the proposed algorithm steps per user

The result of applying the algorithm on the environment shown in Figure 1 will be moving the users to the data centers in which most of their friends exist as shown in Figure 4.

5. Implementation

The discussed algorithm needs to be tested on a social network environment where users have friends and can write data and read data of friends. A JAVA model was built in order to simulate the environment on which the algorithm will be applied. In this model, three main objects were created: the user object, the server object, and the data center object.

Figure 4: Moving the user data to the optimum location according to the user's friends (moves shown by arrows from the initial location to the destination)

The aim of the user object was to simulate the presence of a real user in the simulation. Therefore, the following properties were created for being able to describe a user: a unique username, the location of the stored user's data, the current location of the user, the rate at which the user reads data of her friends, the rate at which the user writes new data, the required RAM size, the required storage size, and the CPU capability.

As discussed earlier, there was an urge to simulate servers in the environment since they are the ones responsible for processing and overloading the servers was not a valid option. For this purpose, a server object was created. It was simply represented by only two main parameters: The RAM and the CPU where the RAM describes the RAM size of the server and the CPU describes the CPU capability of the server.

The last and one of the most important objects in this environment was the data center. The object was created with the four main properties which describe a data center. These properties are the location of the data center, a list of the servers connected to that data center, a list of the storage arrays of that data center, and a list of users having their data stored in that data center.

After simulating the standalone nodes in the environment, the simulation of the overall system environment was created by creating different instances of these nodes and creating links between them. This was done by generating four instances of the data center object. Each data center was located in a different country: the first one is located in Egypt, the second in USA, the third in Germany and the fourth in China. For each data center, two server objects were attached.

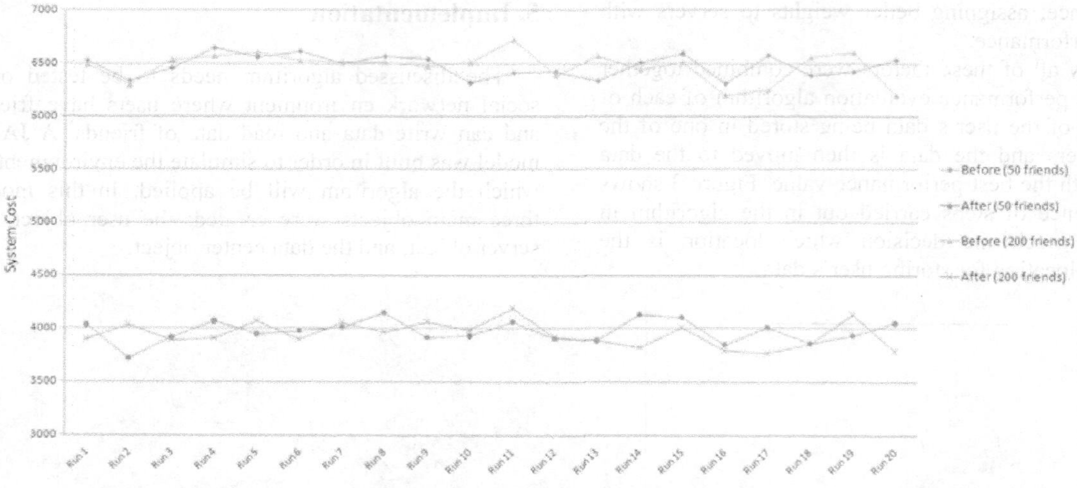

Figure 5: The cost values before and after running the algorithm with 500 users

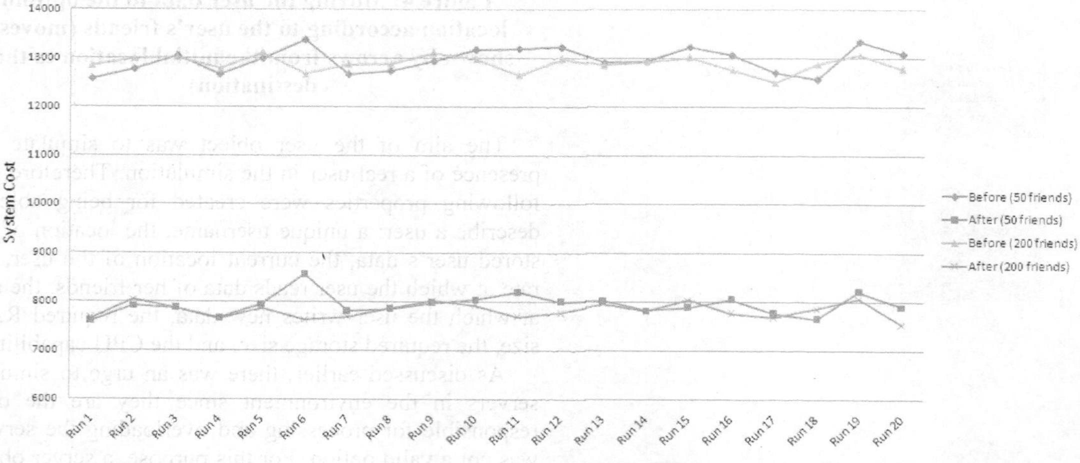

Figure 6: The cost values before and after running the algorithm with 1000 users

Table II shown below presents an overview of the simulation settings that were used when setting up the environment. Users were created randomly using the uniform distribution function *math.rand()* and were also randomly placed in different locations such that initially their data is stored in the nearest data center. Finally, to simulate the idea of a user having friends, a friendship matrix is created indicating which user is friend with which other users.

The last step here was to run the simulation and start collecting results. The results were collected by calculating the cost efficiency using the equations presented in the Problem Formulation section before and after applying the algorithm. To estimate the real impact of the algorithm, the environment is simulated more than once and each time the conditions of the environment run were changed for example the number of users on the system and the number of friends for each user. For each simulation, the process of collecting results was done. The results obtained from the different simulations are presented in the next section.

	Data center				User
	EG	CH	US	DE	
Storage	10TB	15TB	20TB	10TB	10-50 MB
RAM	2x8GB	2x8GB	2x8GB	2x8GB	10MB
CPU	2x22 GHz	2x22 GHz	2x22 GHz	2x22 GHz	10-50 MHz

Table II: The simulation settings

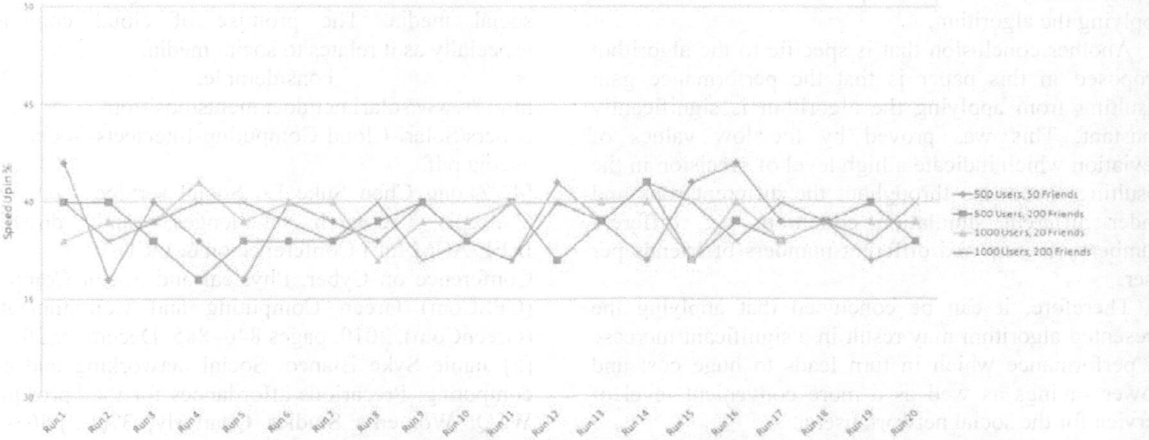

Figure 7: The speed up values calculated from the 4 different system simulations

5. Experimental Results

After the simulation model was complete, some tests were carried out to evaluate the performance of the algorithm. These tests were carried out by calculating the total usage cost for all of the users in the system as shown in the problem formulation section twice; once before running the algorithm when users were assigned to random data centers according to their initial location, and once after running the algorithm when the users data location changed according to the friends location. Dividing the first number by the latter gives the speed up that resulted from the algorithm. These tests were repeated for different number of users with different numbers of friends.

Looking deeper into the simulation results of running the system with 500 users where each user has 50 friends, these simulations yielded speed up results with interesting speed up values ranging from 36% to 42% with an average of 39% and a standard deviation of 1.8. Repeating the same test but with 200 friends per user, the speed up results were also around the same values. Figure 5 shows the cost values before and after running the algorithm.

Increasing the number of users in the system to 1000 users where each user has 50 friends yielded speed up results ranging from 37% to 41% with an average of 39.15% and standard deviation of 1.03. Increasing the number of friends per user to 200 friends, the speed up results were also almost the same. Figure 6 shows the cost values before and after running the algorithm using different numbers of friends per user.

It is of course very logical that the values of cost in the simulation with 500 users as shown in Figure 5 is significantly less than those shown in Figure 6 with 1000 users. The reason is that as mentioned previously, the total cost of the system is the sum of costs of each user in the system. This implies that the cost of the system is directly proportional to the number of users in the simulation.

Having a broad look on the speed up values in Figure 7, it can be noticed that the different runs under several different conditions resulted in speed up values with high precision within the range of 36-42%. This gives an indication that the algorithm is not affected by increasing numbers of users and that applying this algorithm on the huge numbers of social networks users will give more or less 35-40% improvement in the overall system performance.

Moreover, Figure 7 shows that although it was expected that the increasing number of friends will increase the probability of not having a lot of friends in the same location, the algorithm showed a constant response even with the presence of complex friendship matrix between the users.

7. Conclusion

In this paper, the target was to present an algorithm which optimizes the choice of data location for a certain user according to the location of her friends in the social network. To test the efficiency and speed up of the suggested algorithm, a social network environment was simulated and the performance before and after applying the algorithm was calculated.

The results presented in the previous section led to some interesting conclusions. The first and most general conclusion was that locating the friends' data according to her friends' location can be a good approach to optimize the performance of the whole social networking system. This was proved by the approximately 40% speed up that was achieved after applying the algorithm.

Another conclusion that is specific to the algorithm proposed in this paper is that the performance gain resulting from applying the algorithm is significantly constant. This was proved by the low values of deviation which indicate a high level of precision in the resulting speed ups throughout the different runs and under different simulation conditions e.g. different numbers of users and different numbers of friends per user.

Therefore, it can be concluded that applying the presented algorithm may result in a significant increase in performance which in turn leads to huge cost and power savings as well as a more convenient level of service for the social network users.

8. Limitations and Future Work

The research presented in this paper had some limitations which can be targeted for future research. For example, the maximum number of users used for simulation in this research was 1000 users. Therefore, more tests targeting a larger number of social networks users which in reality exceed millions can be carried out.

Another limitation was that the simulations were carried out on only four data centers with two servers. These numbers do not represent real simulation parameters since in reality the number of servers per data center are definitely more than two servers and there may exists more than four data centers. Therefore, a possible future research is to use an accurate number of data centers and servers as well as using real specification description, e.g. RAM and CPU frequency.

In this research it was assumed that users belong to the countries in which the data centers exist. This assumption led to some location constraints thus some common cases were not thoroughly tested in the performed simulation. Therefore, a target for future research may be extending the simulation model to research more cases like allowing users from all countries not just the ones in which a data center exists.

9. References

[1] Soumitra Dutta Matthew Fraser. The business advantages of social networking. Finance and Management, (168), July/August 2009.

[2] Jeff Bullas. 12 major business benefits of the social media revolution, 2012. http://www.jeffbullas.com/2011/02/14/12-major-benefits-of-the-social-media-revolution/

[3] Rich Maggiani. Cloud computing intersects with social media. The promise of cloud computing, especially as it relates to social media, is considerable, 2012. http://www.solari.net/documents/position-papers/Solari-Cloud-Computing-Intersects-Social-Media.pdf.

[4] Zhong Chen Suke Li. Social services computing: Concepts, research challenges, and directions. IEEE/ACM Int'l Conference on & Int'l Conference on Cyber, Physical and Social Computing (CPSCom) Green Computing and Communications (GreenCom), 2010, pages 840–845, December 2010.

[5] Jamie Syke Bianco. Social networking and cloud computing: Precarious affordances for the "prosumer". WSQ: Women's Studies Quarterly, 37(1,2):303–309, 2009.

[6] EMC Education Services G. Somasundaram, Alok Shrivastava, editor. Information Storage and Management. Storing, Managing, and Protecting Digital Information. Wiley Publishcing, Inc., 2009.

[7] N. Markatchev R. Simmonds Tan Tingxi M. Arlitt B. Walker R. Curry, C. Kiddle. Facebook meets the virtualized enterprise. EDOC '08. 12th International IEEE Enterprise Distributed Object Computing Conference, 2008, pages 286– 292, September 2008.

[8] Ashish S. Prasad. Cloud computing and social media: Electronic discovery considerations and best practices. The Metropolitan Corporate Counsel, pages 26–27, February 2012.

[9] M. Sato. Creating next generation cloud computing based network services and the contributions of social cloud operation support system (oss) to society. WETICE '09. 18th IEEE International Workshops on Enabling Technologies: Infrastructures for Collaborative Enterprises, 2009, July 2009.

[10] O. Rana K. Bubendorfer K. Chard, S. Caton. Social cloud: Cloud computing in social networks. IEEE 3rd International Conference on Cloud Computing (CLOUD), 2010, pages 99–106, July 2010.

[11] K. Chard A. M. Thaufeeg, K. Bubendorfer. Collaborative eresearch in a social cloud. IEEE 7th International Conference on E-Science (e- Science), 2011, pages 224–231, 2011.

[12] Rajkumar Buyya, Rajiv Ranjan, and Rodrigo Calheiros. Intercloud: Utility-oriented federation of cloud computing environments for scaling of application services. In Ching-Hsien Hsu, Laurence Yang, Jong Park, and Sang-Soo Yeo, editors, Algorithms and Architectures for Parallel Processing, volume 6081 of Lecture Notes in Computer Science, pages 13–31. Springer Berlin / Heidelberg, 2010.

[13] Paul Butler. Visualizing friendships, December 2010. http://www.facebook.com/note.php?note id=469716398919.

SESSION

VIRTUAL MACHINES AND CLOUD COMPUTING

Chair(s)

Prof. Hamid Arabnia
University of Georgia

A Fast Live Migration Algorithm of Virtual Machine with CPU Scheduling

Jia Zhao[1], Liang Hu[1], Gaochao Xu[1], Decheng Chang[1], Yan Ding[1,*], and Xiaodong Fu[1]
[1]Department of Computer Science and Technology, Jilin University, Changchun, Jilin, China
[*]Corresponding author

Abstract - *Live migration of virtual machine (VM) is one of the most important virtualization technologies to facilitate the management and improve the performance of data centers. In this paper, we propose a fast convergent live migration approach called FMC. It is a self-adaptive method which synchronizes the state of the VM migrated between the source and target host by log tracing and replaying instead of dirty memory pages transferring. First, the mechanisms of fine-grained log files division, replay time units feedback and dynamic variable step K are presented. Second, we introduce the CPU scheduling mechanism into FMC to adjust the CPU timeslices in order to reduce the log data size when the network bandwidth is too low. Experimental results show that FMC can significantly reduce migration overheads compared with Pre-copy algorithm in a fast network bandwidth. Identically, the migration downtime of FMC is less than that of CR/TR-Motion in a low network bandwidth. The overheads are also acceptable even in low network bandwidth.*

Keywords: Virtual Machine, Live Migration, CPU scheduling, Checkpoint, Replay, Virtualization

1 Introduction

Virtualization is an abstraction of computer resources which subdivides the ample resources of a modern computer [1] or aggregates servers, storage, network, etc. as an entirely. It has been employed as the basic management technology for consolidation, automated management and isolation, etc. in data centers or Cloud Computing environment. In addition, Hardware assisted virtualization accelerates the development of virtualization [2]. Live migration of VM is one of the most important technologies of virtualization technology. Live migration of VM migrates a running VM among distinct physical hosts while making sure that applications running on the VM not affected. It allows administrators to consolidate system load, perform maintenance, and flexibly reallocate cluster-wide resources on-the-fly [3]. To provide benefits for administrators of data centers or clusters, a fast and transparent live migration strategy is necessary. Our research focuses on improving migration speed and reducing migration overheads. A live migration algorithm can be evaluated in these performance metrics: total migration time, downtime, total data transmitted and application degradation [4]. Total migration time is the time taken from the start of migration to the time the migrated VM gets a consistent state with the original one. Downtime is defined as the duration for which a VM's CPU execution is fully suspended during live migration [4]. Total data transmitted is the data transferred while synchronizing the VMs' state. Application degradation means the extent that the applications running within the migrating VMs slow down because of the operation of live migration.

To make further optimization on live migration, we propose a fast convergent live migration approach with CPU scheduling mechanism, namely, FMC. Our prototype is implemented based on ReVirt [5] which is a full system trace and replay system. Make a checkpoint first for rolling forward via the log later. Non-deterministic events are recorded in log files. The fine-grained log files division mechanism is applied on the source host. A log file is generated every time unit if non-deterministic events happen. Log files are transferred from the source host to the target host iteratively. The replay time units feedback mechanism is applied on the target host. The number of log files transferred each round is determined by the replaying time units of previous round on the target host. By this way, we make more use of the computing power of target host to speed up replaying. Our strategy also introduces CPU scheduling mechanism in the phase of iterative logs transferring to adjust the log growth rate. When the log transfer rate is slower than the log growth rate, the CPU timeslices allocated for the VM are reduced to decrease the log growth rate.

The rest of this paper is organized as follows. In Section 2, we give a brief introduction of related work about current live migration methods. In Section 3, a prerequisite that should be satisfied is pointed out. The design and implementation of FMC are presented in detail. We also discuss its benefits. In Section 4, experiments undertaken and results obtained are shown, demonstrating that it provides an effective solution. Finally, in Section 5 we conclude the paper.

2 Related works

Pre-copy is a predominantly used approach in the state of the art for live migration. XenMotion [6] and VMotion [7] which are the most influential methods for live migration employ pre-copy algorithm. Pre-copy first copies the memory state over multiple iterations followed by a final transfer of the processor state [8]. Pre-copy mainly considers the migration of VM's physical memory because it affects the migration downtime as a main factor.

Many optimized solutions for pre-copy algorithm have been proposed. First, some optimizations can be classified as memory compression. H. Jin et al. proposed MECOM in [9]. MECOM compresses memory based on memory page characteristics, memory pages of different characteristics adopt corresponding different compression algorithm. Delta Compression stores data in the form of changes between versions instead of the full data sets [10]. It computes the delta page by applying XOR on the current and previous version of a page, and then compresses the delta page by binary Run Length Encoding compression algorithm. Second, some solutions try to change the order of transferring dirty memory pages. Pages modified frequently should be transferred at last to reduce re-transfers. Rapid Page Dirtying transfers pages dirtied in the previous round that have not been dirtied again at the time they are scanned [6]. Dynamic page transfer reordering [11] is another method dynamically adapts the transfer order of VM memory pages during live migration. Third, some other solutions take advantage of the HPC networks. A high performance VM migration with RDMA over Modern Interconnects is proposed in [12]. It significantly improves the efficiency of VM migration. However, most of them mentioned above adapt to the memory writing passively. There are also some other solutions adjust memory writing speed in an active way. Stunning Rogue Processes [6] limits each process to a certain number of write faults and stun processes that make migration difficult. But it is not fit for complex environment. Optimized pre-copy by CPU scheduling is proposed in [13]. By introducing CPU scheduling mechanism, rate of dirty memory pages can be reduced via adjusting the CPU timeslices allocated to the VM being migrated. It is a compatible method with other optimization methods, but it may sacrifice the performance of application running in VM.

In contrast to the classic pre-copy algorithm, post-copy first suspends the migrating VM at the source host, copies minimal processor state to the target host, resumes the virtual machine, and begins fetching memory pages over the network from the source [3, 8]. Some technologies can also be adopted in post-copy for optimization [3]: demand paging, active push, pre-paging and dynamic self-ballooning. Duplicate page transmissions may be eliminated via adaptive pre-paging while the transfer of free memory pages can be eliminated via dynamic self-ballooning.

Other live migration methods include opportunistic replay [14] that replays user actions on a target site to recreate VM state and minimizes the overhead of VM migration. However, it is implemented only at the GUI level and not in a live fashion. Another novel approach CR/TR-Motion is proposed by H. Liu et al. in [15] to provide fast and transparent live migration. It is based on checkpointing/recovery [16] and trace/replay [5, 17, 18] technology which transfers log files recording system events instead of dirty memory pages. Obviously, dirty memory pages consume more network bandwidth than log files.

In many cases, pre-copy needs to transfer a large amount of data. As for post-copy, the latency of fetching pages from the source host causes extended downtime. However, the optimized methods for pre-copy and post-copy are worth learning from. For example, CPU scheduling adopted in pre-copy algorithm can be introduced to other live migration methods to increase the adaptability. Furthermore, CR/TR-Motion may greatly decrease the amount of the data transferred while synchronizing the two VM's running states, so are the downtime and total migration time. But the requirement that the log transfer rate is faster than the log growth rate should be satisfied. Considering the characteristics of these live migration methods, the proposed method FMC employs the technologies similar to these adopted in CR/TR-Motion and combines with CPU scheduling to achieve better live migration.

3 The proposed algorithm

Here we propose a fast convergent live VM migration with CPU scheduling approach named FMC. It combines checkpointing, logging, and roll-forward recovery with CPU scheduling which can reduce migration overheads compared with pre-copy algorithm. The main idea of our algorithm is that VM to be migrated on the source host generates log files continuously which record non-deterministic system events like external input every time unit, these log files are transferred to the target host in sequence while the target host replays with the received log files. A log file will be generated every time unit. Each round, after the received log files have been consumed, the time units used for replaying are counted as value *K*. Then a request is sent to the source host for *K* log files which will be transferred in the next round. We also come up with an interesting idea that adopts CPU scheduling mechanism, aim to reduce the timeslices allocated to the VM if the log grow rate is faster than the log transfer rate. The VM's CPU timeslices will be recovered if the log grow rate is slowed down in order to balance application performance and migration downtime.

3.1 Prerequisites

In this paper, we assume that the replay speed on target host is fast enough. Generally, the log replay rate is higher than the log growth rate. This rule has been explained in [15]. During replay the events that may cause a process block waiting for them such as I/O events can be immediately replayed. For instance, if the VM is running a daily use workload, the log replay rate is 33 times larger than the log growth rate according to the experiment in [5]. Replay skips over periods of idle time such as that encountered during the non-working hours of the daily use workload. In many cases, the VM will be very likely migrated to a host providing better performance which may speed up the replay speed. Another limitation for FMC should also be satisfied. The log transfer rate should be faster than the log growth rate, otherwise the log files will accumulate on the source and our method will get no benefit. However, according to the characteristics of our method such as the CPU scheduling mechanism, FMC is a general method which can be applied even in low network bandwidth. Hence, we need not consider the relationship between the log transfer rate and the log growth rate.

3.2 Live migration process of FMC

In this section, we describe the specific process of FMC as shown in Figure 1. Details are as follows:

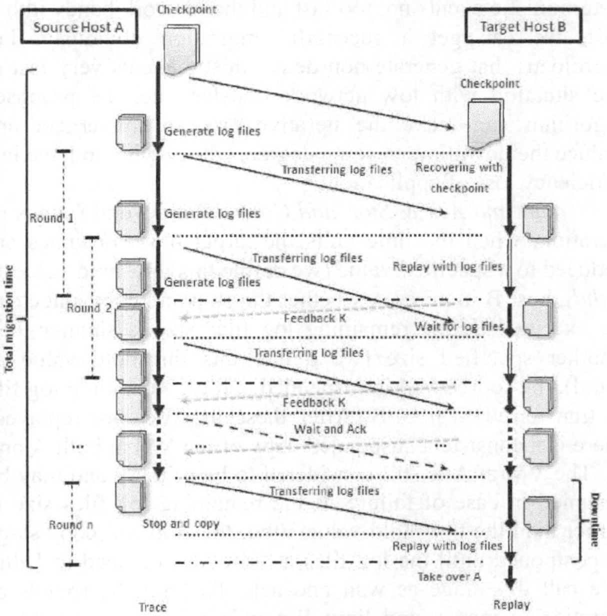

Figure 1. Live VM migration process

(1) *Make and transfer checkpoint* When the preparation is ready, make a checkpoint on host A. After checkpointing, transfer the checkpoint file to host B. During the transferring, log files will be generated.

(2) *Overlapping iterative log files transfer* To achieve fast convergent live migration, the proposed algorithm adopts fine-grained log files division and replay time units feedback mechanisms in the iterative process. Furthermore, a novel method dynamic variable step K is applied to the mechanism of replay time units feedback in the iterative process, aim to control the log files transferred number from the source host to the target host.

The iterative process is conducted after the previous three steps. During the first round of transferring, the log files generated in the course of checkpoint file transferring are copied from host A to B, while VM on host A is continuously running and recording non-deterministic system events in log files according to time unit. Simultaneously, the log files are replayed on host B once it had recovered from the checkpoint and received these log files. When the received log files are consumed, the time units for replaying are counted. We make a key decision that adopts replay time units feedback mechanism and dynamic variable step K method right here. Then a specific number of log files will be transferred to the host B in the next round. Subsequent iterations repeat the process similar to the first round.

Our algorithm employs the form $[V_1, V_2 \ldots V_K]$ to indicate the continuous log files to be transferred in each round. Here, V represents a log file. Every log file is assigned to a serial number according to its generated order. The subscript i of V_i indicate the serial number of the current log file. As shown in Figure 2, K_1, K_2 and K_3 represent the sizes of step from round 1 to round 3 respectively. We also use E_1 and E_2 to represent the serial numbers of the last log files generated in round 1 and round 2.

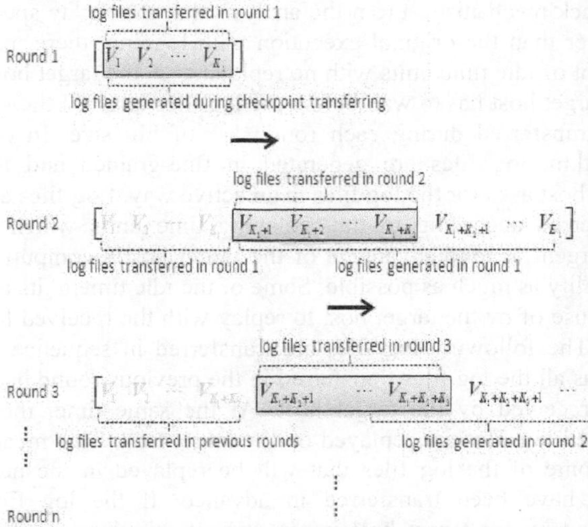

Figure 2. Log files generated and transferred in each round

Let us introduce dynamic variable step K mentioned above. We can obtain the replay time units each time after the replay of the current round. The value of K is set equal to the replay time units. Obviously, K is variable in each iteration round. Then K is sent to the source host as a request that the source should copy K log files to the target host in next round. The source host transfers log files continuously according to the log generated sequence. The first log file to be transferred follows the last log file that had just been received. The next K-1 log files will be transferred in the same round. In fact, some of these K log files in previous may have been sent out or even received by the target host. Therefore, a duplicate period of time may exist in two adjacent rounds of the iterative process. In the iteration rounds of our algorithm, except for the first round, the continuous log files transferred number is determined by K, just like a step whose size is changeable. Here, we describe about the mechanisms adopted in our algorithm.

(a) Fine-grained log files division mechanism. It is noteworthy that the fine-grained log files division mechanism is one of the key points of the proposed algorithm. The log files are generated in fine granularity, which means non-deterministic events happened in two time units are recorded in two different log files. Figure 3 shows the relationship between log files and time units. When the network bandwidth is low, it is faster to transfer several small files than to transfer a large file with the same size. For this reason, the proposed method can reduce the time consumed on the network to some extent, and reduce the total time for generating log files on the source host. From another perspective, it is an improvement on the log transfer rate.

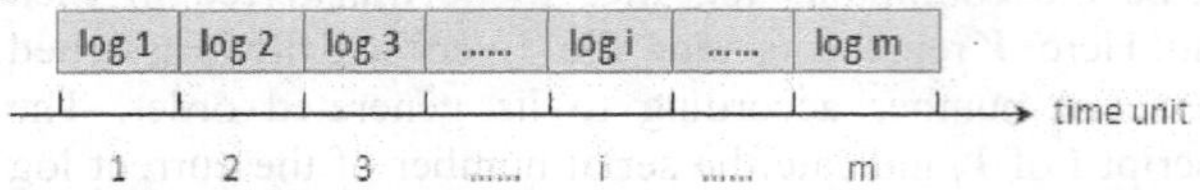

Figure 3. Relationships between log files and time units

(b) Replay time units feedback mechanism. Another key point of the proposed algorithm is the replay time units feedback mechanism. From the analysis that the replay speed is faster than the original execution with logging, there may be a lot of idle time units with no replaying on the target host. The target host has to wait before the log files arrive if the log files transferred during each round are of big size. In our algorithm, log files are generated in fine-grained and the target host asks for the log files in an active way. Log files are transferred according to the replaying time units which is convergent to take advantage of the target host's computing capability as much as possible. Some of the idle time units are made use of by the target host to replay with the received log files. The following log files are transferred in sequence as soon as all the log files transferred in the previous round have been received by the target host. At the same time, these received log files are replayed on the target host. This means that some of the log files that will be replayed in the next round have been transferred in advance. If the log files received by the target host in the current round are no less than the replay time units, these received log files can be replayed at once. Therefore, there will be little interval time between the two replay processes. As a result, the time units for the source host to generate log files are reduced. The proposed algorithm can speed up the convergence of the iterative process.

(c) CPU scheduling mechanism. In this part, we describe the CPU scheduling mechanism employed in the iterative log transferring stage in detail. When the network bandwidth is too low, the log growth rate may be faster than the log transfer rate. As a result, the downtime of migration and the total log data transferred will increase. According to an experiential rule that a certain VM's execution speed of system events increases when the CPU timeslices allocated to the VM increase, the conclusion that the log growth rate decreases with the decreasing VM's CPU timeslices can be drawn. Based on above conclusion, the CPU scheduling mechanism is introduced into the iterative log transferring stage to solve the problems that we have put forward. The log growth rate and the log transfer rate are updated in every round of transferring and the CPU timeslices that just may be allocated to the VM is also computed. If the log growth rate is faster than the log transfer rate, it can be slowed down by reducing the CPU timeslices for the VM being migrated in the next round of log transferring so that the iterative process is convergent. For the reason that the allocated CPU timeslices for VM determines the VM's running speed and the log generating speed, it should balance these two factors. If its value is too small, the performance of application in the VM will be unbearable even though we get a successful live migration. Reduce the allocated CPU time only when it is necessary in order to get a good performance of application. So a constant S is saved all the time. In the case that the CPU timeslices have been reduced, the CPU timelices allocated to the VM in the next round are resumed to the original value S if the log growth rate is slower than the log transfer rate. In this way, our optimized live migration algorithm can be applied in wide range. For the workloads which generate non-deterministic events not too fast and the network bandwidth is fast, we can get a successful migration obviously. For workloads that generate non-deterministic events very fast or the situation with low network transfer rate, the proposed algorithm can make the iterative process convergent and reduce the downtime to some degree, while trying to have less efficiency loss of application.

(3) *Wait and Ack & Stop and Copy* After several rounds of iteration, when the time units the target host consumes are reduced to a specified value (we define this threshold value as *Kthd*), host B inquires A whether the stop and copy stage can be executed. If the remaining log files size is smaller than another specified size (we define this threshold value as Vthd), the source VM is suspended and the remaining log file is transferred to host B. After these log files are replayed, there is a consistent suspended copy of the VM at both A and B. The VM at A is still considered to be primary and may be resumed in case of failure. If the remaining log files size is larger than the threshold value Vthd, the stop and copy stage is postponed until the log files at host A is reduced to Vthd. We call this stage as wait and ack. To limit the rounds of iteration, a max round limit Rmax is set in our algorithm. When the next round is the last one, the iteration will be stopped.

From a direct perspective, the proposed method is an iterative process. From another perspective, the proposed method can be regarded as a Markov process. A Markov process [19] is a stochastic process which satisfies the Markov property and undergoes transitions from one state to another, between a finite or countable number of possible states. It is a discrete-time random process that the next state depends only on the current state and not on the sequence of events that preceded it. The proposed algorithm is in line with the characteristics of Markov property. First, like the state transitions of Markov process, the CPU timeslices allocated for the VM may be altered to another value in each round to adjust the log growth rate. Second, we calculate the CPU timeslices for the next round only based on the current round's CPU timeslices, just the same as a Markov process that the next state depends only on the current state. And the value we get in our algorithm is discrete. Third, the CPU timeslices of each round are equal or less than the initial value and the combination of these values can be treated as a countable set defined in Markov process. In summary, the proposed algorithm is a Markov process indeed.

Starting from this intuition on the classic pre-copy and CR/TR-Motion algorithms, we came up with the FMC

proper adjustment solution for *K*. In addition, we conduct the experiments in a local area network in this paper. We will extend our approach to a wide area network in the future.

6 References

[1] P. Barham, B. Dragovic, K. Fraser, S. Hand, T. Harris, A. Ho, R. Neugebauer, I. Pratt and A. Warfield. "Xen and the Art of Virtualization"; Proc. of the 19th ACM Symposium on Operating Systems Principles (SOSP'03), 164-177, 2003.

[2] J. Nakajima, Q. Lin, S. Yang, M. Zhu, S. Gao, M. Xia, P. Yu, Y. Dong, Z. Qi, K. Chen and H. Guan. "Optimizing Virtual Machines Using Hybrid Virtualization"; Proc. of the 2011 ACM Symposium on Applied Computing (SAC'11), 573-578, 2011.

[3] M. R. Hines, U. Deshpande and K. Gopalan. "Post-Copy Live Migration of Virtual Machines"; Operating Systems Review (ACM), vol.43, no.3, 14-26, 2009.

[4] U. Deshpande, X. Wang, and K. Gopalan. "Live Gang Migration of Virtual Machines"; Proc. of the IEEE International Symposium on High Performance Distributed Computing, 135-146, 2011.

[5] G. W. Dunlap, S. T. King, S. Cinar, M. A. Basrai and P. M. Chen. "ReVirt: Enabling Intrusion Analysis through Virtual-Machine Logging and Replay"; ACM SIGOPS Operating Systems Review - OSDI '02: Proc. of the 5th symposium on Operating systems design and implementation, vol.36, no.SI, 211-224, 2002.

[6] C. Clark, K. Fraser, S. Hand, J. G. Hansen, E. Jul, C. Limpach, I. Pratt, and A. Warfield. "Live Migration of Virtual Machines"; Proc. of the 2nd conf. on Symposium on Networked Systems Design & Implementation, vol.2, 273-286, 2005.

[7] M. Nelson, B. H. Lim, and G. Hutchins. "Fast Transparent Migration for Virtual Machines"; Proc. of USENIX Annual Technical Conference (USENIX'05), 391-394, 2005.

[8] M. R. Hines and K. Gopalan. "Post-Copy Based Live Virtual Machine Migration Using Adaptive Pre-Paging and Dynamic Self-Ballooning"; Proc. of the 2009 ACM SIGPLAN/SIGOPS International Conf. on Virtual Execution Environments, 51-60, 2009.

[9] H. Jin, L. Deng, S. Wu, X. Shi and X. Pan. "Live Virtual Machine Migration with Adaptive Memory Compression"; Proc. of International Conf. on Cluster Computing and Workshops(CLUSTER '09), 1-10, 2009.

[10] P. Svärd, B. Hudzia and J. Tordsson. "Evaluation of Delta Compression Techniques for Efficient Live Migration of Large Virtual Machine"; Proc. of the 2011 ACM SIGPLAN/SIGOPS International Conf. on Virtual Execution Environments, 111-120, 2011.

[11] P. Svärd, J. Tordsson, B. Hudzia and E. Elmroth. "High performance live migration through dynamic page transfer reordering and compression"; Proc. of the 3rd IEEE International Conf. on Cloud Computing Technology and Science, 542-548, 2011.

[12] W. Huang, Q. Gao, J. Liu and D. K. Panda. "High Performance Virtual Machine Migration with RDMA over Modern Interconnects"; Proc. of International Conf. on Cluster Computing, 11-20, 2007.

[13] H. Jin, W. Gao, S. Wu, X. Shi, X. Wu and F. Zhou. "Optimizing the live migration of virtual machine by CPU scheduling"; Journal of Network and Computer Applications, vol.34, no.4, 1088-1096, 2011.

[14] A. Surie, H. A. Lagar-Cavilla, E. de Lara and M. Satyanarayanan. "Low-Bandwidth VM Migration via Opportunistic Replay"; Proc. of the 9th Workshop on Mobile Computing Systems and Applications (HotMobile'08), 74-79, 2008.

[15] H. Liu, H. Jin, X. Liao, L. Hu and C. Yu. "Live Migration of Virtual Machine Based on Full System Trace and Replay"; Proc. of the 18th ACM International Symposium on High Performance Distributed Computing (HPDC'09), 101-110, 2009.

[16] B. Cully, G. Lefebvre, D.T. Meyer, A. Karollil, M.J. Feeley, N.C. Hutchinson and A. Warfield. "Remus: High Availability via Asynchronous Virtual Machine Replication"; Proc. of the 5th Symp. Networked Systems Design and Implementation (NSDI '08), 2008.

[17] M. Xu, V. Malyugin, J. Sheldon, G. Venkitachalam and B. Weissman. "ReTrace: Collecting Execution Trace with Virtual Machine Deterministic Replay"; Proc. of Third Ann. Workshop Modeling, Benchmarking and Simulation, 2007.

[18] D.A.S. de Oliveira, J.R. Crandall, G. Wassermann, S.F. Wu, Z. Su, and F.T. Chong. "ExecRecorder: VM-Based Full-System Replay for Attack Analysis and System Recovery"; Proc. of Workshop Architectural and System Support for Improving Software Dependability (ASID '06), 66-71, 2006.

[19] http://en.wikipedia.org/wiki/Markov_process. 2012.

[20] S. T. King. "Operating System Extensions to Support Host Based Virtual Machines". Technical Report CSE-TR-465-02, University of Michigan, 2002.

[21] K. Buchacker and V. Sieh. "Framework for Testing the Fault-Tolerance of Systems Including OS and Network Aspects"; Proc. of the 6th IEEE International High Assurance Systems Engineering Symposium (HASE'01), 95-105, 2001.

[22] L. Cherkasova, D. Gupta and A. Vahdat. "Comparison of the Three CPU Schedulers in Xen"; ACM SIGMETRICS Performance Evaluation Review, vol.35, no.2, 42-51, 2007.

[23] R. Bradford, E. Kotsovinos, A. Feldmann, and H. Schioeberg. "Live Wide-Area Migration of Virtual Machines Including Local Persistent State"; Proc. of the 3rd International Conf. on Virtual Execution Environments, 169-179, 2007.

[24] H. Liu, H. Jin, X. Liao, C. Yu and C.-Z. Xu. "Live Virtual Machine Migration via Asynchronous Replication and State Synchronization"; IEEE Transactions on Parallel and Distributed Systems, vol.22, no.12, 1986-1999, 2011.

A Fuzzy Predictable Load Balancing Approach in Cloud Computing

Fahimeh Ramezani, Jie Lu, Farookh Hussain
Decision Systems & e-Service Intelligence Lab, Centre for QCIS
School of Software, Faculty of Engineering and IT, University of Technology, Sydney
PO Box 123, Broadway NSW 2007 Australia
Fahimeh.Ramezani@student.uts.edu.au, {Jie.Lu, Farookh.Hussain}@uts.edu.au

***Abstract*— Cloud computing is a new paradigm for hosting and delivering services on demand over the internet where users access services. It is an example of an ultimately virtualized system, and a natural evolution for data centers that employ automated systems management, workload balancing, and virtualization technologies. Live virtual machine (VM) migration is a technique to achieve load balancing in cloud environment by transferring an active overload VM from one physical host to another one without disrupting the VM. In this study, to eliminate whole VM migration in load balancing process, we propose a Fuzzy Predictable Load Balancing (FPLB) approach which confronts with the problem of overload VM, by assigning the extra tasks from overloaded VM to another similar VM instead of whole VM migration. In addition, we propose a Fuzzy Prediction Method (FPM) to predict VMs' migration time. This approach also contains a multi-objective optimization model to migrate these tasks to a new VM host. In proposed FPLB approach there is no need to pause VM during migration time. Furthermore, considering this fact that VM live migration contrast to tasks migration takes longer to complete and needs more idle capacity in host physical machine (PM), the proposed approach will significantly reduce time, idle memory and cost consumption.**

Keywords—cloud computing, load balancing, virtual machine migration, workload prediction.

I. INTRODUCTION

Cloud computing is a style of computing where flexible high-performance, pay-as-you-go, and on-demand offering service are delivered to external customers using Internet technologies. Cloud computing services are divided into three classes, according to the abstraction level of the capability provided and the service model of providers, namely Infrastructure as a Service (IaaS), Platform as a Service (PaaS) and Software as a Service (SaaS) [1]. The key underlying technology in cloud infrastructures is virtualization. Virtualization is a technique for hiding the physical characteristics of computing resources and allows servers and storage devices to be shared and utilization be increased. This simulated environment is called a virtual machine (VM) that is a software abstraction with the looks of a computer system's hardware (real machine) [2].

Cloud computing platform achieves dynamic balance between the servers applying virtualization technology for resource management. In virtualized cloud environment, applying online VM migration technology can achieve online remapping of VMs and physical resources, and dynamic whole system load balancing [3]. In particular, VM migration has been applied for flexible resource allocation or reallocation, by moving VM from one physical machine to another for stronger computation power, larger memory, fast communication capability, or energy savings [4].

Although a significant amount of research has been done to achieve system load balancing [4, 5], more improvement is still needed as most of these approaches tried to migrate VMs, when they became overload. In addition, in most of them predicting VMs' migration time is missed. Considering this fact that the whole VM migration takes much more times and cost in comparison with tasks migration, we propose a fuzzy load balancing method which migrates tasks from overloaded VMs instead of migration VMs to achieve load balancing in cloud environment. We also propose an algorithm to solve the problem of migrating these tasks to new VMs host which is a multi-objective problem subject to minimizing cost, minimizing execution and transferring time. To solve this problem we apply multi-objective genetic algorithm (MOGA). Furthermore, to accelerate load balancing process and reduce response time, we develop a fuzzy prediction method to predict VM workload situation and its migration time.

The rest of this paper is organized as follows. Section II presents the related works about VM migration techniques and VM workload prediction methods. Section III explains the basic concept of expert systems and neural networks, and genetic algorithm. In Section IV, we develop a Fuzzy Prediction Method (FPM) to predict VM migration time. In Section V, we propose a conceptual model and the algorithm of Fuzzy Predictable Load Balancing (FPLB) approach for solving the problem of overloaded VMs by optimal tasks migration from overloaded VMs. Our developed algorithm for solving multi-objective tasks scheduling problem and completing FPLB algorithm, is described in Section VI. The proposed approach is evaluated in Section VII. Finally we present the conclusion and future works in Section VIII.

II. RELATED WORKS

A. VM Migration Thechniques

Virtualization technique has improved utilization and system load balancing by enabling VM migration, and provided significant benefits for cloud computing [6]. Several methods have been developed to migrate a running instance of a VM from one physical host to another to optimize cloud utilization. Primary migration relies on process suspend and resume. Many systems [7, 8] just pause the VM and copy the state data, then resume the VM on the destination host. This forces the migrated application to stop until all the memory states have been transferred to the migration destination where it is resumed. These methods cause the application to become unavailable during the migration process. ZAP [9] could achieve lower downtime of the service by just transferring a process group, but it still uses stop-and-copy strategy. To reduce the migration downtime and move the VM between hosts in local area network without disrupting it, VMotion [10] and Xen [11] utilize pre-copy migration technique to perform live migration and support seamless process transfer. In pre-copy migration technique, VMs migrate by pre-copying the generated run-time memory state files from the original host to the migration destination host. If the rate for such a dirty memory generation is high, it may take a long time to accomplish live migration because a large amount of data needs to be transferred. In extreme cases, when dirty memory generation rate is faster than pre-copy speed, live migration will fail. Considering this fact, Jin et al. presented the basic pre-copy model of VM live migration and proposed an optimized algorithm to improve the performance of live migration by limiting the speed of changing memory through controlling the CPU scheduler of the VM monitor [4]. Lin et al. believe that most of the proposed methods for on-demand resource provisioning and allocation, focused on the optimization of allocating physical resources to their associated virtual resources and migrating VMs to achieve load balance and increase resource utilization. Unfortunately, these methods require the suspension of the executing cloud computing applications due to the mandatory shutdown of the associated VMs [12]. To overcome this drawback, they proposed a threshold-based dynamic resource allocation scheme for cloud computing that dynamically allocate the VMs among the cloud computing applications based on their load changes. In their proposed method, they determined when migration should be done but they did not specify the details of how the reallocation will occur.

A fundamental drawback of the most existing researches is that they consider complete VM migration to overcome overload VM and achieve system load balance. In addition, predicting VMs' workload situation and their migration time, are not considered in most of traditional load balancing approaches. In this paper, we propose a new Fuzzy Predictable Load Balancing (FPLB) approach which predicts VMs' workload situation, and transfers tasks from overloads VMs instead of whole VM migration to achieve system load balancing. The proposed approach not only eliminates the suspend and resume process during VM migration, but also omits pre-copy mechanism and producing dirty memory in live VM migration.

B. Workload Prediction Methods

Resource provisioning in compute clouds often requires an estimate of the required capacity for VMs. The estimated VM size is essential for allocating resources commensurate with demand [13]. Meng et al. proposed an algorithm for estimating the aggregate size of multiplexed VMs. They decoupled VM workload into regular and irregular fluctuating components. To forecast regular workload, they simply assumed that the regular patterns will preserve in the future, e.g., a steadily increasing trend keeps increasing at the same rate. On the other hand, for forecasting irregular workload, they performed a time series forecasting technique based on historic workload patterns [13]. Nagothu et al. proposed a new method for load prediction. They separated load prediction into linear and non-linear prediction algorithms categories. They believed a linear prediction algorithm can either involve 1-Dim observation sequences or d-Dim observation space signals [14].

Most of the existing researches in this area have applied prediction methods such as neural networks and linear regression to forecast VMs workload in cloud environment. These prediction methods predict future workload applying previous workload patterns in time slot *t*. In IaaS where VMs are assigned to customers; VMs' workload is affected by customers' behavior and decisions, and significantly changes in seconds. Therefore, upcoming VMs' workload in cloud environment could be independent from their previous workload pattern. To overcome this problem we propose a workload prediction method applying a neural network and an expert system with the specific parameters that control and monitor recent changes in VMs' workload pattern.

III. BACKGROUND

A. Expert Systems

The basic idea behind expert systems (ES) is simply that expertise, which is the vast body of task-specific knowledge, is transferred from a human to a computer. This knowledge is then stored in the computer and users call upon the computer for specific advice as needed. The computer can make inferences and arrive at a specific conclusion. Then like a human consultant, it gives advices and explains, if necessary, the logic behind the advice. A rule-based ES is defined as one, which contains information obtained from a human expert, and represents that information in the form of rules, such as IF–THEN. The rule can then be used to perform operations on data to inference in order to reach appropriate conclusion. These inferences are essentially a computer program that provides a methodology for reasoning about information in the rule base or knowledge base, and for formulating conclusions [15, 16].

B. Neural Networks

A neural network (NN) consists of a number of layers: the input layer has a number of input neurons $X =$

$\{x_1, ..., x_m\}$; the output layer has one or more output neurons $O = \{o_1, ..., o_n\}$ and several hidden layers with hidden neurons $H = \{h_1, ..., h_l\}$ in between. In a fully-connected NN, the neurons at each layer are connected to the neurons of the next layer; these connections are known as synapses. Each synapse is associated with a weight, which is to be determined during training. During the training phase, the NN is fed with input vectors and random weights are assigned to the synapses. After presentation of each input vector, the network generates a predicted output $\hat{y}$. The generated output is then compared with the actual output y; the difference between the two is known as the error term which is then used as a feedback to correct the synaptic weights of the network. The training of the NN continues until a specific criterion is met, e.g. the sum of squared errors falls below a certain threshold [17].

C. A Multi Objective Genetic Algorithm

A multi-objective genetic algorithm (MOGA) is concerned with the minimization of multiple objective functions that are subject to a set of constraints. In MOGA for solving multi-objective optimization problems, first initial population whose scale is *N* is generated randomly. The first generation child population is gained through non-dominated sorting [18] and basic operations such as selection, crossover and mutation. Then, from the second generation on, the parent population and the child population will be merged and sorted based on fast non-dominated. Calculate crowding distance among individuals on each non-dominated layer. According to non-dominant relationship and crowding distance among individuals, select the appropriate individuals to form a new parent population. Finally, new child population is generated through basic operations of genetic algorithm and so on, until the conditions of the process end can be met [19].

IV. A Fuzzy Prediction Method for Determining the VM Migration Time

Considering this fact that future VMs' workload could be independent from their previous workload pattern, we propose a Fuzzy Prediction Method (FPM) that not only applies neural network to predict workload patterns in VMs, but also applies an expert system to control near future changes in workload patterns for every VM, and determine the time that VMs will be overloaded and need to be migrated. To design the FPM, we first determine the conditions which lead to a VM to be overloaded. Then the ES rules are extracted from determined conditions. We run FPM every 5 minutes and control VM workload situation for the past 2 minutes.

A. VM Migration Conditions

If VM_{wc} be the VM workload capacity and $VM_{et}(t)$ be the number of executing tasks in the VM as a time series in time slot *T*, then the VM will be overloaded at the time *x* when:

$$\lim_{t \to x} VM_{et}(t) = VM_{wc} \quad (1)$$

and Equation 1 could have an answer for variable *x* during next 2 minutes, if following conditions be satisfied where *ct* is current time, and $t_i \in T = \{ct - (120\ seconds), ct\}$:

Condition 1: Time series $VM_{et}(t)$ rises one or more times during *T*. It means:

$$VM_{et}(t_i) < VM_{et}(t_i + 1), \exists \{t_i\} = T^* \subset T \quad (2)$$

It means: $VM'_{et}(t_i) \geq 0, \exists \{t_i\} = T^* \subset T$

Condition 2: There would be overloading time for the VM if: $VM_{wc} - \max_{t_i \in T} VM_{et}(t_i) < 2 \quad (3)$

Condition 3: Rao (2011) proposed a metric of Productivity Index (PI) and use it to measure the system processing capability. He defined PI as:

$$PI\ (t) = \frac{CW(t)}{CC\ (t)} \quad (4)$$

where $CW(t)$ is the amount of completed work and $CC(t)$ is the amount of resource (CPU) consumed during the time slot *t*. An overloaded system means that its *cost* keeps increasing but with stagnated or compromised *yield*. Virtual machine will be overloaded if PI begins to drop. Although Rao believes that for online identification, the single PI metric is not enough to identify system state because any change of *PI* can be either due to the system capacity or the input load change [20]. Considering this fact, to control VM's workload situation during *T*, We determine following conditions that show PI drops during T:

$$PI(t_i) > PI(t_i + 1), \exists \{t_i\} = T^+ \subset T \quad (5)$$

It means:

$$PI'(t_i) \leq 0, \exists \{t_i\} = T^+ \subset T$$

In addition, the time series $PI(t)$ has a decreasing trend:

$$PI(ct - 120s) > PI(ct) \quad (6)$$

Condition 4: Time series $VM_{et}(t)$ has a raising trend:

$$VM_{et}(ct - 120\ s) < VM_{et}(ct) \quad (7)$$

B. The Variables of Fuzzy Prediction Method

The *input* variables of proposed FPM are defined as follows: the number of executing tasks in the VM at current time as $VM_{et}(ct)$, the maximum number of executing tasks in VM during *T* as $\max_{t_i \in T} VM_{et}(t_i)$, the change in number of executing tasks in the VM at random time $t_r \in T^*$ as $VM_{et}(t_r + 1) - VM_{et}(t_r)$, the $VM_{et}(ct) - VM_{et}(ct - 120\ s)$ that shows $VM_{et}(t)$ raised during *T*, the amount of completed tasks in the VM till current time as $CW(ct)$, the amount of CPU consumed till current time as $CC(ct)$, the change in productivity index at random time $t_r \in T^+$ as $PI(t_r) - PI(t_r + 1)$, the $PI(ct - 120s) - PI(ct)$ that shows PI(t) decreased during *T*. In addition, in this approach a neural network model is trained, given the previous historic workload patterns (training data set) to predict VM workload pattern. The neural network prediction results $NN_R(t)$ (desired output of neural network) will be applied by proposed FPM as an input variable. The FPM's *output* variable is defined as $VM_{WL}(t)$ that denotes the predicted VM workload situation in near future. The FPM's variables membership functions are defined as follow:

TABLE I. FUZZIFICATION OF $VM_{et}(t)$ AND $\text{MAX}_{t_i \in T} VM_{et}(t_i)$: INPUT

Set	Linguistic term	α level cuts	
		1-level cut	0-level cut
VL	Very Low	0	$0.25 * VM_{wc}$
L	Low	$0.25 * VM_{wc}$	$0, 0.5 * VM_{wc}$
M	Medium	$0.5 * VM_{wc}$	$0.25 * VM_{wc}, 0.75 * VM_{wc}$
H	High	$0.75 * VM_{wc}$	$0.5 * VM_{wc}, 1 * VM_{wc}$
VH	Very High	$1 * VM_{wc}$	$0.75 * VM_{wc}$

Universe of discourse: (0, VM_{wc})

TABLE II. FUZZIFICATION OF $VM_{et}(t_i + 1) - VM_{et}(t_i), t_i \in T^*$ AND $VM_{et}(ct - 120s) - VM_{et}(ct)$: INPUT

Set	Linguistic term	α level cuts	
		1-level cut	0-level cut
VL	Very Low	-1	-0.5
L	Low	-0.5	-1,0
M	Medium	0	-0.5,0.5
H	High	0.5	0,1
VH	Very High	1	0.5

Universe of discourse: (-1,1)

TABLE III. FUZZIFICATION OF $CW(t)$: INPUT

Set	Linguistic term	α level cuts	
		1-level cut	0-level cut
VL	Very Low	0	$0.25 * CU$
L	Low	$0.25 * CU$	$0, 0.5 * CU$
M	Medium	$0.5 * CU$	$0.25 * CU, 0.75 * CU$
H	High	$0.75 * CU$	$0.5 * CU, 1 * CU$
VH	Very High	$1 * CU$	$0.75 * CU$

Universe of discourse: (0, 100% Virtual CPUs utilization=CU)

Note: Virtual CPUs determines how many physical CPUs can be used by a VM. The number of virtual CPUs together with the scheduler credit determine the total CPU resource allocated to a VM [20].

TABLE IV. FUZZIFICATION OF $CC(t)$: INPUT

Set	Linguistic term	α level cuts	
		1-level cut	0-level cut
VL	Very Low	0	$0.3 * N$
L	Low	$0.25 * N$	$0, 0.5 * N$
M	Medium	$0.5 * N$	$0.25 * N, 0.75 * N$
H	High	$0.75 * N$	$0.5 * N, 1 * N$
VH	Very High	$1 * N$	$0.75 * N$

Universe of discourse: (0, Total number of executed tasks during T=N)

TABLE V. FUZZIFICATION OF $PI(t_i + 1) - PI(t_i), t_i \in T^+$ AND $PI(ct - 120s) - PI(ct)$: INPUT

Set	Linguistic term	α level cuts	
		1-level cut	0-level cut
VL	Very Low	-1	-0.5
L	Low	-0.5	-1,0
M	Medium	0	-0.5,0.5
H	High	0.5	0,1
VH	Very High	1	0.5

Universe of discourse: (-1, 1)

TABLE VI. FUZZIFICATION OF $NN_R(t)$: INPUT

Set	Linguistic term	α level cuts	
		1-level cut	0-level cut
U	Underload	0,0.3	0.7
O	Overload	0.7,1	0.3

Universe of discourse: (0,1)

TABLE VII. FUZZIFICATION OF $VM_{WL}(t)$: OUTPUT

Set	Linguistic term	α level cuts	
		1-level cut	0-level cut
U	Underload	0,0.3	0.7
O	Overload	0.7,1	0.3

Universe of discourse: (0,1)

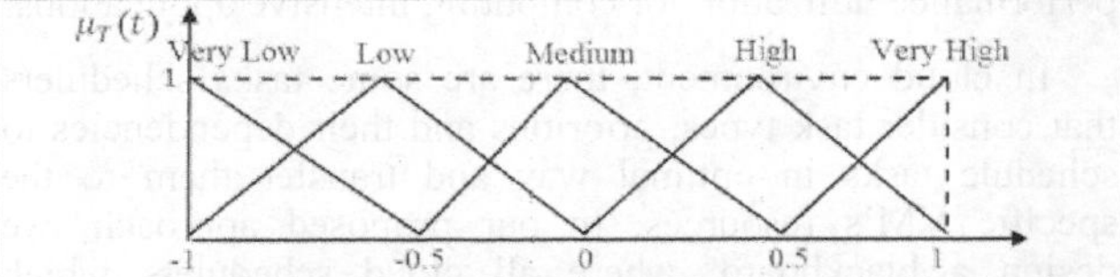

Fig. 1. The Membership Function of Input Variables of Tables 2 and 5

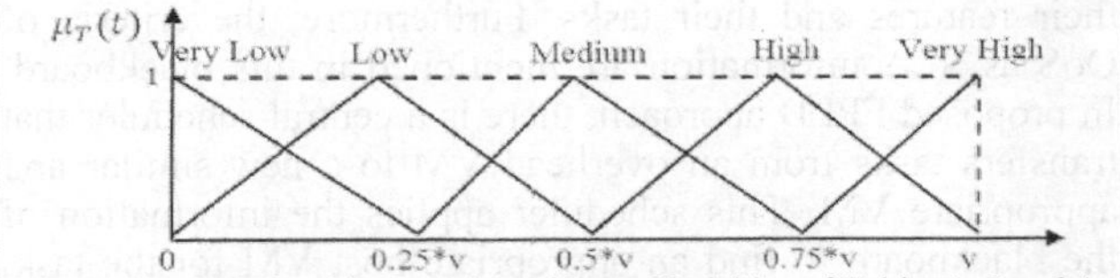

Fig. 2. The Membership Function of Input Variables of Tables 1, 3 and 4

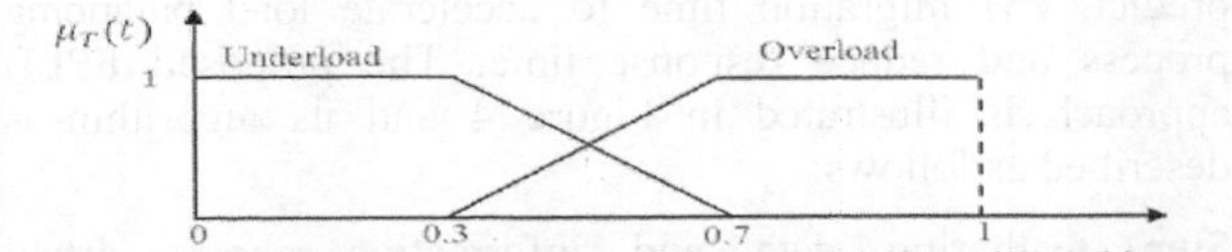

Fig. 3. The Membership Function of Output Variable and $NN_R(t)$

C. The Expert System Rules

We determine the ES rules base on aforementioned conditions to control VM's workload changes and predict the time of VM migration. The two main rules are described as follows. For random $t_r \in T$ and $\forall\, t_i \in T$ and *ct* as current time:

- **If** $NN_R(ct) = H$ **and** $VM_{et}(ct) = H$ **and** $\max_{t_i \in T} VM_{et}(t_i) = H$ **or** $VM_{et}(t_r + 1) - VM_{et}(t_r) = H$ **and** $CW(ct) = VH$ **and** $CC(ct) = H$ **or** $PI(t_r) - PI(t_r + 1) = L$ and $PI(ct - 120s) - PI(ct) = L$ and $VM_{et}(ct) - VM_{et}(ct - 120\ s) = \boldsymbol{H}$ **then** $VM_{WL} = O$
- **If** $NN_R(ct) = H$ **and** $VM_{et}(ct) = VL$ **and** $\max_{t_i \in T} VM_{et}(t_i) = H$ **or** $VM_{et}(t_r + 1) - VM_{et}(t_r) = VL$ **and** $CW(ct) = L$ **and** $CC(ct) = VL$ **or** $PI(t_r) - PI(t_r + 1) = H$ and $PI(ct - 120s) - PI(ct) = H$ and $VM_{et}(ct) - VM_{et}(ct - 120\ s) = VL$ **then** $VM_{WL} = U$

V. A FUZZY PREDICTABLE LOAD BALANCING APPROACH

In this section, we propose a FPLB approach. This approach contains a conceptual model and an algorithm which are designed to achieve system load balancing by migrating tasks from overloaded VMs. In addition, in this approach to decrease energy consumption and costs, we avoid choosing idle PMs as a new PM host, because if we transfer tasks to an idle PM, we have to turn it on and this action will increase energy consumption and costs [5].

The complex applications in cloud environment are classified into two groups: (1) computing intensive, and (2) data intensive applications. To transfer data intensive applications, the scheduling strategy should decrease the data movement to reduce the transferring time; but for transferring computing intensive tasks, the scheduling strategy should schedule the data to the high performance computer [21]. In this paper, we consider bandwidth as a variable to minimize the tasks transferring time for data intensive applications. In addition we consider new host PM's properties (memory, hard disk, etc) to enhance performance utilization for computing intensive applications.

In cloud environment, there are some tasks schedulers that consider task types, priorities and their dependencies to schedule tasks in optimal way and transfer them to the specific VM's resources. In our proposed approach, we design a blackboard, where all cloud schedulers which manage VMs on clouds, share their information about VMs, their features and their tasks. Furthermore, the criteria of QoS as SLA information are mentioned in this blackboard. In proposed FPLB approach, there is a central scheduler that transfers tasks from an overhead VM to a new similar and appropriate VM. This scheduler applies the information of the blackboard to find an appropriate host VM for the task. In addition, the proposed FPM is used in FPLB approach to predict VM migration time to accelerate load balancing process and reduce response time. The proposed FPLB approach is illustrated in Figure 4 and its algorithm is described as follows:

Step1- Gathering data and information about virtual machine managers (VMMs), VMs, PMs and SLA information, in the global blackboard as inputs:
1. VMs tasks information:
   1.1. The number of executing tasks
   1.2. Tasks' execution time and locations
   1.3. Tasks' required resources (number of required processors)
2. PMs' Criteria (total/current)
   2.1. CPU (number and speed of the processors)
   2.2. Free Memory and Free Hard disk
   2.3. Bandwidth
   2.4. PM situation: Idle or active
   2.5. Its host VMM
3. SLA information
4. The objectives of the tasks migration optimization model and their information:
   4.1. Minimizing cost
      4.1.1. Cost policy information
   4.2. Minimizing execution time and transferring time
      4.1.2. Execution information
      4.1.3. Bandwidth information

Step2- Monitoring data and information to determine VMs' workflow information

Step3- Predicting VM migration time applying proposed FPM:
1. Determining $\{t_i\} = T^* \subset T$ when $VM'_{et}(t_i) \geq 0$
2. Determining $\{t_i\} = T^+ \subset T$ when $PI'(t_i) \leq 0$
3. Determining $\max_{t_i \in T} VM_{et}(t_i)$
4. Determining NN results about VMs' workload situation (Input for FPM)
5. Calculating other FPM input variables
6. Determining overloaded VMs and their migration time applying proposed FPM

Step4- Determining the list of tasks which should be migrated from overloaded VM's, and the list of candidate VMs to be the new host

Step5- Finding optimal homogeneous VMs as a new host for executing the tasks of the overloaded VMs, which is a multi-objective task migration problem, applying MOGA (this step will be described in Section VI).

Step6- Considering obtained optimal tasks migration schema, determining following information as the outputs:
1. New optimal cost and optimal execution time
2. Current VMs properties (Executing tasks, CPU, etc.)

Step7- Transferring tasks and their corresponding data to the determined optimal host VMs

Step8- Updating blackboards and schedulers' information according to the outputs of Step 4.

Step9- End.

VI. An Algorithm for Solving Multi-Objective Tasks Migration Problem Using MOGA

In this section, we describe a sub-algorithm to complete the Step 5 of FPLB algorithm and solve the multi-objective tasks migration problem. This sub-algorithm determines an optimal tasks scheduling model to assign tasks from overloaded VMs to the new host VMs applying MOGA. Among different MOGA methods, we apply Deb's NSGAII [19]. NSGAII not only has good convergence and distribution mechanism, but also has higher convergence speed. This sub-algorithm applies data and information which are determined in Steps 1 to 4 of the FPLB algorithm as its inputs, then finds the optimal schema to assign arrival tasks from overloaded VMs to host VMs, conducting following steps:

Step5.1. Determining candidate host VMs set by choosing the set of VMs which satisfy the constraints about host VMs' properties as $VM_{set} = \{vm_1, \ldots, vm_m\}$

Step5.2. Eliminating the list of overloaded VMs (which are determined in Step 2 applying proposed FPM) from candidate host VMs set.

Step5.3. Determining the set of tasks which should migrate from overloaded VMs as immigrating tasks set: $T_{set} = \{t_1, \ldots, t_n\}$

Step5.4. Applying MOGA to solve the multi-objective problem and assign the immigrating tasks to the optimal host VMs to minimize execution and transferring time and processing cost, conducting following steps:

Step5.4.1. Initializing population P_0 which is generated randomly

Step5.4.2. Assigning rank to each individual based on non-dominated sort

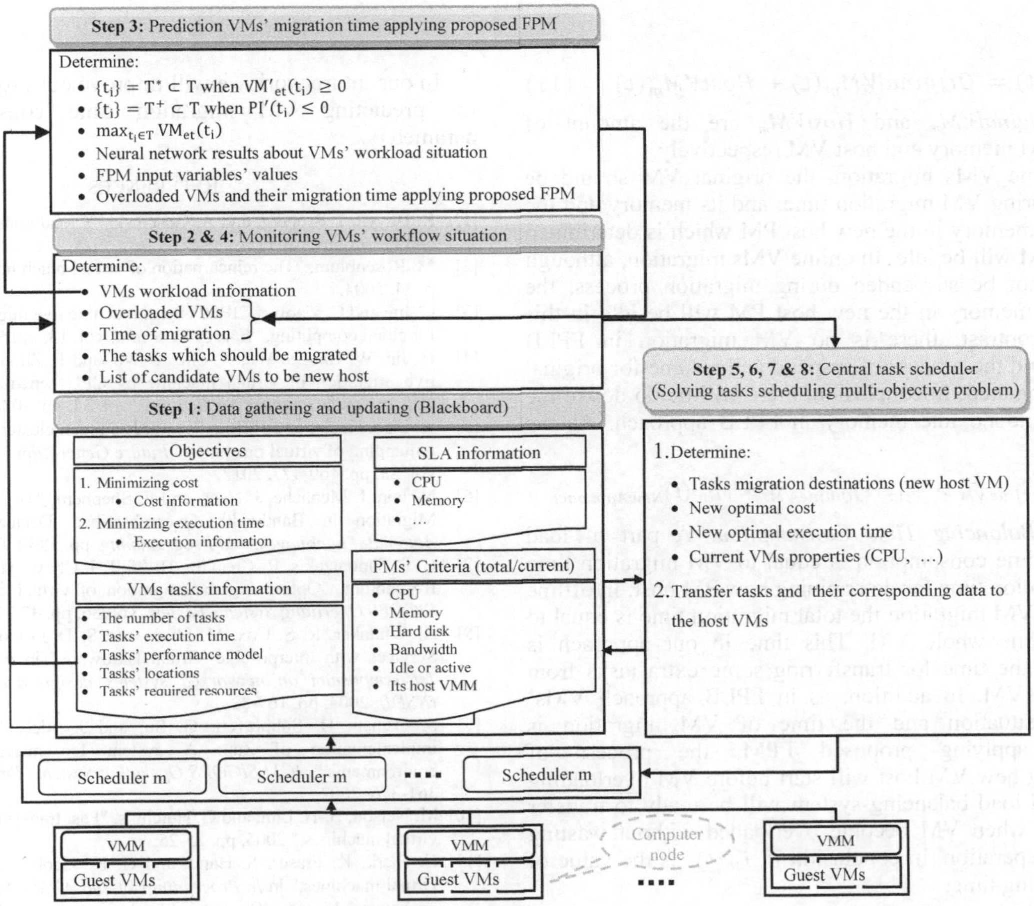

Fig. 4. The Conceptual Model of FPLB Approach

Step5.4.3. Implementing binary tournament selection, crossover and mutation on the initial population and creating a new population Q_0 and set $t=0$.

Step5.4.4. Merging the parent P_t and the child Q_t to form a new population $R_t = P_t \cup Q_t$.

Step5.4.5. Adopting non-dominated relationship to sort population and calculate the crowding distance among population on each layer.

Step5.4.6. Selecting the former N individuals as the parent population, namely $P_{t+1} = P_{t+1}\,[1:N]$ (Elite strategy).

Step5.4.7. Implementing reproduction, crossover and mutation on population P_{t+1} to form population Q_{t+1}.

Step5.4.8. If the termination conditions are met, output results as optimal tasks migration schema; otherwise, update the evolutionary algebra counter $t=t+1$ and go to step 5.4.4.

VII. Evaluation

A system prototype is being developed based on the proposed FPLB and will be evaluated against the determined features. However, in this paper, the evaluation is presented by comparison of the proposed FPLB approach with traditional whole VM migration methods applying three parameters:

(1) Power Consumption: considering this fact that the less number of active PM means the less power consumption [5], we applied following ratio to compare power consumption after load balancing applying FPLB approach:

$$R_{pc} = \frac{number\ of\ active\ PM}{number\ of\ overloaded\ VMs} \tag{10}$$

In proposed approach, to transfer extra tasks from overloaded VM, we just need to find a new similar VM on an active PM as a new host and there will be no need to turn a new PM on. In contrast, for whole VM migration, more hardware capacity is needed and it is impossible for every case to avoid choosing idle PM. Therefore, R_{pc} in FPLB approach compare to VM migration technique has lower value. Therefore, we have less "power consumption" after load balancing using FPLB approach and:

$$R_{pc_{Offline\ VM}} \geq R_{pc_{Online\ VM}} > R_{pc_{NewApproach}}$$

(2) Idle Memory: to compare the efficiency of FPLB approach, we apply idle memory that is prepared during the load balancing process as:

$$M_{im}(t) = OriginalVM_m(t) + HostVM_m(t) \quad (11)$$

where $OriginalVM_m$ and $HostVM_m$ are the amount of original VM memory and host VM respectively.

In offline VMs migration, the original VM should be suspend during VM migration time, and its memory and the amount of memory in the new host PM which is determined for host VM will be idle. In online VMs migration, although VM will not be suspended during migration process, the amount of memory in the new host PM will be idle in this time. In contrast, there is no VM migration in FPLB approach and the process of suspend and resume for original VM is eliminated. In conclusion, there will be no downtime for VMs and no idle memory in FPLB approach. As the results:

$$M_{im}(t)_{Offline\,VM} > M_{im}(t)_{Online\,VM} > M_{im}(t)_{NewApproach}$$

(3) Load Balancing Time Consumption: A part of load balancing time consumption is equal to VM migration time and preparation time for determining new PM host. In offline and online VM migration the total migration time is equal to migration one whole VM. This time in our approach is reduced to the time for transferring some extra tasks from overloaded VM. In addition, as in FPLB approach VMs' workload situation and the time of VM migration is predicted applying proposed FPM, the process of determining new VM host will start before VM overloading happen and load balancing system will be ready to transfer extra tasks when VM become overloaded without wasting time for preparation, in conclusion if $T_{lb}(t)$ is the value of load balancing time:

$$T_{lb}(t)_{Offline\,VM} > T_{lb}(t)_{Online\,VM} > T_{lb}(t)_{FPLB\,Approach}$$

VIII. Conclusion and Future Work

VM migration technique has been applied for elastic resource allocation, by migrating overload VM from one PM to another to achieve stronger computation power, larger memory, fast communication capability, or energy savings.

This paper proposed a new FPLB approach to achieve system load balancing by migrating arrival tasks from overloaded VM to another homogeneous VM instead of whole VM migration. The proposed approach has ability to determine overloaded VMs and predict their migration time. This approach also contains a multi-objective tasks migration model subject to minimizing cost, execution time and transferring time. In proposed approach there is no need to pause VM during migration time. In addition, the proposed approach will significantly reduce time, memory and cost consumption, because unlike tasks migration, VM live migration takes longer to complete and needs more idle capacity in host PM. Furthermore, proposed approach decreases energy consumption by avoiding choosing idle PMs as a new host PM. This approach also accelerates load balancing process and reduces response time applying proposed FPM.

In our future work we will improve our proposed method for predicting VM migration time considering SLA parameters.

References

[1] R. Buyya, J. Broberg, and A. Goscinski, "Cloud computing, Principles and Paradigms," 2011.

[2] M. Rosenblum, "The reincarnation of virtual machines," *Queue,* vol. 2, p. 34, 2004.

[3] C. Jun and C. xiaowei, "IPv6 virtual machine live migration framework for cloud computing," *Energy Procedia,* vol. 13, pp. 5753-5757, 2011.

[4] H. Jin, W. Gao, S. Wu, X. Shi, X. Wu, and F. Zhou, "Optimizing the live migration of virtual machine by CPU scheduling," *Journal of Network and Computer Applications,* vol. 34, pp. 1088-1096, 2011.

[5] X. Liao, H. Jin, and H. Liu, "Towards a green cluster through dynamic remapping of virtual machines," *Future Generation Computer Systems,* vol. 28, pp. 469-477, 2012.

[6] N. Jain, I. Menache, J. Naor, and F. Shepherd, "Topology-Aware VM Migration in Bandwidth Oversubscribed Datacenter Networks," *Automata, Languages, and Programming,* pp. 586-597, 2012.

[7] C. P. Sapuntzakis, R. Chandra, B. Pfaff, J. Chow, M. S. Lam, and M. Rosenblum, "Optimizing the migration of virtual computers," *ACM SIGOPS Operating Systems Review,* vol. 36, pp. 377-390, 2002.

[8] A. Whitaker, R. S. Cox, M. Shaw, and S. D. Gribble, "Constructing Services with Interposable Virtual Hardware," in *Proceedings of the 1st symposium on networked systems design and implementation (NSDI)*, 2004, pp. 169-82

[9] S. Osman, D. Subhraveti, G. Su, and J. Nieh, "The design and implementation of Zap: A system for migrating computing environments," *ACM SIGOPS Operating Systems Review,* vol. 36, pp. 361-376, 2002.

[10] M. Nelson, B. H. Lim, and G. Hutchins, "Fast transparent migration for virtual machines," 2005, pp. 25-25.

[11] C. Clark, K. Fraser, S. Hand, and G. H. Jacob, "Live migration of virtual machines," in *In Proceedings of 2nd ACM/USENIX Symposium on Network Systems, Design and Implementation (NSDI)*, 2005.

[12] W. Lin, J. Z. Wang, C. Liang, and D. Qi, "A Threshold-based Dynamic Resource Allocation Scheme for Cloud Computing," *Procedia Engineering,* vol. 23, pp. 695 – 703, 2011.

[13] X. Meng, C. Isci, J. Kephart, L. Zhang, E. Bouillet, and D. Pendarakis, "Efficient resource provisioning in compute clouds via vm multiplexing," in *Proceeding of the 7th international conference on Autonomic computing*, 2010, pp. 11-20.

[14] K. M. Nagothu, B. Kelley, J. Prevost, and M. Jamshidi, "Ultra low energy cloud computing using adaptive load prediction," in *World Automation Congress (WAC), 2010*, 2010, pp. 1-7.

[15] M. Naderpour and J. Lu, "Supporting situation awareness using neural network and expert system," in *International Conference on uncertainty Modeling in Knowledge Engineering and Decision Making (FLINS 2012)* Turkey, Istanbul, 2012, pp. 993-998.

[16] M. Naderpour and J. Lu, "A fuzzy dual expert system for managing situation awareness in a safety supervisory system," in *2012 IEEE International Conference on Fuzzy Systems (FUZZ-IEEE)*, Australia, Brisbane, 2012, pp. 1-7.

[17] S. Islam, J. Keung, K. Lee, and A. Liu, "Empirical prediction models for adaptive resource provisioning in the cloud," *Future Generation Computer Systems,* vol. 28, pp. 155–162, 2012.

[18] N. Srinivas and K. Deb, "Muiltiobjective optimization using nondominated sorting in genetic algorithms," *Evolutionary computation,* vol. 2, pp. 221-248, 1994.

[19] Y. Zhang, C. Lu, H. Zhang, and J. Han, "Active vibration isolation system integrated optimization based on multi-objective genetic algorithm," in *Computing, Control and Industrial Engineering (CCIE), 2011 IEEE 2nd International Conference on*, 2011, pp. 258-261.

[20] J. Rao, "Autonomic management of virtualized resources in cloud computing," 2011.

[21] L. Guo, S. Zhao, S. Shen, and C. Jiang, "Task Scheduling Optimization in Cloud Computing Based on Heuristic Algorithm," *Journal of Networks,* vol. 7, pp. 547-553, 2012.